Index to the
Public Official Bonds
of
Sonoma County, California

1850–1892

Steven M. Lovejoy

HERITAGE BOOKS
2018

HERITAGE BOOKS

AN IMPRINT OF HERITAGE BOOKS, INC.

Books, CDs, and more—Worldwide

For our listing of thousands of titles see our website
at
www.HeritageBooks.com

Published 2018 by
HERITAGE BOOKS, INC.
Publishing Division
5810 Ruatan Street
Berwyn Heights, Md. 20740

International Standard Book Number
Paperbound: 978-0-7884-5805-7

Contents

Index to the Public Official Bonds
of Sonoma County, California, 1850–1892

Bonds guaranteeing the faithful performance of the duties of their offices have been required of Californian public officials since the formation of the state. One of the first statutes passed by the California legislature was "An Act Concerning the Official Bonds of Officers."[1] Composed of twenty-five sections, this act set out the basic law governing bonds of both state and county public officials. Before taking office, a public official, known as the "principal" of the bond, was required to pledge a certain amount of money, $100 to $100,000 depending on the office, which would be forfeited to the State of California should the public official not faithfully perform the duties of his or her office. Two or more other persons, the "sureties" of the bond, usually the principal's friends or family, were required to pledge at least an equal amount. After approval by the County Court judge (later the Superior Court judge or judges), the bonds were to be filed and recorded in the office of the County Clerk or Recorder.

Preparation of this Index

In early 2017, a large number of Sonoma County public official bonds and other types of documents contained in two cardboard boxes erroneously labeled "Bonds of Law Enforcement Officials, 1851–1892" were found in the Sonoma County Archives. After the removal of the rusting paper clips and decomposing rubber bands holding them together, the documents were sorted by document type. Each public official bond, after the extraction of its data for this publication, was placed in an individual acid-free file folder labeled with the bond principal's name. All of the public official bonds for each year were then placed in an acid-free manila file folder, and the individual bond file folders were arranged alphabetically by surname within this manila file folder for ease of locating. These manila file folders are now housed in ten flip-top archival boxes in the Sonoma County Archives.

The information extracted from each public official bond for this index includes the bond principal's name, the sureties' names, the amount and date of the bond, the office to which the public official was appointed or elected, any relevant information contained in the text of bond, and the book and page(s) in which the bond was recorded. Information within the appropriate books of three series of volumes of Sonoma County recorded bonds (entitled "Bonds," "Bonds and Agreements," and "Official Bonds") was also extracted, capturing public official bonds for which no originals were found in the Sonoma County Archives. Over 2,300 bonds of public officials dated from 1850 through 1892 are indexed in this publication.

---

[1] *The Statutes of California, Passed at the First Session of the Legislature. Begun the 15th Day of Dec. 1849, and Ended the 22d Day of April, 1850, at the City of Pueblo de San José. With an Appendix and Index* (San José: J. Winchester, State Printer, 1850), pp. 74–76, chap. 21, "An Act Concerning the Official Bonds of Officers."

County offices for which bonds were required include:

Clerk	Recorder	Sheriff
Assessor	Treasurer	Under Sheriff
Deputy Assessor	Coroner	Deputy Sheriff
Tax Collector	Surveyor	Auctioneer
Public Administrator	District Attorney	Road Overseer/Road Master
Notary Public	Justice of the Peace	Superintendent of Public Schools
Constable	Supervisor	Commissioner of Highways
Deputy Constable	Auditor	County Physician

Format of the Bonds

Public official bonds of the 1850s were entirely handwritten. By the 1860s pre-printed forms were starting to be used, and by the 1880s and 1890s almost all public official bonds were fill-in-the-blank pre-printed forms. No matter whether handwritten or pre-printed form, public official bonds generally followed the same format. In the first section of the bond, the bond principal and his sureties were named along with the bond amount and the date of the bond. The next section stated the conditions of the bond, that is, it named the office to which the bond principal had been elected or appointed and bound the bond principal to faithfully perform the duties of his office. Many times, this section gave the exact date of election or appointment and the length of term. In the case of an appointment, the person or entity who appointed the public official may have been named. An example of an early Sonoma County public official bond is shown in Figure 1. Charles M. Hudspeth, a farmer born in Tennessee, was elected Sonoma County's first coroner on 1 April 1850 and executed this bond on 9 April 1850 along with his sureties James Cooper and James M. Hudspeth. Note that the bond preparer erroneously names Charles as "Charles N. Hedspeth." In later bonds, another section was added in which the bond sureties certified that their financial net worth was at least the amount for which they had bound themselves. Various notations appear on the reverse of the bonds or on separate pieces of paper associated with each bond indicating the bond's approval by the County or Superior Court judge(s), the date the bond was filed and/or recorded, and, if recorded, the book and page of its recording. Some public officials posted more than one bond at the same time. For example, sheriffs sometimes posted one bond for their faithful discharge of that office, but also another bond for the faithful discharge of the office of tax collector.

How to Use this Index

Bonds for each individual public official are listed alphabetically by the bond principal's name in the far-left column of the index. Once a bond of interest has been identified by the researcher, the original bond, if available, should be consulted by contacting the Sonoma County Archivist (currently the manager of the Sonoma County History and Genealogy Library in Santa Rosa). The original bond will be located in the Sonoma County Archives and brought to the Sonoma County History and Genealogy library for the researcher's use. Bonds, if recorded, as clerk's copies can be found on the pages of the appropriate bound volumes shown in the two far-right columns of the index. For those bonds in which the bond principal's name has been asterisked in the index, such as Burnett, Albert G.*, no original bond was located in the Sonoma County Archives. The recorded clerk's copy of these bonds should be consulted by requesting the appropriate bound volume from the Sonoma County Archivist or the Sonoma County Recorder.

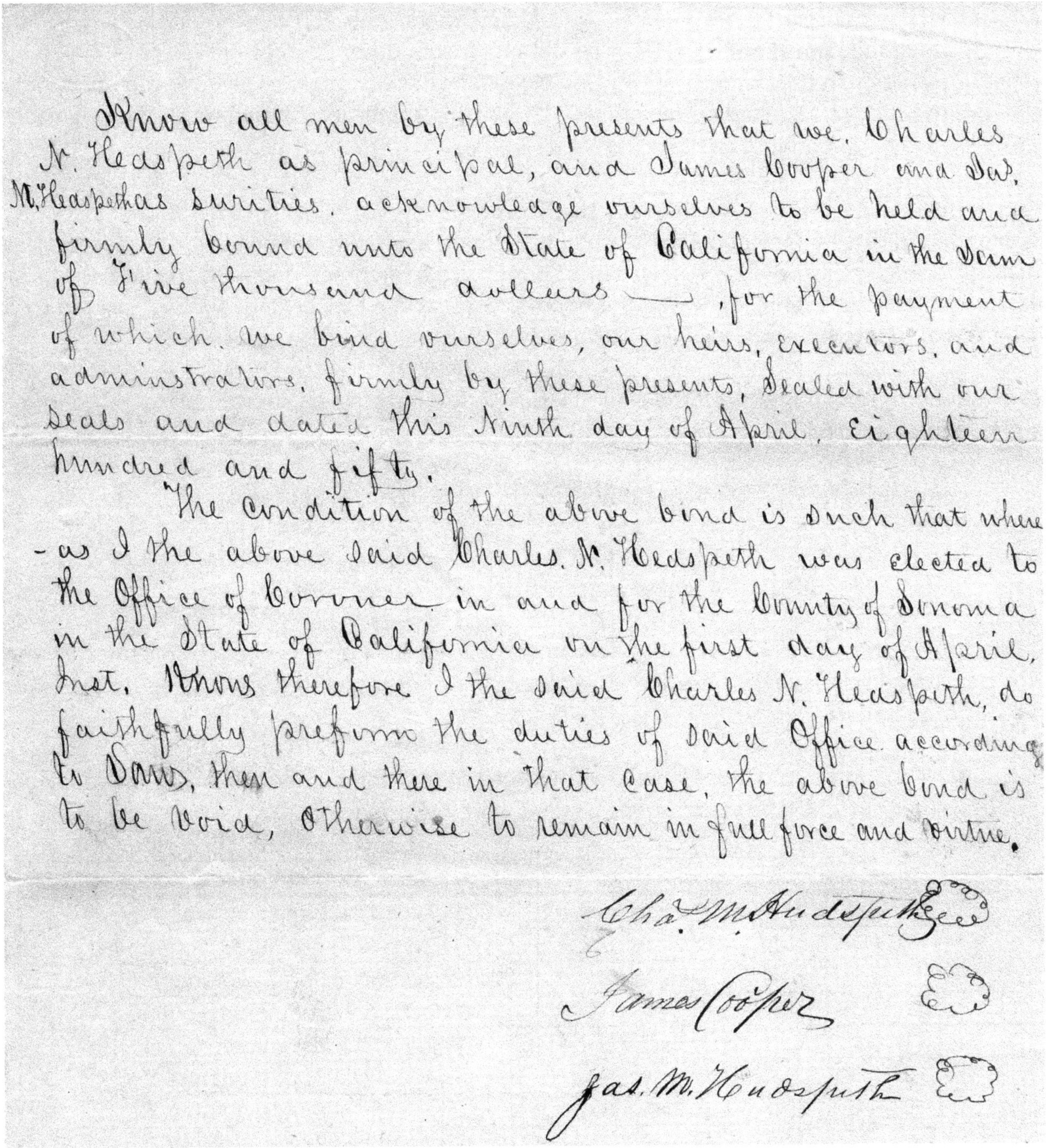

Know all men by these presents that we, Charles N. Hedspeth as principal, and James Cooper and Jas. M. Hedspeth as surities, acknowledge ourselves to be held and firmly bound unto the State of California in the Sum of Five thousand dollars —, for the payment of which we bind ourselves, our heirs, executors, and administrators, firmly by these presents, Sealed with our seals and dated this Ninth day of April, Eighteen hundred and fifty.

The condition of the above bond is such that where-as I the above said Charles N. Hedspeth was elected to the Office of Coroner in and for the County of Sonoma in the State of California on the first day of April, Inst. Know therefore I the said Charles N. Hedspeth, do faithfully preform the duties of said Office according to Laws, then and there in that case, the above bond is to be void, Otherwise to remain in full force and virtue.

Chas. M. Hudspeth

James Cooper

Jas. M. Hudspeth

Figure 1. Public official bond of Charles M. Hudspeth (1850)

Spelling in the 19th century was not standardized. Names can be spelled a variety of ways within each bond. The spelling of the names in this index is generally that used by the bond principals or sureties themselves in their signatures. Researchers are advised to look for all possible variations of a name for which they are searching in the index.

A question mark within square brackets ([?]) indicates that the pertinent information was not given in the bond, and that it could not be obtained from other sources or was not implied by other information in the bond. Thus, [?] Nov 1856 indicates no date was given in the bond, only the month and year. Similarly, Constable ([?] Township) indicates the name of the Township was not given in the bond.

Text within square brackets, such as [by the Board of Supervisors] or [vice W. J. Cunninghame, resigned], indicates information not stated in the bond itself, but obtained from other sources such as *The Sonoma Democrat* newspaper. Bonds are sometimes undated. In these cases, a date of filing or recording, if given in the bond, is used as the bond's date and is indicated by a date within square brackets, such as [21 Dec 1865].

The names of the months of the year in this index have been shortened to three-letter abbreviations as follows:

Jan	January	May	May	Sep	September
Feb	February	Jun	June	Oct	October
Mar	March	Jul	July	Nov	November
Apr	April	Aug	August	Dec	December

Witnesses to the signatures or the marks of bond principals or sureties are indicated in the Notes column in the index. These witnesses are usually notary publics, clerks, deputy clerks, or justices of the peace.

In the Book column of the index, the letters (some bolded) and numbers indicate the following bound volumes in which bonds of public officials were recorded:

Book	Bound Volume
A	Official Bonds, volume A
A (bold A)	Bonds & Agreements, volume A
B	Official Bonds, volume B
B (bold B)	Bonds & Agreements, volume B
C	Bonds, volume C
1	Official Bonds, volume 1
2	Official Bonds, volume 2
3	Official Bonds, volume 3
4	Official Bonds, volume 4

More information about each of the individual bound volumes is given in the "Records Utilized in the Assembly of this Index" section below.

Records Utilized in the Assembly of this Index

1. Original Sonoma County public official bonds, 1850-1892, as found among the collection entitled "County Documents, 1850-1899" in the 1982 Inventory of Records of the Sonoma County Clerk's Office stored in the Sonoma County Archives in Santa Rosa, California.[2] These original bonds had been microfilmed sometime before 1982, and the images, erroneously labeled "Bonds of Law Enforcement Officials, 1851-1892," are contained on microfilm reels 11–13 of the collection entitled "Old Miscellaneous Sonoma County Records, 1850-1958" in the 1982 Inventory of Records.[3] These microfilms are housed in the Sonoma County Clerk-Recorder's Office in Santa Rosa, California.

2. Index to Official Bonds. This bound volume, inventory number 19 in the 1982 Inventory of Records of the Sonoma County Clerk's Office and Sonoma County Archives accession number 1629, is stored in the Sonoma County Archives in Santa Rosa, California.[4] It indexes the bonds of Sonoma County public officials that are recorded in volumes A and B of Official Bonds by surname, not strictly alphabetically. Volume A of Official Bonds is missing and has been since at least 1919 when Owen C. Coy inventoried all of California's counties' records.[5]

3. Official Bonds, volume B. This bound volume, inventory number 18 in the 1982 Inventory of Records of the Sonoma County Clerk's Office and Sonoma County Archives accession number 1626, is stored in the Sonoma County Archives in Santa Rosa, California.[6] It contains 638 pages of recorded Sonoma County public official bonds and a few other miscellaneous bonds dated from 1859 to 1869. Page numbers 637-638 are blank.

4. Bonds, volume C. This bound volume, inventory number 21 in the 1982 Inventory of Records of the Sonoma County Clerk's Office and Sonoma County Archives accession number 1625, is stored in the Sonoma County Archives in Santa Rosa, California.[7] It contains 620 pages. Recorded on page numbers 1–169 are Sonoma County public official bonds and a few other miscellaneous bonds dated from 1869 to 1872. Recorded on page numbers 170–620 are Sonoma County Probate bonds (Administrator, Executor, and Guardian) dated from 1874 to

---

[2] Sonoma County Records Inventory Project, *Inventory of Records, 1847-1980, Office of the Clerk, Sonoma County, California* ([Santa Rosa, California]: Sonoma County Historical Records Commission, 1982), 73. These documents are inventory number 182.

[3] Ibid., 67. These microfilms are inventory number 180.

[4] Ibid., 7.

[5] Owen C. Coy, "Sonoma County," *Guide to the County Archives of California* (Sacramento: California Historical Survey Commission, 1919), 522–533.

[6] Sonoma County Records Inventory Project, *Inventory of Records, 1847-1980, Office of the Clerk, Sonoma County, California* ([Santa Rosa, California]: Sonoma County Historical Records Commission, 1982), 7.

[7] Ibid., 8.

1881. There is a surname index of the bond principals in the front of the volume. Page numbers 254–255 are blank and glued together.

5. Bonds & Agreements, volumes A and B. These bound volumes, part of inventory number 174 in the 1979 Inventory of Records of the Sonoma County Recorder's Office, are stored in the Sonoma County Clerk-Recorder's Office in Santa Rosa, California.[8] Digital images of the pages of these bound volumes are also available on the public-use computers of the Sonoma County Clerk-Recorder's Office.

Volume A records various types of bonds, including bonds of public officials, and agreements dated from 1857 to 1875. It contains 360 pages. Page numbers 19, 21, 24, 47, 285–288, and 313–321 are blank, while page numbers 25–46 and 289–312 have been removed and noted as having been blank before removal. Page numbers 322–360 contain a surname index of the bond principals which also notes the type of bond and the bond's date of filing. No documents were recorded in this bound volume from 30 October 1861 to 8 May 1874.

Volume B records various types of bonds, including bonds of public officials, and agreements dated from 1861 to 1887. It contains 883 pages. Page numbers 639 and 640 are blank.

6. Official Bonds, volumes 1–4. These bound volumes, part of inventory number 177 in the 1979 Inventory of Records of the Sonoma County Recorder's Office, are stored in the Sonoma County Clerk-Recorder's Office in Santa Rosa, California.[9] Digital images of the pages of these bound volumes are also available on the public-use computers of the Sonoma County Clerk-Recorder's Office.

Volume 1 records bonds of public officials, and a few agreements, dated from 1873 to 1886, mostly 1873 to 1880. It contains 601 pages.

Volume 2 records bonds of public officials dated from 1880 to 1888, mostly 1880 to 1886. It contains 560 pages.

Volume 3 records bonds of public officials dated from 1886 to 1901. It contains 640 pages.

Volume 4 records bonds of public officials dated from 1888 to 1898. It contains 406 pages of one-page pre-printed bond forms.

---

[8] Sonoma County Records Inventory Project, *Inventory of Records, 1834-1986, Office of the Recorder, Sonoma County, California* (1979; reprint, [Santa Rosa, California]: Sonoma County Recorder's Office and Sonoma County Historical Records Commission, 1987), 40–41.
[9] Ibid., 41–42.

Acknowledgments

The author thanks Katherine Rinehart, manager of the Sonoma County History and Genealogy Library, and Deva Proto, Chief Deputy County Clerk-Recorder, for access to the original Sonoma County public official bonds and bound volumes held at the Sonoma County Archives and Sonoma County Clerk-Recorder's Office.

About the Author

Steven M. Lovejoy is a retired chemist living in Sebastopol, Sonoma County, California. He is currently (2018) the president of the Sonoma County Genealogical Society and a Sonoma County Historical Records Commissioner. He holds a Certificate in Genealogical Research from Boston University and can be contacted at stevelov@comcast.net.

Principal Name	Sureties	Amount ($)	Date	Office	Notes	Book	Page(s)
Abell, Sidney	Hendley, John; Arnold, G. W.	1,000	10 May 1861	Justice of the Peace (Santa Rosa Township)	Appointed May Term 1861 by the Board of Supervisors in place of D. D. Myers, resigned	B	153
Abell, Sidney	Shattuck, Frank W.; Hoen, Berthold	1,000	18 Sep 1861	Justice of the Peace (Santa Rosa Township)	Elected 4 Sep 1861	B	210
Abraham, Isidore	Ink, W. P.; Sink, Daniel	1,000	10 Sep 1891	Justice of the Peace (Cloverdale Township)	Appointed 7 Sep 1891 by the Board of Supervisors, vice J. F. Hoadley, Sr., deceased	4	192
Abraham, Isidore*	Rosenberg, W.; Clack, John	5,000	16 Feb 1888	Notary Public	Appointed & commissioned 13 Feb 1888 by R. W. Waterman, Governor of California	2	559-560
Abraham, Isidore*	Abraham, Casper; Ink, W. P.; Brush, William T.	5,000	19 Dec 1890	Notary Public	Appointed & commissioned 15 Dec 1890 by R. W. Waterman, Governor of California	3	352-354
Acker, R. W.	Taylor, Despard; Clark, James	10,000	22 Nov 1876	Supervisor (District No. 4)	Elected 7 Nov 1876	1	279-280
Acker, R. W.	Goodman, L. S.; Clark, James; Johnson, Andrew; Gleason, William	10,000	25 Sep 1879	Supervisor (District No. 4)	Elected 3 Sep 1879	1	540-541
Acker, R. W.	Rien, Samuel; Clark, James	1,000	3 Feb 1874	Road Overseer (Bodega Road District)	Appointed 3 Feb 1874 by the Board of Supervisors		
Acker, R. W.	Rien, Samuel; Hoag, O. H.	1,000	4 Jan 1876	Road Master (Bodega Township, District No. 1)	Appointed 4 Jan 1876 by the Board of Supervisors	1	196-197
Acker, R. W.*	Clark, James; Stump, James	500	30 Dec 1874	Road Overseer (Bodega Township)	Appointed 4 Jan 1875 by the Board of Supervisors	1	74-75
Acton, William	Johnson, George A.; Allen, S. I.; Wright, Joseph; Peterson, A.; Jacobs, Eli; Mills, E. T.	5,000	3 Oct 1879	Notary Public	Appointed 26 Sep 1879 by the Governor of California	1	534-535
Adamson, W. H.	Stites, A. H.; Hotchkiss, B.	5,000	20 Dec 1875	Justice of the Peace (Washington Township)	Appointed 8 Dec 1875 by the Board of Supervisors	1	180
Adel, Frank	Bowles, J. M.; Sroufe, D. W.	2,000	16 Sep 1867	Constable (Petaluma Township)	Elected 4 Sep 1867 for the term of two years, witness John Cavanagh	B	575
Adel, Frank	Carpenter, L. F.; Sroufe, D. W.	2,000	16 Sep 1873	Constable (Petaluma Township)	Elected 3 Sep 1873	**B**	717-718
Adel, Frank	Bowles, J. M.; Sroufe, D. W.	2,000	23 Sep 1869	Constable (Petaluma Township)	Elected 1 Sep 1869	B	630
Adel, Frank	Mecham, H.; Bowles, J. M.	2,000	27 Sep 1865	Constable (Petaluma Township)	Elected 6 Sep 1865	B	475
Adel, Frank.	Mecham, H.; Bowles, J. M.	2,000	17 Sep 1875	Constable (Petaluma Township)	Elected 1 Sep 1875	1	129-130
Adrain, John	Wilson, William L.; Linnehen, Jerry; Kavanaugh, Nicholas; Munday, B. B.; Ryan, Mortimer	1,000	24 Sep 1861	Constable (Sonoma Township)	Elected 4 Sep 1861	B	171-172
Aikin, Mathew	Overton, A. P.	11,000	14 Jun 1881	Treasurer	Elected 3 Sep 1879, a supplemental bond substituting A. P. Overton for Alma Phelps and Bartholomew Tuomey (both removed from California) as surety on Mathew Aikin's original bond dated 17 Sep 1879, includes several Superior Court documents relating to this matter	1	596-598

1

Principal Name	Sureties	Amount ($)	Date	Office	Notes	Book	Page(s)
Aikin, Mathew	Kee, James; Doran, W. M.; McCaughey, James; Farrell, Martin; Goodman, L. S.; Hitchcock, Hollis; Fitzgerald, William; Clark, James; Tuomey, Bartholomew; Gallagher, John; Cunningham, John; Estes, H.; Warneky, Christian; Gleason, William; Johnson, Andrew; Phelps, Alma; McCrea, John	80,000	17 Sep 1879	Treasurer	Elected 3 Sep 1879, witness A. D. Laughlin	1	477-480
Aikin, Matthew	Hitchcock, Hollis; Estes, Hickman; Clark, James; Kee, James; Goodman, L. S.; Fitzpatrick, A.; McCrea, John; Gaffney, Miles; Smith, Wash.; Taylor, Despard; Doran, William M.; Farrell, Martin; Quinlan, P. D.; Gallagher, John; Keeff, Nathaniel; Hackett, J. J.; Clark, John; McCaughey, James	80,000	12 Nov 1877	Treasurer	Appointed by the Board of Supervisors to fill a vacancy occasioned by the resignation of T. N. Willis for the unexpired term [to take effect on or after 12 Nov 1877]	1	364-367 & 449-452
Aikin, Matthew	McCrea, John; Hitchcock, Hollis; Watson, James; Doran, W. M.; Goodman, L. S.; McCaughey, James; Stump, Henry; Keefe, Nathaniel; Gallagher, John; Estes, H.; Kee, James; Gleason, William; Johnson, Andrew; Smith, George W.; Clark, James	100,000	17 Nov 1882	Treasurer	Elected 7 Nov 1882	2	160-163
Aikin, Matthew	Hitchcock, Hollis; Estes, Hickman; McCaughey, J.; Quinlan, Patrick D.; McCrea, John; Doran, William M.; Fitzpatrick, A.; Kee, James; Hackett, J. J.; Gaffney, Miles; Gleason, William; Goodman, L. S.; Clark, John; Clark, James; Cunningham, John; Taylor, Despard; Phelps, A.; Peatross, W. W.; Overton, A. P.	80,000	17 Sep 1877	Treasurer	Elected 5 Sep 1877	1	297-301
Akers, Montgomery	Akers, Stephen; Dillon, Charles H.	1,000	19 Oct 1865	Constable (Sonoma Township)	Elected 6 Sep 1865	B	505
Akers, S.	Goodman, Willis; Pauli, G. T.; Dillon, C. H.	2,000	2 Dec 1869	Justice of the Peace (Sonoma Township)	Elected 20 Oct 1869	C	7
Akers, Stephen	Haraszthy, A. F.; Litzins, Lewis	1,000	18 Nov 1880	Justice of the Peace (Sonoma Township)	Elected 2 Nov 1880	2	17-18
Akers, Stephen	Litzius, L.; Lyon, R. B.	1,000	23 Nov 1882	Justice of the Peace (Sonoma Township)	Elected 7 Nov 1882	2	169-170
Akers, Stephen	Pauli, G. T.; Cornelius, George H. H.	1,000	26 Oct 1877	Justice of the Peace (Sonoma Township)	Elected 17 Oct 1877	1	353-355
Akers, Stephen	Warfield, J. B.; Monahan, P.; Oettl, F.; Wiseman, D. J.; McDonell, Angus	2,000	4 Nov 1875	Justice of the Peace (Sonoma Township)	Elected 20 Oct 1875, witness G. L. Wratten	1	181
Akers, Stephen	McDonell, Angus; Adler, Lewis	2,000	8 Nov 1873	Justice of the Peace (Sonoma Township)	Elected 15 Oct 1873, witness Murray Whallon	B	739-740
Albertson, James H. *	Wegner, Edward; Weyl, Henry	1,000	23 Nov 1882	Constable (Sonoma Township)	Elected 7 Nov 1882	2	168-169
Albertson, Joseph	Powell, Ransom; Bloom, David; Grant, John D.; Hassett, John D.	2,000	30 Oct 1863	Justice of the Peace (Mendocino Township)	Elected 21 Oct 1863	B	387

Principal Name	Sureties	Amount ($)	Date	Office	Notes	Book	Page(s)
Alexander, J. H.	Ferguson, Henry O.; Ferguson, John N.	200	3 Oct 1863	Road Master (District No. 1, Washington Township)	Elected [2 Sep 1863], witness David Odell	B	377
Alexander, Rufus	McCaughey, James; Taylor, Despard	2,000	4 Dec 1876	Constable (Bodega Township)	Appointed 16 Nov 1876	1	229-230
Allen, B. B.	Sheridan, Flan; Selling, John; Dougherty, John; McChristian, Patrick; Ragle, George J.	5,000	1 Dec 1873	Notary Public	Appointed 1 Dec 1873	1	3-5
Allen, B. B.	Hudspeth, James M.; McReynolds, James; Crawford, Adam; Harbine, L.; Ragle, George J.	5,000	14 Oct 1871	Notary Public	Appointed 7 Oct 1871 by H. H. Haight, Governor of California	C	90
Allen, B. B.	Walker, John; Hudspeth, James M.; Gannon, James; Ragle, George J.	5,000	15 Apr 1880	Notary Public	Appointed 22 Oct 1879	2	51-52
Allen, B. B.	Walker, John; McChristian, Patrick	5,000	15 Nov 1882	Notary Public	Commissioned 8 Nov 1882	2	143-144
Allen, B. B.	Ragle, George J.; Barnes, Aaron; Dougherty, John; Wilton, Thomas G.; Gannon, James	5,000	24 Nov 1877	Notary Public	[Appointed] 8 Oct 1877	1	372-374
Allen, B. B.	Huntly, G. W.; Gannon, James P.; Walker, John	5,000	6 Dec 1886	Notary Public	Appointed & commissioned 18 Nov 1886 by George Stoneman, Governor of California	3	117-118
Allen, B. B. *	Dougherty, John; Walker, John; Ragle, G. J.; Hudspeth, James M.	5,000	19 Nov 1875	Notary Public	Commissioned 8 Oct 1875	1	177
Allen, Darwin C.	Chamberlain, David; Bryant, William J.	5,000	12 Apr 1882	Notary Public	Appointed & commissioned by the Governor of California	2	129
Allen, Darwin C.	Farmer, E. T.; Murdock, L. A.; Cooper, S. R.; Weeks, S. S.; DeTurk, I.; Campbell, John T.; Glenn, J. H.	15,000	25 Nov 1884	District Attorney	Elected 4 Nov 1884	2	381-382
Allen, George F.	Veale, W. R.; Roberts, Charles; Ellsworth, L.; Higgins, Asa; Ayers, William; Wilsey, Henry	15,000	22 Nov 1884	Supervisor (District No. 2)	Elected 4 Nov 1884	2	427-428
Allen, George F.	Lougee, F. W.; Whitney, A. P.; Fairbanks, H. T.; Hill, William; Zartman, William	15,000	24 Nov 1882	Supervisor (District No. 2)	Elected 7 Nov 1882	2	184-186
Allen, George F.	Lawrence, Henry E.; Zartman, William; Veale, William R.; Ayers, William; Ellsworth, Lee; Wilsey, H.	15,000	27 Nov 1886	Supervisor (District No. 2)	Elected 2 Nov 1886	3	44-46
Allen, George F.	Hill, William; Fairbanks, H. T.; Whitney, A. P.; Mecham, H.; Lougee, F. W.	10,000	9 Nov 1880	Supervisor (District No. 2)	Elected 2 Nov 1880	2	3-4
Allen, S. I.*	Hitchcock, Hollis; Hardin, James A.; Markham, Andrew; Maddux, J. P.; Taylor, John S.; Hopper, Thomas; McConnell, William E.	50,000	23 Nov 1892	Sheriff	Elected 8 Nov 1892, witness A. D. Laughlin	4	208
Allen, S. I.*	Hitchcock, Hollis; Hardin, James A.; Markham, Andrew; Maddux, J. P.; Taylor, John S.; Hopper, Thomas; McConnell, William E.	50,000	23 Nov 1892	Tax Collector	Elected 8 Nov 1892, witness A. D. Laughlin	4	209
Allen, William T.	Willson, H. M.; Yates, John W.	5,000	2 Oct 1854	Justice of the Peace (Mendocino Township)	Elected 6 Sep 1854	A	88

3

Principal Name	Sureties	Amount ($)	Date	Office	Notes	Book	Page(s)
Ames, C. G.	Hahman, F. G.; Hendley, John; Wise, Henry; Weiss, M.; Martin, R. M.; Shane, Adam; Wilkinson, R.; Gault, Thomas L.; Gray, J. W.; Cocke, W. E.; Holmes, H. P.; Pyatt, Thomas H.; Crane, G. L.	15,000	[?] Feb 1866	Superintendent of Public Schools	Elected 6 Sep 1865	B	536-537
Ames, Charles G.	Crane, G. L.; Hendley, John; Marks, B.; Boyce, J. F.; Wise, Henry; McReynolds, James	10,000	[?] Feb 1868	Superintendent of Public Schools	Elected 4 Sep 1867	B	612
Ames, Charles G.	Hendley, John; Smith, Jacob; Williamson, James R.; Hahman, F. G.; Martin, R. M.; Bostwick, N. W.; Roney, J. M.; Hood, T. B.; Shane, Adam; Boyce, J. F.; Gault, T. L.; Kohle, August; Farmer, E. T.; Marks, B.; Cocke, W. E.; Richardson, J. H.; Wise, Henry; Jacobs, Eli; McClelland, J. J.; Manion, William; Holmes, H. P.; Bowles, J. M.; Heisel, Paul; Crane, G. L.; Gordon, A. J.	22,000	[5 Feb 1864]	Superintendent of Public Schools	Elected 2 Sep 1863	B	430-432
Ames, Charles G.	Martin, R. M.; Pyatt, Thomas H.; Hoen, Berthold; Williamson, Thomas D.; Hood, T. B.; Bostwick, N. W.; Hahman, F. G.; Hendley, John; Smith, Jacob; Wise, Henry; Clark, J. P.; Arnold, G. W.	12,000	10 Mar 1862	Superintendent of Public Schools	Elected 4 Sep 1861	B	254-255
Ames, Charles G.	Barnes, Michael; Smith, Jacob; Hood, Thomas B.; Bostwick, N. W.; Ellis, John J.; Green, E. L.; Crane, G. L.; Davis, G. W.; Hendley, John; Pyatt, Thomas H.; Arnold, G. W.; Hoen, B.; Martin, R. M.; Carrillo, Julio	12,000	21 Sep 1861	Superintendent of Public Schools	Elected 4 Sep 1861	B	189-190
Ames, T. M.	Dougherty, John; Johnson, Levi; Walker, John; Gregson, James	2,000	21 Dec 1863	Justice of the Peace (Analy Township)	Elected 21 Oct 1863, term commences on 1 Jan 1864 and continues until 1 Jan 1866	B	406
Ames, T. M.	Dougherty, John; Johnson, Levi; Walker, John; Gregson, James	2,000	21 Dec 1863	Justice of the Peace (Analy Township)	Elected 21 Oct 1863, term commences on 1 Jan 1864 and continues until 1 Jan 1866	B	408
Ames, T. M.	Marshall, John; McChristian, Patrick	2,000	24 Dec 1863	Justice of the Peace (Analy Township)	Elected 21 Oct 1863, term commences on 1 Jan 1864 and continues until 1 Jan 1866	B	407
Ames, T. M.	Marshall, John; McChristian, Patrick	2,000	24 Dec 1863	Justice of the Peace (Analy Township)	Elected 21 Oct 1863, term commences on 1 Jan 1864 and continues until 1 Jan 1866	B	409
Ames, T. M.	Dougherty, John; Chenoweth, John H.; Olmsted, O. A.; Wilson, William H.; Winkler, Clayton	2,000	6 Nov 1865	Justice of the Peace (Analy Township)	Elected 18 Oct 1865	B	501
Ames, Thaddeus M.	Spratt, James G.; Pierpoint, Robert R.; Hopkins, Robert	5,000	10 Mar 1852	Coroner	Elected 3 Sep 1851	A	59
Andersen, John*	Stengel, Christian; Luttringer, Joseph	1,000	9 Dec 1892	Justice of the Peace (Salt Point Township)	Elected 8 Nov 1892	4	256
Anderson, W. G.	Parks, D. H.; Palmer, C. H.; Percival, W. C.	2,000	[?] Oct 1877	Constable (Analy Township)	Elected 5 Sep 1877	1	352-353
Anderson, William L.	Ross, L.; Farmer, E. T.; Hahman, F. G.; Pauli, G. T.	4,000	8 Jan 1873	Road Master (Analy Road District)	Appointed 8 Jan 1873 by the Board of Supervisors		

Principal Name	Sureties	Amount ($)	Date	Office	Notes	Book	Page(s)
Anderson, William L.*	Bowles, J. M.; Towne, Smith D.; Sroufe, John; Daly, James; Martin, S. M.; Taylor, John; Ellis, John J.; Hardin, James A.; Wright, W. S. M.; Wise, Henry	6,000	[?] Nov 1863	Clerk	Elected 2 Sep 1863	B	76-78
Anderson, William L.*	Hahman, F. G.; Holmes, H. P.; Boyce, J. F.; Wise, M.	6,000	10 Jan 1866	Clerk	Elected 6 Sep 1865, includes oath of office dated 11 Jan 1866	B	203-205
Anderson, William L.*	Jackson, Zadok; Holmes, H. P.; Wright, W. S. M.; Grant, John D.	5,000	20 Nov 1867	Clerk	Elected 4 Sep 1867	B	293-294
Anderson, William L.*	Martin, Silas M.; White, E. F.; Hendley, John; Green, E. L.; Overton, A. P.; Trinque, W. D.; Lovell, H. L.; Hardin, J. A.; Ellsworth, LeGrand	6,000	23 Sep 1861	Clerk	Elected 4 Sep 1861	A	266-268
Armstrong, Albert	Miller, W. R.; Dixon, James	1,000	1 Jan 1872	Justice of the Peace (Salt Point Township)	Elected 18 Oct 1871	C	156-158
Armstrong, Albert*	McMale, Richard; Miller, W. R.	1,000	13 Dec 1869	Justice of the Peace (Salt Point Township)	Elected 20 Oct 1869	C	22
Arnold, W. J.	Story, Stephen C.; Sharp, Charles	1,000	25 Oct 1879	Justice of the Peace (Knight's Valley Township)	Elected 3 Sep 1879	1	548-549
Arnold, W. J.	Clark, James P.; Stanley, William B.	1,000	3 Nov 1877	Justice of the Peace (Knight's Valley Township)	Elected 17 Oct 1877	1	345-346
Aston, George P.*	Nagle, F. G.; Mulgrew, J. F.; McMinn, John, Sr.; Davis, W. S.; Reynolds, W. D.	5,000	5 Jun 1889	Notary Public	Appointed 1 Jun 1889	4	59
Atterbury, William B.	Hendley, John; Maxey, J. B.; Snoddy, B. A.; Boggs, Th. J.; Ewing, W. P.; Nugent, Thomas; Fitch, Frederick; Akers, Stephen; Bright, S. B.; Copeland, William L; Talbot, Coleman; Brockman, Israel	30,000	16 Jul 1855	Public Administrator	Appointed by the Board of Supervisors	A	105
Atterbury, William B.	Hendley, John; Hudson, Martin; Carrillo, Julio; Beaver, Henry; Hartman, J. William; Towne, Smith D.; Edwards, Uriah; Brown, S. C.; Bowles, J. M.; Singley, J.; Rochford, Thomas; Overton, A. P.; Rodgers, A. W.	15,000	2 Dec 1858	Public Administrator	Appointed 24 Nov 1858 by the Board of Supervisors		
Atwater, H. H.*	Whitney, Arthur L.; Knowles, James H.	5,000	20 Apr 1889	Notary Public	Appointed & commissioned 17 Apr 1889 by R. W. Waterman, Governor of California	4	53
Aull, A. B.	Bloom, David; Poor, F. G.	1,000	[16 Sep 1863]	Constable (Mendocino Township)	Elected 2 Sep 1863, includes oath of office dated 16 Sep 1863	B	354-355
Ayers, William	Woods, George; Vestal, L. H.	2,000	15 Jan 1880	Road Overseer (Petaluma Road District No. 1)	Appointed 7 Jan 1880 [by the Board of Supervisors]		
Ayers, William	Cavanagh, John; Davidson, S. E.	100	5 May 1859	Road Overseer (Road District No. 31, Analy Township)	Appointed, witness W. H. Bond	A	374

5

Principal Name	Sureties	Amount ($)	Date	Office	Notes	Book	Page(s)
Baber, R. G.	Adams, John; Lewis, Joshua; Scott, D. P. H.; Root, Jeremiah; Hendley, John; Harris, James H.; Hearn, James; Thompson, Thomas L.; Marks, B.; Hahman, F. G.; Williams, J. S.; Pyatt, Thomas H.; Holmes, H. P.; Wise, Henry; Boyce, J. F.; Goldfish, B.; Lewis, Isaac; Maxwell, J. G.; Harris, James H.; Wilson, H.; Shane, A.; Hood, T. B.	15,000	[3 Mar 1866]	Public Administrator	Elected 6 Sep 1865	B	537-538
Baber, R. G.	Lewis, Joshua; Fulton, James	1,000	16 Sep 1862	Justice of the Peace (Santa Rosa Township)	Elected 3 Sep 1862	B	276
Baber, R. G.	Pugh, James A.; Coulter, S. T.; Lewis, J. N.; Lewis, Joshua; Taylor, John S.; Root, John F.; Burrus, Edmond	5,000	28 Nov 1863	Coroner	Elected 2 Sep 1863	B	400-401
Badger, George W.	Averill, Anson; Whitney, A. P.	5,000	28 Oct 1881	Auctioneer		2	106-107
Baer, George B.*	Chalfant, John E.; Heald, J. G.; Holloway, Lewis; Goetzelman, John; Yordi, Fred	5,000	4 Sep 1891	Notary Public	Appointed 28 Aug 1891 by the Governor of California	4	190
Bagley, H. L.	Bachelder, J. E.; Turner, N. B., Jr.	1,000	25 Nov 1890	Justice of the Peace (Redwood Township)	Elected 4 Nov 1890	4	101
Bagley, H. L.*	Wescott, Oliver; Walker, L. F.; Dietz, G.; Connell, D.	5,000	30 Aug 1890	Notary Public	Appointed & commissioned 26 Aug 1890	4	171
Bagley, J. W.	Bachelder, J. E.; Beaver, Henry; McFadyen, Allan; Torrance, S. H.	1,000	12 Dec 1882	Road Overseer (Redwood Township)	Elected 7 Nov 1882	2	268-270
Bagley, J. W.	Williams, Reuben; Wilson, John	1,000	14 Feb 1877	Road Master (Redwood Township)	Appointed 9 Feb 1877 [by the Board of Supervisors], witness John T. Fortson	1	237-238
Bagley, J. W.	Guerne, George E.; Yarbrough, C. D.	1,000	16 Jan 1875	Road Overseer (Redwood Township)	Appointed 7 Jan 1875 by the Board of Supervisors	1	91-92
Bagley, J. W.	Murphy, Rufus; Brown, Albert	1,000	22 Jan 1885	Road Overseer (Redwood Road District)	Appointed 13 Jan 1885 [by the Board of Supervisors]	2	472-473
Bagley, John W.	Allison, George; Fannin, R. C.	200	18 Feb 1863	Road Master (District No. 2, Mendocino Township)	Appointed, includes oath of office dated 18 Feb 1863	B	339
Bailey, James B.	Campbell, David; Dickinson, H. W.	2,000	20 Jun 1860	Road Overseer (Washington Road District)	Appointed 18 Jun 1860 by the Board of Supervisors for the term of one year	B	89
Bailey, James B.	Morris, John; Campbell, David	1,000	26 Nov 1860	Constable (Washington Township)	Elected 6 Nov 1860	B	112-113
Bailey, R. F.	Weaver, C. W.; Ferguson, H. O.	1,000	20 Dec 1888	Justice of the Peace (Knight's Valley Township)	Elected 6 Nov 1888	4	32
Bailey, R. F.	Ferguson, H. O.; Weaver, C. W.	1,000	25 Nov 1890	Justice of the Peace (Knight's Valley Township)	Elected 4 Nov 1890	4	145

Principal Name	Sureties	Amount ($)	Date	Office	Notes	Book	Page(s)
Bailey, R. F.*	Ferguson, H. O.; Weaver, C. W.	1,000	3 Dec 1892	Justice of the Peace (Knight's Valley Township)	Elected 8 Nov 1892	4	225
Bailhache, John N.	Aull, A. B.; Sondheimer, E.; Engel, H. S.; Hudson, T. W.; Newman, B.; Raney, J. B.; Thurgood, W. S.; Carson, Lindsey; March, W. J.; Hooper, V. C. W.	5,000	13 Oct 1859	Notary Public	Appointed & commissioned 5 Oct 1859, includes oath of office dated 15 Oct 1859	B	56-57
Bailhache, John N.	Grant, John D.; Bloom, David	5,000	22 Jun 1868	Notary Public	Appointed & commissioned 16 Jun 1868 by H. H. Haight, Governor of California, to take effect from 25 Jun 1868, includes oath of office dated 22 Jun 1868	B	615
Bailhache, John N.	Pyatt, Thomas H.; Fike, Nathan; Hill, William McPherson; Bowles, J. M.; Hoen, Berthold	15,000	7 May 1862	Notary Public	Appointed & commissioned 1 May 1862 by Leland Stanford, Governor of California, for the term of two years, includes oath of office dated 7 May 1862	B	258-259
Bailhache, John N.	Norton, L. A.; Hassett, John D.; Thurgood, William S.; Forrister, A. J.; Engel, H. S.; Crane, G. L.	15,000	8 Oct 1861	Notary Public	Commissioned 4 Oct 1861 by John G. Downey, Governor of California	B	220-221
Baker, A. M.	Lambert, C. L.; Capell, C. W.	1,000	22 Nov 1884	Justice of the Peace (Mendocino Township)	Elected 4 Nov 1884	2	415-417
Baker, A. M.	Allen, W. T.; Lambert, W. S.	1,000	4 Dec 1886	Justice of the Peace (Mendocino Township)	Elected 2 Nov 1886	3	104-105
Baker, A. M.*	Barnes, T. J.; Coffman, N. B.	1,000	5 Dec 1892	Justice of the Peace (Mendocino Township)	Elected 8 Nov 1892	4	240
Baker, J. C.	Freeman, John M.	200	4 Nov 1862	Road Overseer (Road District No. 2, Petaluma Township)	Appointed	B	320
Baldwin, O. T.	Fritsch, John; Carpenter, L. F.; Dinwiddie, J. L.; Cassidy, John W.	2,000	22 Nov 1884	Justice of the Peace (Petaluma Township)	Elected 4 Nov 1884	2	420-421
Baldwin, O. T.	Denman, E.; Merritt, John; Bowles, J. M.; Scudder, N. W.; Lawrence, H. E.; Brown, Daniel; Fairbanks, H. T.; Haskell, W. B.	2,000	27 Oct 1877	Justice of the Peace (Petaluma Township)	Elected 17 Oct 1877	1	359-361
Baldwin, O. T.	Perry, A. F.; Fritsch, John; Dinwiddie, J. L.; Veale, W. R.	2,000	4 Dec 1886	Justice of the Peace (Petaluma Township)	Elected 2 Nov 1886	3	98-99
Baldwin, O. T.	Bowles, J. M.; Hahman, F. G.; Fike, Nathan; Hill, William McPherson; Hoen, Berthold	5,000	7 Aug 1862	Notary Public	Appointed & commissioned 1 May 1862 by Leland Stanford, Governor of California, for the term of two years, includes oath of office dated 7 Aug 1862	B	273-274
Baldwin, O. T.	Fritsch, John; Dinwiddie, J. L.	2,000	7 Feb 1889	Justice of the Peace (Petaluma Township)	Appointed 5 Feb 1889 by the Board of Supervisors	4	37
Ball, William P.	Rupe, Samuel H.; Emerson, John P.	2,000	11 May 1871	Constable (Mendocino Township)	Appointed [by the Board of Supervisors]	C	72-73
Banks, J. R.	Norton, L. A.; Amesbury, William	1,000	18 Aug 1890	Pound Master (Tzabaco Pound District)	Appointed 5 Aug 1890 by the Board of Supervisors	4	95
Barham, Aubrey	Barham, H. W.; Lowrey, J. J.; Gray, J. W.	5,000	14 Apr 1887	Notary Public	Appointed & commissioned 1 Apr 1887 by [Washington Bartlett], Governor of California	3	186-187

7

Principal Name	Sureties	Amount ($)	Date	Office	Notes	Book	Page(s)
Barnes, Edwin H.	Boggs, L. W.; Cameron, John	5,000	6 Oct 1851	Justice of the Peace (Russian River Township)	Elected 3 Sep 1851	A	37
Barnes, Jehu	Ormsby, John H.; Hopper, Thomas	1,000	17 Feb 1877	Road Master (Vallejo Township, Northern District)	Appointed 9 Feb 1877 by the Board of Supervisors, witness Frank W. Shattuck	1	245-246
Barnes, Jehu	Munday, B. B.; Tempel, C.	2,000	18 Jan 1873	Road Master (Vallejo Road District)	Appointed 7 Jan 1873 by the Board of Supervisors		
Barnes, Jehu	Patton, R. A.; Lavin, James	1,500	18 Jan 1879	Road Overseer (Vallejo Township [Road District No. 1])	Appointed 8 Jan 1879 [by the Board of Supervisors]		
Barnes, Jehu	Hopper, Thomas; Lawrence, J. A.	1,000	21 Feb 1878	Road Overseer (Vallejo Road District, North)	Appointed 7 Feb 1878 [by the Board of Supervisors], witness Frank W. Shattuck	1	406-407
Barnes, Jehu	Wharff, David; Carr, Mark	1,000	24 Jan 1880	Road Overseer (Vallejo Township North)	Appointed 7 Jan 1880 by the Board of Supervisors		
Barnes, Michael	Barnes, Thomas L.; Henley, William	1,000	26 Sep 1857	Constable (Petaluma Township)	Elected 2 Sep 1857, taking office from 1 Oct 1857 for one year, accepted by W. B. Hagans, Chairman of the Board of Supervisors	A	215-216
Barnett, J. D.*	Burnett, E.; Ragsdale, J. W.	5,000	2 Apr 1891	Notary Public	Appointed 27 Mar 1891 by H. H. Markham, Governor of California	4	187
Barnhardt, C. M.	Harris, Jacob; Warboys, J. W.; Frost, C. W.; Young, J. B.	2,000	23 Nov 1888	Constable (Santa Rosa Township)	Elected 6 Nov 1888	3	299-300
Barnhardt, C. M.*	Frost, C. W.; Doggett, W. J.; Coffey, Henry; Warboys, J. W.	2,000	2 Dec 1890	Constable (Santa Rosa Township)	Elected 4 Nov 1890	4	147
Barnhardt, Christian M.*	Doggett, W. J.; Abendroth, F. C.	1,000	1 Dec 1892	Constable (Santa Rosa Township)	Elected 8 Nov 1892	4	214
Barth, Adam H.	Barth, Adam; Clark, Benjamin	2,000	24 Sep 1877	Constable (Russian River Township)	Elected 5 Sep 1877	1	314-315
Bartley, W. H.	Burns, J. A.; Coon, R. W.	1,000	25 Nov 1890	Justice of the Peace (Redwood Township)	Elected 4 Nov 1890	4	102
Bartley, W. H.	Burns, J. A.; Coon, R. W.	1,000	28 Nov 1888	Constable (Redwood Township)	Elected 6 Nov 1888	3	286-288
Bartley, William H.	Coon, R. W.; Burns, Joshua A.	1,000	17 Oct 1885	Constable (Redwood Township)	Appointed 8 Oct 1885 [by the Board of Supervisors], vice C. S. Hill, resigned	2	497-498
Bartley, William H.	Burns, J. A.; Coon, R. W.	1,000	27 Nov 1886	Constable (Redwood Township)	Elected 2 Nov 1886	3	46-47
Batchelder, Ezra D.	Helmke, F.; Miller, W. R.	500	27 Dec 1862	Constable (Salt Point Township)	Appointed by the Board of Supervisors, witness T. W. Phinney, includes oath of office dated 27 Dec 1862	B	316
Bates, Philip	Porterfield, J. W.; Crigler, William E.	1,000	13 Feb 1871	Constable (Cloverdale Township)	Appointed 6 Feb 1871 by the Board of Supervisors	C	68

Principal Name	Sureties	Amount ($)	Date	Office	Notes	Book	Page(s)
Bates, Philip	Crigler, William E.; Shores, L.	2,000	30 Sep 1871	Constable (Cloverdale Township)	Elected 6 Sep 1871	C	127-129
Baxter, George P. *	Wightman, Chauncy; Morris, Joseph H. P.; Atkinson, Percy Herbert	5,000	25 Apr 1892	Notary Public	Appointed & commissioned 20 Apr 1892 by H. H. Markham, Governor of California	4	199
Beacom, Thomas	Orr, John; Rien, Samuel	1,000	12 Jul 1879	Justice of the Peace (Ocean Township)	Appointed 9 Jul 1879 [by the Board of Supervisors] to fill the unexpired term of A. H. Heffron, removed from Township	1	460-461
Beacom, Thomas	Coolbroth, Samuel W.; Farrell, Martin	2,000	13 Nov 1870	Justice of the Peace (Ocean Township)	Appointed 9 Nov 1870 by the Board of Supervisors	C	62-63
Beacom, Thomas	Rien, Samuel; Sartori, Benjamin	2,000	14 Dec 1871	Justice of the Peace (Ocean Township)	Elected 18 Oct 1871	C	150-152
Beacom, Thomas	Orr, John; Duncan, Alexander; Rien, Samuel; Hammy, George; Dixon, James	10,000	17 Sep 1873	Supervisor [District No. 4]	Elected 3 Sep 1873	B	722-724
Beacom, Thomas	Hammy, George; Orr, John	1,000	19 Sep 1879	Justice of the Peace (Ocean Township)	Elected 3 Sep 1879	1	528-529
Beacom, Thomas	Tupper, G. A.; Roney, J. M.	1,000	5 Dec 1888	Justice of the Peace (Analy Township)	Elected 6 Nov 1888	3	325-326
Beacom, Thomas	Miller, L. W.; Parmeter, John	1,000	7 Jan 1873	Road Master (Ocean Road District)	Appointed 7 Jan 1873 by the Board of Supervisors		
Beacom, Thomas *	Walker, John; Hammy, George	5,000	14 Jan 1889	Notary Public	Appointed 9 Jan 1889 by R. W. Waterman, Governor of California	4	33
Beahan, Dennis *	Pauli, G. T.; Green, John F.	3,000	1 Jul 1863	Trustee (Town of Sonoma)	Elected 18 May 1863	B	50
Beahan, Dennis *	Pauli, G. T.; Ryan, Mortimer	3,000	31 [May] 1862	Trustee (City of Sonoma)	Elected 19 May 1862	B	15
Beam, Jeremiah	Cox, C. B.; Byington, H. W.	1,000	21 Mar 1881	Deputy Assessor	Appointed 21 Mar 1881 by George W. Lewis, Assessor	2	92-93
Beatty, George W. *	Weise, C.; Monahan, P.	1,000	[?] [?] 1892	Constable (Sonoma Township)	Appointed 13 Jul 1892 by the Board of Supervisors, vice C. Weise, resigned	4	203
Beatty, George W. *	Weise, Christian; Monahan, Patrick	1,000	6 Dec 1892	Constable (Sonoma Township)	Elected 8 Nov 1892	4	247
Beaver, Henry	Williamson, William M.; Cook, James G.	1,000	20 Feb 1857	Road Overseer (Santa Rosa Township)	Appointed at the February 1857 session of the Board of Supervisors	A	186-187
Beaver, Henry	Case, James M.; Holman, John H.	5,000	25 Sep 1854	Justice of the Peace (Santa Rosa Township)	Elected 6 Sep 1854, includes oath of office dated 26 Sep 1854	A	40
Bedwell, Franklin	Ormsby, J. S.; Thompson, J. D.	1,000	7 Nov 1856	Road Overseer (Washington Township)	Appointed 7 Nov 1856		
Bedwell, John C.	Bedwell, Thomas J.; Bedwell, Ira	500	8 Dec 1855	Road Overseer (Washington Township, Road District No. 8)	Appointed 8 Nov 1855 by the Board of Supervisors, includes oath of office dated 26 Jan 1856		
Beeson, J. B.	Beeson, Isaac; Moore, Elisha	1,000	29 Nov 1860	Justice of the Peace (Washington Township)	Elected 6 Nov 1860	B	102

Principal Name	Sureties	Amount ($)	Date	Office	Notes	Book	Page(s)
Beeson, J. Brooks	Peckinpah, Rice; Beeson, E. M.	100	[7 Sep 1859]	Road Overseer (Road District No. 19, Washington Township)	Appointed by the Board of Supervisors	B	8
Bell, A. K.	Cunningham, F. Z.; Powell, R.	1,000	1 Dec 1888	Road Overseer (Healdsburg Road District)	Elected 6 Nov 1888	3	292-292
Bell, A. K.	Mead, James A.; Miller, George T.	1,000	9 Feb 1888	Road Overseer (Healdsburg Road District in Mendocino Township)	Appointed 9 Feb 1888	3	221-222
Bell, G. R.	Richardson, Achilles; Hartman, J. W.	1,000	25 Sep 1854	Constable (Santa Rosa Township)	Elected 6 Sep 1854	A	36
Bell, George R.	Duglass, Barton H.; King, William O.	2,000	16 Sep 1851	Constable (Santa Rosa Township)	Elected 3 Sep 1851	A	29
Bell, George R.	Piner, Stephen; McCluer, N. H.	2,000	7 Oct 1853	Constable (Santa Rosa Township)	Elected 7 Sep 1853	A	56
Bell, Henry	Lewis, Seveir; Lewis, H. H.	1,000	8 Oct 1855	Constable (Russian River Township)	Elected 5 Sep 1855	A	147
Bell, J. S.	Hassett, Aaron; Brown, H. K.	2,000	20 Sep 1879	Constable (Mendocino Township)	Elected 3 Sep 1879	1	484-485
Bell, J. S.	Board, William; Hassett, J. D.	1,000	6 Dec 1884	Constable (Mendocino Township)	Elected 4 Nov 1884	2	407-408
Bell, J. S.	Bloom, David; Capell, C. W.; Clack, John W.	2,000	6 Oct 1871	Constable (Mendocino Township)	Elected 6 Sep 1871	C	81
Bell, J. W.	Vaughan, J. H.; Bell, J. S.; Hassett, J. D.; Hassett, Aaron; Bell, A. K.	10,000	15 Apr 1874	Collector (Healdsburg & Pine Flat Road District)	Elected 3 Apr 1874 at a special election held in Mendocino Township	1	20-21
Bell, John W.	Hassett, John D.; Bell, James S.	2,000	15 Sep 1873	Constable (Mendocino Township)	Elected 3 Sep 1873	B	707-708
Bell, William	Vann, P. W.; Godwin, A. C.	5,000	2 Oct 1854	Justice of the Peace (Washington Township)	Elected 6 Sep 1854	A	89
Bell, William S.	Solomon, J.; Sondheimer, M.; Davis, D. S.	3,000	9 Dec 1875	Justice of the Peace (Mendocino Township)	Elected 20 Oct 1875	1	175
Benson, J. H.	Benson, Henry; Tempel, C.	1,000	15 Feb 1887	Justice of the Peace (Vallejo Township)	Elected 2 Nov 1886, witness H. P. Brainerd	3	146-147
Benson, J. H.	Veale, W. R.; Roach, Thomas	1,000	6 Dec 1888	Justice of the Peace (Vallejo Township)	Elected 6 Nov 1888	4	12
Benson, Josiah H.	Wiers, James; Cralle, L. J.	2,000	18 Mar 1872	Constable (Vallejo Township)	Appointed 6 Feb 1872 by the Board of Supervisors, [vice Joab Powell, resigned]	C	168-169
Benson, Josiah H.	Lynch, John; Overton, J. H.	1,000	24 Nov 1884	Justice of the Peace (Vallejo Township)	Elected 4 Nov 1884	2	382-384

Principal Name	Sureties	Amount ($)	Date	Office	Notes	Book	Page(s)
Berry, B. B.	Hudspeth, J. M.; Walker, John; Wilson, William H.; Emerson, Henry	2,000	11 Dec 1869	Justice of the Peace (Analy Township)	Elected 20 Oct 1869	C	18
Berry, B. B.	Crawford, Adam; Emerson, Henry; Gannon, James; Walker, John	2,000	13 Dec 1871	Justice of the Peace (Analy Township)	Elected 18 Oct 1871	C	117-119
Berry, B. B.	Walker, John; Joy, Benjamin	2,000	2 Feb 1874	Road Overseer (Analy Township)	Appointed 7 Jan 1874 by the Board of Supervisors		
Berry, B. B.	Dougherty, John; McChristian, Patrick; Solomon, C.; Walker, John; Dougherty, B. G.	2,000	25 Nov 1873	Justice of the Peace (Analy Township)	Elected 15 Oct 1873	B	737-739
Berry, B. B.	Allen, Otis; Walker, John	1,000	26 Nov 1884	Justice of the Peace (Analy Township)	Elected 4 Nov 1884	2	384-385
Berry, B. B.	Walker, John; Solomon, Charles	1,000	26 Nov 1886	Justice of the Peace (Analy Township)	Elected 2 Nov 1886	3	94-95
Berry, B. B.	Walker, John; Ragle, G. J.; Dougherty, B. G.; Jones, J. S.	1,000	27 Sep 1879	Justice of the Peace (Analy Township)	Elected 3 Sep 1879	1	532-533
Berry, B. B.	Walker, John; Dougherty, John; Seeley, David; Ragle, George J.	1,000	29 Nov 1880	Justice of the Peace (Analy Township)	Elected 2 Nov 1880	2	35-36
Berry, B. B.	Dougherty, John; Brown, John A.; Riddle, David M.; Wilton, Thomas G.	1,000	6 Nov 1877	Justice of the Peace (Analy Township)	Elected 17 Oct 1877	1	369-371
Berry, B. B.	Walker, John; Ragle, George J.	1,000	9 Dec 1882	Justice of the Peace (Analy Township)	Elected 7 Nov 1882	2	259-260
Berry, B. B. *	Dougherty, John; Gannon, James; Dougherty, B. G.; McGuire, C.	2,000	9 Nov 1875	Justice of the Peace (Analy Township)	Elected 20 Oct 1875	1	172
Berry, Baxter B.	Gault, Thomas L.; Moffett, Henry	500	28 May 1862	Justice of the Peace (Annally Township)	Appointed	B	269
Berry, J. H.	Emerson, Henry; McGuire, Cornelius	2,000	20 Sep 1873	Constable (Analy Township)	Elected 3 Sep 1873	B	725-726
Berry, John H.	Lee, William G.; Berry, B. B.	1,000	25 Sep 1854	Constable (Analy Township)	Elected 6 Sep 1854	A	18
Berry, John H.	Joyce, Thomas; Legg, Thomas	2,000	3 Feb 1873	Constable (Analy Township)	Appointed 3 Feb 1873 by the Board of Supervisors	B	618-619
Berry, W. A.	Burris, David; Carriger, N.	2,000	[?] Nov 1873	Justice of the Peace (Sonoma Township)	Elected 15 Oct 1873	B	746-747
Berry, W. A.	Williams, Joseph A.; Oettl, F.	2,000	24 Dec 1875	Justice of the Peace (Sonoma Township)	Elected 20 Oct 1875	1	182
Berry, W. A.	Agnew, S. J.; McDonell, Angus; Monahan, Patrick; Adler, Lewis; Cornelius, G. H. H.; Burris, William	5,000	9 Mar 1876	Notary Public	Appointed & commissioned 28 Jan 1876 by William Irwin, Governor of California	1	214-215
Berry, W. P.	McReynolds, James; Hudspeth, James M.; Orender, Joel	1,000	20 Feb 1866	Constable (Annally Township)	Appointed 12 Feb 1866 by the Board of Supervisors	B	523
Berry, William A.	Townsend, William M. A.; Carriger, Nicholas	2,000	27 Nov 1871	Justice of the Peace [Sonoma Township]	Elected 18 Oct 1871	C	110-111

Principal Name	Sureties	Amount ($)	Date	Office	Notes	Book	Page(s)
Berry, William A.	Stanley, Solomon; McHarvey, Charles	2,000	8 May 1871	Justice of the Peace [Sonoma Township]	Appointed 2 May 1871 by the Board of Supervisors [to fill the vacancy occasioned by the resignation of William Ellis]	C	71
Binns, Joseph D.	Crawford, John; Seaman, Jesse F.	1,000	21 Sep 1861	Constable (Mendocino Township)	Elected 4 Sep 1861	B	170
Birchett, Joseph M.	Johnson, J. J.; Whitman, J. H.	1,000	25 Sep 1861	Constable (Cloverdale Township)	Elected [4 Sep 1861], witness James Ramey	B	172
Bishop, T. C.	Powell, R.; Hall. L. J.; Barnes, E. H.; Hassett, J. D.; Norton, L. A.; Samuels, James	60,000	13 Nov 1884	Sheriff	Elected 4 Nov 1884	2	431-432
Bishop, T. C.	Farmer, E. T.; McReynolds, James; Maddux, John P.; Overton, A. P.; Taylor, John S.	50,000	15 Nov 1884	Tax Collector	Elected 4 Nov 1884	2	429-430
Bishop, T. C.	Norton, L. A.; Barnes, E. H.; Powell, R.; Hall, L. J.; Moffet, John; Hassett, A.; St. Clair, F. C.; Young, M.; Kennedy, G. H.; Hassett, J. D.; Nalley, A. B.; Hendricks, M. C.; Grant, John D.; Stites, A. H.; Samuels, James; Fox, Henry	50,000	25 Nov 1882	Tax Collector	Elected 7 Nov 1882	2	198-201
Bishop, T. C.	Overton, A. P.	10,000	27 May 1884	Tax Collector	Elected 7 Nov 1882, A. P. Overton to replace John Moffat and F. C. St. Clair, both deceased, on original bond dated 25 Nov 1882	2	323-324
Bishop, Tennessee*	Willson, H. M.; Norton, L. A.; Cunningham, F. Z.; Cohn, Samuel; Meyer, S.; Brown, H. K.; Truitt, John R.; Cox, N. H.; Mead, James A.; Truitt, R. K.; Hassett, J. D.; Nalley, A. B.; Powell, R.; Wisecarver, J. R.; Allen, W. T.; Long, Isaac; Grant, John D.; Stites, A. H.; Samuels, James; Barnes, E. H.; Fox, Henry	60,000	17 Nov 1882	Sheriff	Elected 7 Nov 1882	2	202-205
Black, George H.	Crigler, William E.; Gibbens, A. H.	1,000	28 Jan 1885	Road Overseer (Cloverdale Road District)	Appointed 13 Jan 1885 [by the Board of Supervisors]	2	489-490
Black, George H.	Black, William H.; Davis, G. V.	1,500	5 Dec 1882	Road Overseer (Cloverdale Township)	Elected 7 Nov 1882	2	247-248
Blackford, E.	Orr, John; Beacom, Thomas	1,000	2 Nov 1877	Justice of the Peace (Salt Point Township)	Elected 17 Oct 1877	1	371-372
Blackford, Edwin	Call, George W.; Bolden, Samuel	2,000	18 May 1876	Justice of the Peace (Salt Point Township)	Appointed 10 May 1876 [by the Board of Supervisors to fill the vacancy occasioned by the resignation of J. D. Burdick]	1	217
Blackford, Edwin	Schroyer, Aaron; Call, G. W.	1,000	23 Dec 1882	Justice of the Peace (Salt Point Township)	Elected 7 Nov 1882	2	271-273
Blackford, Edwin	Stockhoff, John Henry; Tomasini, G.	1,000	27 Sep 1879	Justice of the Peace (Salt Point Township)	Elected 3 Sep 1879	1	535-536

12

Principal Name	Sureties	Amount ($)	Date	Office	Notes	Book	Page(s)
Blair, John	Shoemake, Omer; Keaton, John J.	1,000	15 Aug 1890	Pound Master (Guerneville Pound District, Redwood Township)	Appointed 5 Aug 1890 by the Board of Supervisors	4	96
Blake, Joseph	Holmes, Calvin; McDonnell, William	200	9 May 1863	Road Master (St. Helena District, St. Helena Township)	Appointed	B	346
Blakeney, J. C.	Leiding, C. F.; Pauli, G. T.	1,000	16 Sep 1862	Constable (Sonoma Township)	Elected 3 Sep 1862, includes oath of office certification dated 16 Sep 1862	B	300
Blakney, Jacob C.	Kamp, Harold Lud.; Pauli, G. T.	1,000	22 Sep 1854	Constable (Sonoma Township)	Elected 6 Sep 1854, includes oath of office dated 22 Sep 1854	A	41
Blaney, A. J.	Chenoweth, John H.; Robinson, David	1,000	16 Dec 1882	Justice of the Peace (Bodega Township)	Elected 7 Nov 1882	2	265-266
Blaney, Andrew J.	Howard, William; Robinson, David	1,000	1 Dec 1886	Justice of the Peace (Bodega Township)	Elected 2 Nov 1886	3	102-103
Blaney, Andrew J.	Chenoweth, J. H.; Brown, William; Taylor, G. C.	1,000	20 Nov 1880	Justice of the Peace (Bodega Township)	Elected 2 Nov 1880	2	33-35
Blaney, Andrew J.	Taylor, Godfrey C.; Chenoweth, John H.	1,000	6 Dec 1884	Justice of the Peace (Bodega Township)	Elected 4 Nov 1884	2	405-406
Blaney, Andrew J.	Markham, Andrew; Chenoweth, John H.	1,000	6 Dec 1888	Justice of the Peace (Bodega Township)	Elected 6 Nov 1888	4	11
Blaney, Andrew J.*	Jones, William; Gaver, A. P.	5,000	11 Dec 1890	Coroner	Appointed 4 Dec 1890 by the Board of Supervisors, vice John Tivnen, deceased	4	161
Blaney, Andrew J.*	Jones, William; Gaver, A. P.	5,000	11 Dec 1890	Coroner	Elected 4 Nov 1890	4	163
Blaney, Andrew J.*	Jones, William; Gaver, A. P.	30,000	11 Dec 1890	Public Administrator	Appointed 4 Dec 1890 by the Board of Supervisors, vice John Tivnen, deceased	4	162
Blaney, Andrew J.*	Jones, William; Gaver, A. P.	30,000	11 Dec 1890	Public Administrator	Elected 4 Nov 1890	4	164
Blaney, John W.	Glynn, F. B.; Howard, William	1,000	17 Feb 1887	Constable (Bodega Township)	Appointed 9 Feb 1887	3	180-181
Blazer, John S.	Willson, H. M.; Mead, James A.; Bell, J. W.; Hassett, Aaron	1,000	15 Jan 1875	Road Overseer ([?])	Appointed 7 Jan 1875 by the Board of Supervisors	1	84-86
Blazer, John S.	Brown, H. K.; Vaughan, J. H.	1,000	25 Feb 1876	Road Overseer (Mendocino Road District)	Appointed [7 Jan 1876] by the Board of Supervisors, witness H. M. Willson, includes oath of office dated 25 Feb 1876	1	195-196

13

Principal Name	Sureties	Amount ($)	Date	Office	Notes	Book	Page(s)
Bledsoe, Anthony C.	Heald, H. G.; McKinnon, A. C.; Yancey, R. J.; McManus, John G.; White, Wilson; Pool, Henry J.; Fannin, Robert C.; Carson, Lindsey; Thompson, John D.; Gordon, Joseph; Potter, William; Gordon, A. J.; Wilkerson, William C.; Capell, B. B.; March, William J.; Aull, A. B.; Dow, S. G.; Willson, H. M.; Cavanagh, John; Campbell, J. A.; Ormsby, John S.	25,000	22 Sep 1855	Sheriff	Elected 5 Sep 1855	A	154-155
Bliss, William D.	Towne, Smith D.; McCune, James N.; Haydon, S. C.	5,000	13 May 1862	Notary Public	Appointed & commissioned 1 May 1862 by Leland Stanford, Governor of California, for the term of two years, includes oath of office dated 13 May 1862	B	263
Bliss, William D.	Huie, J. Thompson; Cavanagh, John; McCune, Alexander; Schmitt, George; Ordway, William	5,000	5 May 1864	Notary Public	Appointed 2 May 1864 by the Governor of California, witness F. D. Colton, includes oath of office dated 5 May 1864	B	454
Bliss, William D.	Denman, E.; Tuttle, B. F.; Case, A. B.; Schmitt, George	5,000	9 Mar 1867	Notary Public	Commissioned 4 Mar 1867 by Frederick F. Low, Governor of California, includes oath of office dated 9 Mar 1867	B	559
Blume, F. G.	Vanderlieth, John; Cerini, John	1,000	23 Sep 1879	Justice of the Peace (Bodega Township)	Elected 3 Sep 1879	1	519-521
Blume, F. G.	Kohle, A.; Vanderlieth, John	2,000	25 Oct 1873	Justice of the Peace (Bodega Township)	Elected 15 Oct 1873	B	740-741
Blume, F. G.	Vanderlieth, John; Caseres, Cero	1,000	26 Oct 1877	Justice of the Peace (Bodega Township)	Elected 17 Oct 1877	1	336-337
Blume, F. G.	Cerini, John; Doran, W. M.	1,000	29 Nov 1882	Justice of the Peace (Bodega Township)	Elected 7 Nov 1882	2	210-212
Blume, F. G.	Goodman, L. S.; Crayne, Daniel	1,000	29 Nov 1886	Justice of the Peace (Bodega Township)	Elected 2 Nov 1886	3	54-55
Blume, F. G.	Roney, J. M.; Doran, W. M.	1,000	3 Dec 1888	Justice of the Peace (Bodega Township)	Elected 6 Nov 1888	3	306-307
Blume, F. G. *	Goodman, L. S.; Stump, James	2,000	[3 Nov 1875]	Justice of the Peace (Bodega Township)	Elected 20 Oct 1875	1	164-165
Blume, Julius	Gwinn, John E.; Hasbrouck, H. B.	1,000	10 Sep 1869	Secretary of the Board of Fire Delegates of the City of Petaluma	Elected 21 Aug 1869 for the term of one year	C	31
Boggs, A. L.	McManus, John G.; Bishop, T. C.; Barron, M. D.	1,000	18 Aug 1860	Constable (Mendocino Township)	Appointed [?] August 1860 by the Board of Supervisors	B	91
Boggs, A. L.	McManus, J. G.; Bloom, David	1,000	9 May 1865	Constable (Mendocino Township)	Appointed, witness Joseph Albertson	B	471
Boggs, A. Leonard	McManus, J. G.; Barron, M. D.; McLaughlin, Hugh	1,000	20 Nov 1860	Constable (Mendocino Township)	Elected 6 Nov 1860	B	94
Boggs, James B.	Price, J. A.; Bright, S. B.; Maxey, J. B.; Boggs, Abiel Leonard	5,000	28 Jan 1856	Notary Public	Appointed	A	116

14

Principal Name	Sureties	Amount ($)	Date	Office	Notes	Book	Page(s)
Boggs, James B.	Griffith, John G.; Shattuck, Frank W.	5,000	30 Sep 1853	Justice of the Peace (Sonoma Township)	Elected 7 Sep 1853	A	73
Boggs, W. M.	Wilson, William L.; Leiding, C. F.	1,000	24 Sep 1861	Justice of the Peace (Sonoma Township)	Elected 4 Sep 1861, witness William Ellis	B	206
Boggs, William M.	Boggs, L. W.; Maupin, R. A.	5,000	26 Apr 1850	Recorder	Elected 1 Apr 1850	A	80
Boggs, William M.	Coleman, Charles; Reynolds, W. J.	2,000	30 Nov 1860	Justice of the Peace (Sonoma Township)	Elected 6 Nov 1860, includes oath of office certification dated 23 Nov 1860	B	118-119
Boileau, Kirk P.	Orr, John; Shaw, George P.	1,000	18 Jan 1887	Road Overseer (Ocean Road District comprising all of Ocean Township)	Appointed 5 Jan 1887	3	177-178
Bond, William H.	Hopper, Thomas; Forsyth, Robert	2,500	12 Nov 1869	Recorder & ex officio Auditor	Elected 1 Sep 1869	C	4
Bond, William H.	Boyce, John F.; Spencer, Thomas; Crane, George L.; Wright, Winfield S. M.	5,000	12 Nov 1869	Recorder	Elected 1 Sep 1869	C	3
Bond, William H.	Boyce, John F.; Marks, B.	2,500	21 Sep 1867	Recorder & ex officio Auditor	Elected 4 Sep 1867	B	590
Bond, William H.	Boyce, John F.; Wright, Winfield S. M.; Marks, B.; Hahman, F. G.; Crane, George L.	5,000	21 Sep 1867	Recorder	Elected 4 Sep 1867	B	592
Bond, William H.	Ames, C. G.; Farmer, E. T.	2,500	23 Sep 1871	Recorder & ex officio Auditor	Elected 6 Sep 1871	C	78-79
Bond, William H.	Wise, Henry; Holmes, H. P.; Abelbeck, F. D.; Willis, T. N.	5,000	23 Sep 1871	Recorder	Elected 6 Sep 1871	C	76-77
Bond, William Hammet	Tupper, G. A.; Wise, Henry; Davis, E. L.; Hahman, F. G.	5,000	9 May 1874	Notary Public	Commissioned 1 May 1874	A	271-272
Bond, William Hammet	Byington, H. W.; Neblett, E.; White, J. M.; Petit, A. P.	5,000	9 May 1876	Notary Public	Commissioned 2 May 1876 by William Irwin, Governor of California	1	211-212
Bonham, B. B.	Davidson, J. E.; Crane, Joel	3,000	12 Oct 1855	Superintendent of Public Instruction	Elected 5 Sep 1855	A	139
Borton, J. W.	Wood, W. B.; Lefebvre, O. M.	1,000	27 Nov 1863	Constable (Analy Township)	Elected [2 Sep 1861], includes oath of office dated 5 Dec 1863	B	401-402
Borton, J. W.	Arthur, C. R.; Kuffel, Isaac	1,000	29 Sep 1862	Constable (Anally Township)	Elected 3 Sep 1862	B	305
Bowles, Joseph M.	Swift, G. P.; Sroufe, John; Delaney, James; Hill, William; Charles, James M.; McCune, James N.; Carder, D.D.; Powell, John	25,000	16 Sep 1861	Sheriff	Elected 4 Sep 1861	B	179-180
Bowles, Joseph M.	Southworth, E. C.; Atterbury, W. B.; Ayers, William, Sr.; Fine, J. H.; Henderson, J. W.; Alberding, Frederic H.; Edwards, Thomas; Brown, S. C.; Roberts, William M.; Hendley, John; Mahoney, W. P.; Ordway, William; Overton, A. P.; Swetland, O.	20,000	25 Sep 1861	Tax Collector	Authorized and empowered by an Act of the California State Legislature entitled "An Act to Provide Revenue for the Support of the Government of this State" approved 17 May 1861 to collect the County and State taxes	B	180-181
Box, Reuben F.	Shattuck, Frank W.; Beasley, J.	5,000	29 Sep 1853	Assessor	Elected 7 Sep 1853	A	24

Principal Name	Sureties	Amount ($)	Date	Office	Notes	Book	Page(s)
Boyce, J. F.	Hendley, John; Farmer, E. T.	1,200	28 Dec 1864	Physician and Surgeon in the Hospital of Sonoma County at Santa Rosa	Awarded a contract by the Board of Supervisors to attend to the indigent sick for the sum of $600 for the term of one year from 1 Jan 1865	B	464-465
Boyce, J. F.*	Noonan, George P.; Farmer, E. T.; Hahman, F. G.; Sebring, Thomas	5,000	30 Dec 1865	Physician & Hospital Steward	Appointed 17 Nov 1865 by the Board of Supervisors for the term of one year commencing 1 Jan 1866	B	515
Boyce, John F.	Atterbury, William B.; Lane, J. J.	2,000	19 Jan 1867	Surgeon of the County Hospital	Appointed 17 Jan 1867	B	556
Boyd, Samuel	McCaughey, James; Doran, W. M.	1,000	29 Nov 1884	Constable (Bodega Township)	Elected 4 Nov 1884	2	404-405
Boyd, William H.	Vance, E. H.; Seymour, L. B.; Millerick, M.; Fisk, John C.	1,000	13 Jan 1875	Road Overseer (Salt Point Township)	Appointed 4 Jan 1875 by the Board of Supervisors	1	83-84
Boyd, William H.	Fletcher, Duncan; Houser, S. R.; Seawell, David R.	1,000	2 Feb 1880	Road Master (Salt Point Road District [No. 2])	Appointed 2 Feb 1880 [by the Board of Supervisors]		
Boyd, William H.	Fisk, John C.; Byrne, James; Richardson, H. A.	1,000	22 Nov 1879	Road Overseer (Salt Point Township Road District No. 2)	Appointed 5 Nov 1879 [by the Board of Supervisors to fill the vacancy caused by the removal of Eliel Ogden from the Township]		
Boyden, C. W.	Potter, Samuel, Jr.; Hartman, William	1,000	2 Oct 1854	Constable (Bodega Township)	Elected 6 Sep 1854	A	34
Brackett, James	Farland, H. L.; Leavy, James	1,000	24 Nov 1860	Constable (Vallejo Township)	Elected 6 Nov 1860	B	101
Brackett, James	Linus, John; Graham, James Ross	1,000	28 Sep 1859	Constable (Vallejo Township)	Elected 7 Sep 1859 for the term of one year	B	44
Bradford, George W.	Bradford, Philip B.	5,000	6 Feb 1857	Public Auctioneer		A	185
Brainerd, H. P.	Hill, William; Dinwiddie, J. L.	5,000	22 Nov 1887	Notary Public	Appointed & commissioned 17 Nov 1887 by R. W. Waterman, Governor of California	3	209-210
Brainerd, H. P.*	Hill, William; Dinwiddie, J. L.	5,000	22 Nov 1889	Notary Public	Appointed & commissioned 20 Nov 1889 by R. W. Waterman, Governor of California	4	68
Brainerd, Henry P.	Dinwiddie, J. L.; Carpenter, L. F.; Roberts, Charles; Haskins, T. J.; Van Doren, J. S.	5,000	3 Nov 1885	Notary Public	Commissioned 30 Oct 1885 [by George Stoneman, Governor of California]	2	504-506
Bransford, Z. W.	McGuire, A.; Munday, B. B.	1,000	1 Oct 1869	Constable (Vallejo Township)	Elected 1 Sep 1869, witness F. W. Shattuck	B	633
Bray, Harold	Coulter, S. T.; Berry, John	100	8 Feb 1858	Road Overseer (Road District No. 8, part of Santa Rosa Township lying south of Santa Rosa Creek)	Appointed 7 Dec 1857 by the Board of Supervisors	A	295
Breitenbach, F.	Weyl, H.; Schocken, S.; Cornelius, G. H. H.; Hope, V.	5,000	2 Feb 1885	Notary Public	Appointed 27 Jan 1885 by George Stoneman, Governor of California	2	463-464
Breitenbach, F.	Clewe, F.; Weyl, Henry	1,000	21 Nov 1884	Justice of the Peace (Sonoma Township)	Elected 4 Nov 1884	2	417-418

16

Principal Name	Sureties	Amount ($)	Date	Office	Notes	Book	Page(s)
Breitenbach, F.	Cornelius, G. H.; Fochetti, Julius	1,000	23 Nov 1882	Justice of the Peace (Sonoma Township)	Elected 7 Nov 1882	2	172-173
Breitenbach, F.	Burris, David; Clewe, F.	1,000	24 Sep 1879	Justice of the Peace (Sonoma Township)	Elected 3 Sep 1879	1	514-515
Breitenbach, F.	Weyl, Henry; Schocken, S.; Litzius, Louis; Duhring, F.	5,000	26 Jan 1887	Notary Public	Appointed & commissioned 20 Jan 1887	3	131-133
Breitenbach, F.	Weyl, Henry; Schocken, S.	5,000	3 Dec 1880	Notary Public	Appointed & commissioned 26 Nov 1880	2	40-41
Breitenbach, F.	Weyl, Henry; Engler, George; Duhring, F.	5,000	8 Dec 1882	Notary Public	Appointed & commissioned 6 Dec 1882 by George C. Perkins, Governor of California	2	255-257
Breitenbach, F.*	Weyl, Henry; Schocken, Solomon	5,000	19 Jan 1891	Notary Public	Commissioned 15 Jan 1891	3	358-359
Breitenbach, F.*	Weyl, Henry; Schocken, Solomon	5,000	19 Jan 1891	Notary Public	Commissioned 15 Jan 1891	4	181
Breitenbach, F.*	Schocken, S.; Cornelius, G. H. H.	5,000	22 Jan 1889	Notary Public	Appointed 14 Jan 1889	4	34
Brewster, John A.	Hendley, John; Maupin, R. A.	5,000	[?] Sep 1851	Justice of the Peace (Sonoma Township)	Elected 3 Sep 1851, includes oath of office dated 17 Sep 1851	A	42-43
Brewster, John A.	Leavenworth, T. M.; Funston, M. H.; Boggs, James B.	5,000	29 Sep 1853	Surveyor	Elected 7 Sep 1853	A	25
Brewster, John A.	Maupin, R. A.; Hendley, John; Brockman, Israel; Boggs, Thomas J.; Carson, Lindsey; Shattuck, D. O.; Randolph, I. N.; Hooker, Joseph; McCord, James H.; Ewing, W. P.; McKamy, James W.; Reynolds, James A.; Hudspeth, James M.; Thompson, DeWitt C.; Hereford , William A.	30,000	30 Nov 1852	Public Administrator	Elected 2 Nov 1852	A	60-61
Brockman, Israel	McNair, John E.; Ellis, John J.; Smith, Robert E.; Harris, Jacob; McKinnon, A. C.; Mize, Merrill; Bishop, T. C.; McMinn, Joseph; Finley, S. J.; Matthews, C. W.; Pyatt, Thomas H.; Quesenbery, Moses; Ingram, John; Gallagher, Jacob M.; Tate, Marion; Case, J. M.; Cameron, H. E.; Stiles, John H.; Branstetter, H. M.; Cockrill, H.; Hoen, Berthold; Campbell, J. A.; Carrillo, Julio; Fulkerson, Richard; Williams, John S.; Myers, D. D.; Hartman, J. William	25,000	14 Jun 1855	Sheriff	Elected [?] Sep 1853, the Board of Supervisors required Brockman to enter into a new bond with additional security 3 May 1855	A	101-102
Brockman, Israel	Kamp, Harold Lud.; Brunner, Christ.	25,000	30 Sep 1853	Sheriff	Elected 7 Sep 1853	A	82-83
Brockman, Israel	Lewis, John; Ames, Thaddeus M.; Carriger, Nicholas; Mason, Edmund	10,000	9 Apr 1850	Sheriff	Elected 1 Apr 1850	A	83
Brockman, Israel	Brunner, Christian; Blakney, J. C.	20,000	9 Jun 1853	Auctioneer	Includes oath of office dated 10 Jun 1853	A	65-66
Brockman, Israel	Cooke, Martin E.; Boggs, William M.	25,000	9 Sep 1851	Sheriff	Elected 3 Sep 1851	A	76-77
Brooks, John S.	Ruoff, John; Bohan, Myles	1,000	1 Dec 1890	Justice of the Peace (Salt Point Township)	Elected 4 Nov 1890	4	146
Brooks, John S.	Walk, Andrew J.; Miller, George	1,000	17 Feb 1873	Justice of the Peace (Salt Point Township)	Appointed 4 Feb 1873 by the Board of Supervisors	B	619-621

Principal Name	Sureties	Amount ($)	Date	Office	Notes	Book	Page(s)
Brooks, John S.	McMale, Richard; Liebig, Frederick	2,000	3 Jan 1874	Justice of the Peace (Salt Point Township)	Elected 15 Oct 1873	B	767-769
Brooks, John S.	Morgan, George W.; Durand, Victor	1,000	30 Nov 1886	Justice of the Peace (Salt Point Township)	Elected 2 Nov 1886	3	82-83
Brooks, John S.	McMale, Richard; Ruoff, John	1,000	4 Dec 1884	Constable (Salt Point Township)	Elected 4 Nov 1884	2	437-438
Brooks, John S.	Ruoff, John; Sposite, Peter	1,000	6 Dec 1888	Justice of the Peace (Salt Point Township)	Elected 6 Nov 1888	4	30
Brooks, John S.	McMale, Richard; Tomasini, G.	1,000	8 Jan 1881	Justice of the Peace (Salt Point Township)	Appointed 5 Jan 1881 [by the Board of Supervisors in place of Howard Foster who failed to qualify]	2	58-59
Brookshire, E.	Holmes, Calvin H.; Holmes, Hen P.	2,000	26 Dec 1863	Justice of the Peace [St. Helena Township)	Elected 21 Oct 1863	B	416
Brookshire, E.	Holmes, C. H.	500	3 Mar 1862	Road Master (Knight's Valley [Road] District)	Appointed, witness T. H. White, includes oath of office dated 3 Mar 1862		
Brookshire, E.	Sensibaugh, George A.; Farmer, E. T.	1,000	5 Nov 1867	Justice of the Peace (St. Helena Township)	Elected 16 Oct 1867	B	572
Brookshire, Elijah	Clark, J. P.; Hahman, F. G.	1,000	29 Jan 1866	Justice of the Peace [St. Helena Township]	Elected 18 Oct 1865	B	539
Brown, A. M.	Gird, Henry S.; Bedwell, William (Bedwell, John C. signed for him)	1,000	1 Oct 1855	Constable (Washington Township)	Elected 5 Sep 1855	A	118
Brown, D. H.	Parks, D. H.; Fowler, James E.	1,000	29 Nov 1860	Justice of the Peace (Bodega Township)	Elected, witnesses L. D. Cockrill & James L. Springer	B	131-132
Brown, George*	Armstrong, J. B.; Lewis, R. E.	1,000	8 Dec 1892	Constable (Redwood Township)	Elected 8 Nov 1892	4	252
Brown, Harry C.*	Allen, S. I.; Jewell, S. R.; Proctor, Thomas A.; Davis, Walter S.	5,000	18 Apr 1889	Notary Public	Appointed 17 Apr 1889	4	52
Brown, Henry R.	Reynolds, W. B.; Emerson, P. N.; Bostwick, N. W.; Allen, O. S.; Hughes, H. M.; Thompson, R. A.; Rippeto, I. M.; Thomson, F. M.; Murphy, Rufus; Thomson, J. W.	5,000	23 Dec 1875	Auctioneer		1	186-187
Brown, James W.	Thompson, Thomas L.; Jackson, Zadok	1,000	5 Nov 1866	Constable (Anally Township)	Appointed	B	554
Brown, John	Roney, J. M.; Fitzpatrick, A.	2,000	1 Dec 1886	Justice of the Peace (Santa Rosa Township)	Elected 2 Nov 1886	3	78-79
Brown, John	Carrillo, Julio; Atterbury, William B.; Hendley, John; Williamson, W. M.; Hood, William	5,000	10 Oct 1861	Notary Public	Commissioned 4 Oct 1861 by John G. Downey, Governor of California	B	221-222
Brown, John	Wright, Joseph; Anderson, William L.; Farmer, J. A.; Davisson, D. D.	2,000	17 Dec 1873	Justice of the Peace (Santa Rosa Township)	Elected 15 Oct 1873	B	736-737
Brown, John	Shea, Cornelius; Fitzpatrick, Andrew	2,000	20 Nov 1884	Justice of the Peace (Santa Rosa Township)	Elected 4 Nov 1884, witness A. D. Laughlin	2	351-352 & 357-358

Principal Name	Sureties	Amount ($)	Date	Office	Notes	Book	Page(s)
Brown, John	Hoen, Berthold; Carrillo, Julio; Green, C.C.; Atterbury, William B.; Gallagher, Jacob M.	5,000	21 Sep 1859	Notary Public	Appointed & commissioned 10 Sep 1859 by the Governor of California for the term of two years	B	11
Brown, John	Tupper, George A.; Abelbeck, F. D.	2,000	23 Dec 1869	Justice of the Peace (Santa Rosa Township)	Elected 20 Oct 1869, includes undated oath of office	C	29
Brown, John	Farmer, E. T.; Morris, W. H.	2,000	23 Nov 1882	Justice of the Peace (Santa Rosa Township)	Elected 7 Nov 1882	2	158-159
Brown, John	Wright, Joseph; Farmer, C. C.	2,000	25 Sep 1879	Justice of the Peace (Santa Rosa Township)	Elected 3 Sep 1879	1	522-523
Brown, John	Roney, J. M.; Noonan, George P.	2,000	26 Nov 1890	Justice of the Peace (Santa Rosa Township)	Elected 4 Nov 1890	4	103
Brown, John	Roney, J. M.; Boyce, J. F.	2,000	26 Oct 1875	Justice of the Peace (Santa Rosa Township)	Elected 20 Oct 1875	1	155-156
Brown, John	Williams, James M.; Label, H.; Wright, W. S. M.	2,000	27 Nov 1880	Justice of the Peace (Santa Rosa Township)	Elected 2 Nov 1880	2	32-33
Brown, John	Davisson, D. D.; Latapie, E.	2,000	27 Oct 1877	Justice of the Peace (Santa Rosa Township)	Elected 17 Oct 1877	1	355-356
Brown, John	Tupper, George A.; Boyce, John F.	2,000	29 Oct 1867	Justice of the Peace (Santa Rosa Township)	Elected 16 Oct 1867	B	563
Brown, John	Hoen, Berthold; Bledsoe, A. C.; Atterbury, William B.; Treadway, Griffin; Hood, William; Carrillo, Julio; Leary, William	5,000	3 Oct 1857	Notary Public	Appointed 26 Sep 1857 by the Governor of California, includes oath of office dated 9 Oct 1857, accepted by W. B. Hagans, Chairman of the Board of Supervisors	A	236-239
Brown, John	Roney, J. M.; Tupper, G. A.	2,000	30 Nov 1888	Justice of the Peace (Santa Rosa Township)	Elected 6 Nov 1888	3	302-303
Brown, John	Roney, J. M.; Abelbeck, F. D.	2,000	6 Nov 1871	Justice of the Peace (Santa Rosa Township)	Elected 18 Oct 1871	C	100
Brown, John	Weis, M.; Tupper, G. A.	2,000	8 Nov 1865	Justice of the Peace (Santa Rosa Township)	Elected 18 Oct 1865	B	503
Brown, John*	Doyle, M.; Ross, H. J.	2,000	28 Nov 1892	Justice of the Peace (Santa Rosa Township)	Elected 8 Nov 1892	4	212
Brown, W. M.	Tighe, Kelly; Gwinn, J. E.; Merker, John; Merritt, John	2,000	8 Apr 1880	Constable (Petaluma Township)	Elected 3 Sep 1879, new bond required as some of the sureties on the first bond applied to the Superior Court of Sonoma County to be released from the bond	1	574-575
Brown, William M.	Prescott, A. A.; Main, William W.	1,000	[?] Feb 1867	Secretary of the Board of Fire Delegates of the City of Petaluma	Elected 13 Nov 1866 to hold office until 1 Aug 1868 or until his successor in office shall have been elected		
Brown, William M.	Pfau, John; Steitz, Henry; Van der Noot, Alexander; Savage, John	2,000	10 May 1878	Constable (Petaluma Township)	Elected 5 Sep 1877, witness J. P. Rodgers	1	426-428

19

Principal Name	Sureties	Amount ($)	Date	Office	Notes	Book	Page(s)
Brown, William M.	Gwinn, John E.; Pfau, John; Fritsch, John; Steitz, Henry	2,000	21 Sep 1877	Constable (Petaluma Township)	Elected 5 Sep 1877, includes a petition dated 23 Apr 1878 by John Fritsch and John E. Gwinn to J. G. Pressley, County Judge, requesting to be released from this bond because of William M. Brown's "excessive use of intoxicating liquors," also several Sonoma County Court papers relating to this matter	1	304-306
Brown, William Melville	Gwinn, John E.; Hess, Fred; Merker, John; Hynes, James	2,000	26 Sep 1879	Constable (Petaluma Township)	Elected 3 Sep 1879	1	530-531
Bruner, Daniel	McReynolds, Jacob, Jr.; White, William H.	2,000	15 Nov 1871	Justice of the Peace (Analy Township)	Elected 18 Oct 1871	C	103
Brush, D. C.	Kier, H.; Shores, Leander	2,000	1 Nov 1875	Justice of the Peace (Cloverdale Township)	Elected 20 Oct 1875	1	157-159
Brush, D. C.	Heald, J. G.; Gerkhardt, H. F.	2,000	17 Dec 1867	Justice of the Peace (Cloverdale Township)	Elected 16 Oct 1867	B	564
Brush, D. C.	Gerkhardt, H. F.; Kier, H.	1,000	19 Sep 1879	Justice of the Peace (Cloverdale Township)	Elected 3 Sep 1879	1	485-486
Brush, D. C.	Kleiser, J. A.; Whitman, J. H.	1,000	25 Nov 1865	Justice of the Peace (Cloverdale Township)	Elected 18 Oct 1865	B	511
Brush, D. C.	Kier, H.; Gerkhardt, H. F.	1,000	27 Oct 1877	Justice of the Peace (Cloverdale Township)	Elected 17 Oct 1877	1	339-340
Brush, D. C.	Kier, Harry; Gerkhardt, H. F.	2,000	28 Dec 1871	Justice of the Peace (Cloverdale Township)	Elected 18 Oct 1871	C	130-131
Brush, D. C.	Kier, Harry; Gerkhardt, H. F.	2,000	3 Jan 1874	Justice of the Peace (Cloverdale Township)	Elected 15 Oct 1873	**B**	763-764
Brush, D. C.	Kier, Henry; Gerkhardt, Fred.	5,000	6 Jul 1874	Notary Public	Appointed	1	24-25
Brush, David C.	Caldwell, William; Brush, W. T.; Stockwell, M. V.; Gerkhardt, H. Frederick; Kier, Harry	5,000	8 Jul 1872	Notary Public	Commissioned 2 Jul 1872 by Newton Booth, Governor of California, includes oath of office dated 18 Jul 1872		
Brush, G. M. *	Cassiday, J. W.; Soldate, Joseph A.	2,000	26 Nov 1890	Constable (Petaluma Township)	Elected 4 Nov 1890	4	105
Brush, George M.	Soldate, J. A.; Fritsch, W. S.	2,000	4 Dec 1888	Constable (Petaluma Township)	Elected 6 Nov 1888	4	1
Brush, George M. *	Soldate, J. A.; Collins, F. M.	1,000	3 Dec 1892	Constable (Petaluma Township)	Elected 8 Nov 1892	4	236
Brush, George W.	Pimm, H.; Cassidy, J. W.; Stratton, W. A. T.; Bryant, C. G.	2,000	30 Nov 1886	Constable (Petaluma Township)	Elected 2 Nov 1886	3	68-69
Brush, William T.	Caldwell, William; Whitman, J. H.	1,000	19 May 1865	Constable (Cloverdale Township)	Appointed 2 May 1865 by the Board of Supervisors, witness T. Goldfish, includes oath of office dated 19 May 1865	B	471
Bryan, F. J.	Spotswood, Andrew; Burns, J. W.	1,000	10 Dec 1888	Constable (Vallejo Township)	Elected 6 Nov 1888	4	17

Principal Name	Sureties	Amount ($)	Date	Office	Notes	Book	Page(s)
Bryant, C. G.	Austin, Amos; Berger, M.	5,000	10 Jan 1870	Auctioneer	Did business along with E. F. Virgin as auctioneers in the City of Petaluma under the name of Bryant & Virgin	C	32
Bryant, D. M.	Helmke, F.; Fisk, J. C.	1,000	30 Nov 1868	Constable (Salt Point Township)	Appointed, witness Thomas Ellis	B	621
Bryant, Daniel S.	Leiding, C. F.; Duhring, F.	500	24 May 1862	Road Overseer (Sonoma Road District No. 2)	Appointed & commissioned May Session 1862 by the Board of Supervisors, includes oath of office dated 24 May 1862		
Bryant, John J.	Hallengren, S. P.; Bryant, W. H.	1,000	28 Feb 1878	Road Overseer (Mendocino Road District No. 2)	Appointed 7 Feb 1878 [by the Board of Supervisors]	1	420-421
Bryant, William C.	Sackett, David A.; Bryant, William S.	1,000	4 Oct 1858	Justice of the Peace (Vallejo Township)	Elected 1 Sep 1858	A	339
Buckland, Marvin	Clark, Charles; Crowley, John W.	1,000	22 Nov 1860	Justice of the Peace (Russian River Township)	Elected 6 Nov 1860, witness G. W. Petray	B	98
Buckles, H. H.	Beaver, Henry; Beasley, Jesse	1,000	8 Oct 1858	Justice of the Peace (Anderson Valley Township)	Elected 1 Sep 1858	A	349
Bullard, William P.	Smith, William R.; Hewett, H. T.	100	1 Dec 1859	Road Overseer (Road District No. 21, Bodega)	Appointed 30 Nov 1859 by the Board of Supervisors	B	61
Burchell, R. M.	Hall, L. J.; Dittemore, J. W.	1,000	14 Nov 1865	Justice of the Peace (Washington Township)	Elected 18 Oct 1865	B	509
Burckhalter, J.	Noonan, George P.; Gray, J. W.	2,000	[6 Feb 1883]	Justice of the Peace (Santa Rosa Township)	Appointed 5 Feb 1883 [by the Board of supervisors, vice Matthew Burnett, resigned]	2	283-284
Burckhalter, J.	McReynolds, John; Fulton, James; Overton, A. P.; McReynolds, James; Johnson, Ewan	5,000	13 Mar 1877	Notary Public	Appointed & commissioned 13 Mar 1877 by William Irwin, Governor of California	1	264-265
Burckhalter, J.	McReynolds, James; Fulton, James; Hood, T. B.; Shane, A.	5,000	14 Mar 1879	Notary Public	Appointed & commissioned 13 Mar 1879 by William Irwin, Governor of California	1	456-457
Burckhalter, J.	Peugh, James A.; Fulton, James; Smith, Henry H.; Shane, Adam; Anderson, James; McReynolds, William; Beam, J.	5,000	20 Apr 1875	Notary Public	Appointed 13 Mar 1875 by R. Pacheco, Governor of California	1	100-102
Burdick, J. D.*	Henry, James; Piver, Leroy	2,000	2 Nov 1875	Justice of the Peace (Salt Point Township)	Elected 20 Oct 1875	1	163-164
Burdick, S. W.*	Rose, J. R.; Walsh, M.	1,000	1 [Dec] 1882	Constable (Vallejo Township)	Elected 7 Nov 1882	2	225-226
Burgess, James F.	Forsyth, B.; Hall, J. W.	1,000	29 Nov 1890	Road Overseer (Santa Rosa Road District, Santa Rosa Township)	Elected 4 Nov 1890	4	148
Burhans, W. D.	Wilson, W. H.; Orr, John	1,000	23 Sep 1862	Justice of the Peace [Analy Township]	Elected 3 Sep 1862	B	284
Burnett, A. G.	Austin, James; Spencer, B. M.; Prindle, William; Warboys, J. W.; Hood, T. B.	15,000	27 Nov 1888	District Attorney	Elected 6 Nov 1888	3	276-278

Principal Name	Sureties	Amount ($)	Date	Office	Notes	Book	Page(s)
Burnett, Albert G.*	Prindle, William; Fisher, A. L.; Hood, T. B.; Warboys, J. W.; Spencer, B. M.	15,000	28 Nov 1890	District Attorney	Elected 4 Nov 1890	4	151
Burnett, J. H.	Parks, D. H.; Estes, H.	1,000	23 Jan 1885	Justice of the Peace (Analy Township)	Appointed 10 Jan 1885 [by the Board of Supervisors]	2	469-470
Burnett, Matt	Talmadge, Samuel; Young, James B.	2,000	20 Nov 1882	Justice of the Peace (Santa Rosa Township)	Elected 7 Nov 1882, includes James B. Young's petition to be released from this bond dated 19 Jan 1883 and Superior Court order declaring the office vacant & releasing James B. Young from the bond dated 2 Feb 1883	2	150-151
Burris, George W.	Hassett, Aaron; Hassett, J. D.	4,000	8 Jan 1873	Road Master (Mendocino Road District)	Appointed 7 Jan 1873 by the Board of Supervisors		
Burriss, Lewis C.	Johnson, R. S.; Hembree, A. T.	2,000	11 Jan 1864	Justice of the Peace (Russian River Township)	Elected 21 Oct 1863	B	411
Burriss, Lewis C.	Smith, Isaac P.; Yates, John W.	1,000	25 Sep 1862	Justice of the Peace (Russian River Township)	Elected 3 Sep 1862	B	287
Burriss, Lewis C.	Mitchell, Robert T.; Yates, J. W.; Pool, Henry J.	3,000	26 May 1860	Road Overseer (Russian River District)	Appointed 10 May 1860 by the Board of Supervisors for the term of one year	B	87
Burrus, G. W.	Powell, R.; Hassett, J. D.	1,000	17 Jan 1885	Road Overseer (Mendocino Township)	Appointed 13 Jan 1885 [by the Board of Supervisors]	2	460-461
Burrus, G. W.	Powell, R.; Hassett, A.	4,000	24 Nov 1882	Road Overseer (Mendocino Township)	Elected 7 Nov 1882	2	229-231
Burrus, G. W.	Hassett, Aaron; Hooten, M. V.	1,000	7 Feb 1878	Road Overseer (Mendocino Road District No. 1)	Appointed 7 Feb 1878 [by the Board of Supervisors]	1	392-393
Burrus, G. W.	Hassett, A.; Powell, R.	1,000	8 Jan 1879	Road Overseer (Mendocino Road District No. 1)	Appointed 7 Jan 1879 [by the Board of Supervisors]		
Burrus, George W.	Powell, Ransom; Hassett, J. D.	4,000	[16 Nov 1880]	Road Overseer (Mendocino Township)	Elected 2 Nov 1880	2	69-70
Burrus, George W.	Hassett, John D.; Hassett, Aaron	4,000	13 Jan 1874	Road Overseer (Mendocino Road District)	Appointed 7 Jan 1874 by the Board of Supervisors		
Burrus, George W.	Hassett, Aaron; Powell, Ransom	1,000	8 Jan 1880	Road Overseer (Road District No. 1, Mendocino Township)	Appointed 7 Jan 1880 [by the Board of Supervisors]		
Bushnell, Amasa	Rambo, Jacob; Dougherty, John; Gannon, James; Ragle, G. J.; Gilliam, M.; Harbine, L.	2,500	14 Dec 1867	Justice of the Peace (Analy Township)	Elected 16 Oct 1867, witness T. M. Ames	B	602-603

Principal Name	Sureties	Amount ($)	Date	Office	Notes	Book	Page(s)
Buster, William A.	Fisher, Fenwick; Ward, W. N.	30,000	[?] Nov 1856	Treasurer	Elected 5 Sep 1855, William Spurr and B. Marks released from original bond	A	164
Buster, William A.	Dorff, William; Reed, E. L.; Buster, F. M.	30,000	13 Dec 1856	Treasurer	Elected 5 Sep 1855, Herald Bray released from original bond	A	178
Buster, William A.	Irwin, N. C.; Taylor, James B.; Merchant, Joel; Stephens, E. J.	30,000	19 Feb 1856	Treasurer	Elected 5 Sep 1855, M. McPeak and Joseph Wright withdrawn from original bond	A	
Buster, William A.	Parker, William; Pyatt, Thomas, H.; Tucker, Preston; Branstetter, Henry M.; Rosenberg, M.; Watts, E. M.; Boyce, J. F.; Crane, James E.; Mynatt, William A.; Grove, David; Pennypacker, Joseph J.	30,000	29 Jan 1856	Treasurer	Elected 5 Sep 1855, witness N. McC. Menefee	A	113
Buster, William A.	Spurr, W. P.; Hendley, John; Davidson, J. E.; Epperly, T. S.; Cook, J. G.; Smith, W.; Caldwell, A.; Talbot, Coleman; Manion, William; Bennett, James N.; Ogan, D. P.; McPeak, Mathew; Riley, Stephen; Valentine, H.; Wright, Joseph; Beardin, Lewis M.; Moore, A. C.; Crane, R.; Means, Thomas J.; Elliott, Emsley	30,000	6 Oct 1855	Treasurer	Elected 5 Sep 1855; John Hendley released as surety 29 Jan 1856	A	107
Buster, William A.	Branstetter, H. M.; Boyce, J. F.; Rosenberg, M.; Crane, James E.; Williams, J. S.; Cockrill, H.; Tucker, Preston; Holman, J. H.; Cook, V. B.; Linville, H. H.	30,000	7 Mar 1856	Treasurer	Elected 5 Sep 1855, supplemental bond, Emsley Elliott and William Manion withdrawn on first bond	A	155-156
Buster, William A.	Branstetter, H. M.; Epperley, Thomas S.; Spurr, W. P; Boyce, J. F.; Rosenberg, M.; Crane, James E.; Williams, J. S.; Collier, Ira; Marks, B.; Cockrill, H.; Tucker, Preston; Ogan, D. P.; Holman, J. H.; Riley, Stephen; Cook, V. B.; Cook, James G.; Linville, H. H.; Myers, D. D.; Grove, David; Bray, Harrel; Irwin, N. C.	30,000	7 Mar 1856	Treasurer	Elected 5 Sep 1855	A	156-157
Butler, R. B.	Cooper, James; Nevill, Joseph N.	6,000	2 Jul 1850	Clerk of the County Court	Elected 1 Apr 1850	A	79
Butler, R. B.	Watkins, Lewis D.; Vasques, Pedro J.	5,000	22 Apr 1851	Notary Public		A	62-63
Butler, R. B.	Cameron, John; Fuller, William M.	5,000	9 Apr 1850	Clerk of the County Court	Elected 1 Apr 1850	A	32
Byrne, James	Carsin, John; Miller, William R.	2,000	23 Jan 1875	Constable (Salt Point Township)	Appointed 5 Oct 1874 by the Board of Supervisors, [vice Theo. Parks, resigned]	1	95-96
Cady, M. K.	Seegelken, E. A.; Roney, J. M.; Howell, O.; Shearer, M. M.; Allen, S. I.; Davis, Walter S.; Brown, Harry C.; Ragsdale, J. W.; Tupper, G. A.; Trowbridge, George T.	15,000	21 Nov 1888	Supervisor (District No. 1)	Elected 6 Nov 1888	3	267-269
Caldwell, C. Y.	Laughlin, J. M.; Warner, J. J.	1,000	3 Dec 1888	Road Overseer (Santa Rosa Road District)	Elected 6 Nov 1888	3	300-302

Principal Name	Sureties	Amount ($)	Date	Office	Notes	Book	Page(s)
Caldwell, Charles Y.	Warner, James; Gale, Otis	1,000	17 Jan 1887	Road Overseer (Santa Rosa Road District comprising all of Santa Rosa Township)	Appointed 15 Jan 1887	3	173-174
Caldwell, John V.	Elliott, A. R.; Brockman, Joseph E.; Dunbar, Alexander; Johnson, C. A.; Miller, G. W.	2,000	26 Jul 1854	Assessor	Appointed 25 Jul 1854 by the Court of Sessions	A	92
Caldwell, William	Brush, William T.; Davis, G. V.	5,000	22 Sep 1886	Notary Public	Appointed 17 Sep 1886 [by Governor Stoneman], witness D. F. Spurr	2	554-555
Caldwell, William	Larison, Samuel; Gibbens, A. H.	1,000	26 Jan 1883	Justice of the Peace [Cloverdale Township]	Appointed 9 Jan 1883 by the Board of Supervisors, [vice C. H. Cooley, failed to qualify], witness D. B. Morgan	2	279-281
Caldwell, William	Brush, William T.; Menihan, Michael	5,000	30 Sep 1884	Notary Public	Commissioned 16 Sep 1884 by George Stoneman, Governor of California	2	332-334
Calhoon, John W.	Thompson, Thomas L.; Ellis, John J.	200	[?] [?] 1861	Road Overseer (District No. 1, Russian River Township)	Appointed 12 Sep 1861 by the Board of Supervisors	B	241
Campbell, George S.*	Graham, J. W.; Hotchkiss, Benoni	1,000	25 Nov 1882	Constable (Russian River Township)	Elected 7 Nov 1882	2	252-254
Campbell, J. T.	Proctor, T. J.; Gray, J. W.	5,000	13 Jan 1882	Notary Public	Appointed 10 Jan 1882 for the term of two years, includes oath of office dated 13 Jan 1882	2	118-120
Campbell, John T.	Warner, James; Bishop, T. C.	5,000	25 May 1885	Notary Public	Appointed & commissioned 22 May 1885 [by George Stoneman, Governor of California]	2	475-476
Campbell, John T.*	Tupper, G. A.; Lewis, G. W.	5,000	26 Dec 1890	Notary Public	Appointed 22 Dec 1890 for the term of 4 years, witness A. D. Laughlin	4	179
Campbell, John Tyler	Caldwell, F. M.; Thompson, Thomas L.; Beam, Jeremiah; Mock, Wesley; Cox, Arthur L.; Fisher, A. L.	5,000	17 Dec 1877	Notary Public	Appointed & commissioned 13 Dec 1877	1	375-377
Campbell, John Tyler	Harris, Jacob; Reed, W. C.; Mills, E. T.; Prindle, William; Ludwig, T. J.	5,000	18 Dec 1879	Notary Public	Appointed & commissioned 13 Dec 1879	1	555-556
Campbell, John Tyler*	Henley, Barclay; Smith, R. Press, Jr.; Roney, J. M.; Farmer, E. T.	5,000	14 Dec 1875	Notary Public	Appointed 10 Dec 1875 by the Governor of California for the term of two years	1	176
Campbell, Peter	Kamp, Harold Lud.; Purcill, Matthew; Gahan, Richard	5,000	[?] Sep 1851	Justice of the Peace	Includes oath of office dated [?] Sep 1851	A	65
Campbell, Peter	Harazthy, Agustine; Vasquez, Pedro J.	5,000	10 May 1859	Notary Public	Appointed 20 Apr 1859 by the Governor of California, includes oath of office dated 10 May 1859	A	377
Campbell, Peter	Brunner, Christian; Cooper, James	5,000	12 Jun 1850	Notary Public	Appointed by the Governor of California, witness R. B. Butler	A	50
Campbell, Peter	Vallejo, M. G.; Ray, John G.; Kamp, Harold Lud.; Morrow, Samuel	10,000	12 Oct 1850	Public Administrator	Appointed by H. A. Green, County Judge and Judge of Probate, includes undated oath of office	A	86
Campbell, Peter	Spriggs, Thomas; McChristian, Patrick	2,000	13 May 1850	Justice of the Peace (Sonoma County)	Elected 9 May 1850, witness J. T. Terrill	A	54-55
Campbell, Peter	Pauli, G. T.; Lewis, John	5,000	13 May 1850	Justice of the Peace (Sonoma County)	Elected 9 May 1850, witness R. B. Butler	A	72

Principal Name	Sureties	Amount ($)	Date	Office	Notes	Book	Page(s)
Campbell, Peter	Vasques, P. J.; Blakney, J. C.	5,000	2 May 1854	Justice of the Peace (Sonoma City & Township)		A	88
Campbell, Peter	Vallejo, M. G.; Hennessy, Daniel; Haraszthy, Gaza	5,000	20 Jun 1861	Notary Public	Appointed 30 May 1861 by the Governor of California for the term of two years, includes oath of office dated 20 Jun 1861	B	168-169
Campbell, Peter	Ray, John G.; Reynolds, William J.	1,000	30 Nov 1859	Justice of the Peace (Sonoma Township)	Elected at a special election on 19 Nov 1859, witness G. L. Wratten	B	60
Canan, W. S.	Heald, Thomas T.; Storey, George; Fike, N.; Brown, A. M.; Grant, John D.; Norton, L. A.; Miller, George; Fitch, William; Clark, Benjamin; Seaman, Jesse F.; Dow, J. G.; Skaggs, Alex; Laymance, Isaac C.; Hassett, John D.; Crawford, John; Powell, R.; Ware, George W.; Peck, John R.; Alexander, Cyrus; Engel, H. S.; Thurgood, William S.	30,000	21 Sep 1861	Public Administrator	Elected 4 Sep 1861	B	213-214
Cannon, J. P.	Roney, J. M.; Hoag, O. H.	1,000	9 Jan 1884	Pound Master (Analy Township, Pound District No. 5)	Appointed 8 Jan 1884 [by the Board of Supervisors]		
Cannon, James P.*	Cannon, L. L.; Knapp, G. W.	1,000	4 Dec 1882	Constable (Analy Township)	Elected 7 Nov 1882	2	260-262
Cannon, John T.	Powers, D. P.; Harris, Jacob	2,000	16 Jan 1875	Justice of the Peace (Santa Rosa Township)	Appointed 6 Feb 1874 by the Board of Supervisors	1	80-81
Cannon, John T.	Hendley, John; Roney, J. M.; Mapes, Ira C.	2,000	9 Feb 1874	Justice of the Peace (Santa Rosa Township)	Appointed 6 Feb 1874 by the Board of Supervisors	1	10-11
Capell, B. B.	Lewis, R. E.; Meredith, Elihu	1,000	25 Jan 1875	Road Overseer [[?]	Appointed 7 Jan 1875 by the Board of Supervisors	1	92-93
Capell, B. B.	Hudson, Thomas W.; Proctor, Ira	1,000	4 Mar 1876	Road Overseer (Mill Creek Road District)	Appointed 10 Jan 1876 [by the Board of Supervisors]	1	209-210
Capell, John J.	Wilkerson, William C.; Gordon, Andrew J.	1,000	22 Sep 1857	Constable (Mendocino Township)	Elected 2 Sep 1857, accepted by W. B. Hagans, Chairman of the Board of Supervisors	A	290-291
Carder, D. D.	Wickersham, I. G.; Maynard, F. T.	5,000	25 Aug 1866	Notary Public	Commissioned 20 Aug 1866 by F. F. Low, Governor of California, witness Frank W. Shattuck, includes oath of office dated 25 Aug 1866	B	551
Carder, D. D.	Bradley, George L.; Dodge, L. C.	5,000	29 Feb 1860	Notary Public	Appointed 23 Feb 1860 by John G. Downey, Governor of California, for a term of two years, includes oath of office dated 29 Feb 1860	B	74
Carder, D. D.	McCune, James N.; Denman, Ezekiel	5,000	5 May 1862	Notary Public	Appointed & commissioned 1 May 1862 by Leland Stanford, Governor of California, for the term of two years, includes oath of office dated 5 May 1862	B	262
Carder, D. D.	Doyle, M.; Pickett, J. L.; May, S.; Wickersham, I. G.; Newman, B.; Towne, Smith D.; Ellis, J. J.; Potter, Samuel, Jr.	5,000	6 Apr 1858	Justice of the Peace (Petaluma Township)	Elected 3 Apr 1858 at a special election for the balance of the term up to 1 Oct 1858	A	306

25

Principal Name	Sureties	Amount ($)	Date	Office	Notes	Book	Page(s)
Carder, D. D.*	Bowles, J. M.; Wickersham, I. G.	5,000	19 Aug 1864	Notary Public	Appointed by F. F. Low, Governor of California, includes oath of office dated 19 Aug 1864	B	458
Carder, D.D.	Bowles, J. M.; Denman, E.	5,000	9 Jul 1874	Notary Public	Appointed & commissioned 7 Jul 1874 by Newton Booth, Governor of California	1	26
Cargen, James B.	Fisk, J. C.; Fisk, A. J.	1,000	28 May 1873	Constable (Salt Point Township)	Appointed 7 Apr 1873 [by the Board of Supervisors]		
Carleton, J. M.	Haupt, Charles; O'Neal, David	1,000	12 Dec 1888	Road Overseer (Salt Point Road District)	Elected 6 Nov 1888	4	29
Carlton, Austin	Mayfield, B. F.	200	1 Nov 1862	Road Master (District No. 2, Annally Township)	Elected 3 Sep 1862	B	330
Carlton, Columbus	Pyatt, Thomas H.; Curtis, Tyler	100	2 Apr 1859	Road Overseer (Road District No. 11 in Bodega Township)	Appointed March Session 1859 by the Board of Supervisors	A	372
Carothers, James H.	Huie, J. Thompson; Foreman, W. H.	2,000	4 May 1865	Constable (Petaluma Township)	Appointed 3 May 1865 by the Board of Supervisors, vice C. B. Rice, failed to qualify, witness William D. Bliss	B	470
Carpenter, W. W.	Cowen, Philip; Whitney, A. P.; Hartman, J. W.	600	2 Dec 1863	Surgeon & Hospital Steward (Branch Hospital, Petaluma)	Appointed, witness F. D. Colton	B	399
Carr, H. D.	McChristian, James; Ruch, Michael; Morris, Joseph H. P.; Gannon, James	1,000	29 Nov 1880	Justice of the Peace (Analy Township)	Elected 2 Nov 1880	2	38-40
Carroll, Patrick	Harris, Richard; Bernhard, Isaac	1,000	17 Jan 1880	Road Overseer (Annally Township No. 1)	Appointed 7 Jan 1880 [by the Board of Supervisors]		
Carroll, Patrick	Tighe, Kelly; Hynes, James	1,000	18 Jan 1879	Road Overseer (Annally Road District No. 1)	Appointed 8 Jan 1879 [by the Board of Supervisors]		
Carroll, Patrick	Noonan, George P.; Mullally, Patrick	1,000	21 Feb 1877	Road Overseer (Analy Road District No. 1)	Appointed 9 Feb 1877 [by the Board of Supervisors]	1	248-249
Carroll, Patrick	Mullally, Patrick; Hoag, O. H.	1,000	4 Mar 1878	Road Master (Analy Township, District No. 1)	Appointed 7 Feb 1878 [by the Board of Supervisors]	1	415-416
Carson, Robert W.	Godwin, A. C.; Harrison, Richard; Grayson, Daniel	5,000	2 Oct 1854	Justice of the Peace (Washington Township)	Elected 6 Sep 1854	A	87
Carter, Seth	Potter, Samuel Jr.; Thurston, J. M.	5,000	2 Oct 1854	Justice of the Peace (Bodega Township)	Elected 6 Sep 1854	A	33
Carter, W. F.	Barnes, E. H.; Petray, R. A.	1,000	29 Sep 1865	Constable (Russian River Township)	Elected 6 Sep 1865	B	494
Carter, William F.	Laughlin, James H.; Philbee, James	1,000	1 Dec 1856	Constable (Russian River Township)	Elected 4 Nov 1856	A	162
Carter, William F.	Smith, Alexander H.; Mynatt, William A.	1,000	1 Oct 1855	Constable (Russian River Township)	Elected 5 Sep 1855	A	144
Carter, William F.	Smith, A. H.; Campbell, J. A.	1,000	21 Sep 1863	Constable (Russian River Township)	Elected 2 Sep 1863	B	366

Principal Name	Sureties	Amount ($)	Date	Office	Notes	Book	Page(s)
Carter, William F.	Thompson, John D.; Rosenberg, M. J.	1,000	25 Sep 1862	Constable (Russian River Township)	Elected 3 Sep 1862	B	308
Caseres, Cero	Goodman, L. S.; McCaughey, J.	1,000	22 Sep 1879	Constable (Bodega Township)	Elected 3 Sep 1879	1	518-519
Caseres, Cero F.*	Goodman, L. S.; McCrea, John	1,000	28 Nov 1890	Constable (Bodega Township)	Elected 4 Nov 1890	4	114
Caseres, Cero*	Goodman, L. S.; McCaughey, James	1,000	23 Nov 1882	Constable (Bodega Township)	Elected 7 Nov 1882	2	183-184
Caseres, Cero*	Furlong, James; Goodman, L. S.	1,000	3 Dec 1892	Constable (Bodega Township)	Elected 8 Nov 1892	4	233
Caseres, Cyrus	McCaughey, James; Goodman, L. S.	2,000	21 Sep 1877	Constable (Bodega Township)	Elected 5 Sep 1877	1	315-316
Casey, L. J.	Worth, Claiborne; Menihan, M.	1,000	24 Nov 1884	Constable (Cloverdale Township)	Elected 4 Nov 1884	2	376-377
Casey, L. J.	Sink, W. D.; Brush, William T.	1,000	30 Nov 1886	Constable (Cloverdale Township)	Elected 2 Nov 1886	3	74-75
Cash, Job	Ogan, D. P. V.; McReynolds, John	200	18 Sep 1862	Road Master (Road District No. 1, Annally District)	Appointed 11 Sep 1862 by the Board of Supervisors, includes oath of office dated 18 Sep 1862	B	322
Cassiday, Samuel	Brackett, Joshua S.; Stockdale, Hugh	5,000	22 Nov 1887	Notary Public	Appointed & commissioned 17 Nov 1887 by R. W. Waterman, Governor of California, includes oath of office dated 22 Nov 1887	3	207-208
Cassiday, Samuel*	Campbell, Joseph; Jones, William	5,000	4 Dec 1889	Notary Public	Appointed & commissioned 30 Nov 1889 by R. W. Waterman, Governor of California	3	339-341
Cavanagh, John	Derby, A. B.; Berger, M.	2,000	1 Nov 1877	Justice of the Peace (Petaluma Township)	Elected 17 Oct 1877	1	335-336
Cavanagh, John	Payran, Stephen; Lodge, J. D.	2,000	11 Nov 1871	Justice of the Peace (Petaluma Township)	Elected 18 Oct 1871	C	108-109
Cavanagh, John	Towne, S. D.; Erwin, N.	5,000	15 Aug 1879	Notary Public	Commissioned 13 Aug 1879 by William Irwin, Governor of California, for the term of two years, witness J. P. Rodgers, includes oath of office dated 15 Aug 1879	1	465-467
Cavanagh, John	Lodge, J. D.; Noel, James	2,000	15 Nov 1873	Justice of the Peace (Petaluma Township)	Elected 15 Oct 1873	B	750-751
Cavanagh, John	Towne, S. D.; Van der Noot, Joseph	5,000	17 Aug 1877	Notary Public	Commissioned 13 Aug 1877 by William Irwin, Governor of California, includes oath of office dated 17 Aug 1877	1	273-275
Cavanagh, John	Lodge, J. D.; Commins, Edward	2,000	18 Sep 1861	Constable (Petaluma Township)	Elected 4 Sep 1861, witness L. C. Reyburn	B	216-217
Cavanagh, John	Lodge, J. D.; Derby, A. B.	2,000	18 Sep 1862	Constable (Petaluma Township)	Elected 3 Sep 1862	B	304
Cavanagh, John	Lodge, J. D.; Derby, A. B.	2,000	18 Sep 1879	Justice of the Peace (Petaluma Township)	Elected 3 Sep 1879	1	480-481

Principal Name	Sureties	Amount ($)	Date	Office	Notes	Book	Page(s)
Cavanagh, John	Derby, A. B.; Lougee, F. W.	2,000	19 Sep 1863	Constable (Petaluma Township)	Elected 2 Sep 1863	B	360
Cavanagh, John	Brackett, J. S.; Cronin, P.	5,000	22 Sep 1887	Notary Public	Appointed & commissioned 19 Sep 1887, includes oath of office dated 22 Sep 1887	3	197-198
Cavanagh, John	Henley, William; Payran, Stephen; Bradley, G. L.	2,000	23 Sep 1859	Constable (Petaluma Township)	Elected 7 Sep 1859, witness L. C. Reyburn	B	31
Cavanagh, John	Lodge, J. D.; Gerckens, H.	5,000	27 Aug 1883	Notary Public	Appointed 21 Aug 1883	2	298-299
Cavanagh, John	Biggins, James; Lodge, J. D.	2,000	30 Oct 1875	Justice of the Peace (Petaluma Township)	Elected 20 Oct 1875	1	159-160
Cavanagh, John	Lodge, J. D.; Derby, A. B.	5,000	4 Sep 1885	Notary Public	Appointed & commissioned 31 Aug 1885 by George Stoneman, Governor of California, witness J. P. Rodgers	1	599-600
Cavanagh, John*	Lodge, J. D.; Ward, Porter	5,000	24 Sep 1889	Notary Public	Appointed & commissioned 21 Sep 1889 by R. W. Waterman, Governor of California, witness Frank K. Lippitt, includes oath of office dated 24 Sep 1889	3	334-337
Cavanagh, John*	Case, A. B.; Sroufe, John	2,000	4 Nov 1865	Justice of the Peace (Petaluma Township)	Elected 18 Oct 1865	B	502
Chadbourn, Howard	Henderson, J. W.; Whitman, J. H.	1,000	25 [Sep] 1862	Constable (Cloverdale Township)	Elected [3 Sep 1862], witness J. Ramey	B	310
Chambers, A. K.	Fulkerson, John; Healey, W. E.; Harris, Jacob	2,000	30 Nov 1888	Constable (Santa Rosa Township)	Elected 6 Nov 1888	3	283-285
Chambers, T. K	Case, A. B.; Derby, A. B.	1,000	10 Apr 1862	Justice of the Peace (Vallejo Township)	Appointed 7 Apr 1862 by the Board of Supervisors	B	257
Chambers, T. K.	Peter, Jordan; Rohrer, Cyrus	1,000	19 Sep 1861	Justice of the Peace [Vallejo Township]	Elected 4 Sep 1861, witness J. Chandler; Cyrus Rohrer was released from all liability on the bond 7 Mar 1862. T. K. Chambers failed to give good and ample surity within ten days. County Judge William Churchman declared T. K. Chambers' office to be vacant.	B	202
Chandler, Josiah	Lawler, P.; Bowles, J. M.; Fairbanks, H. T.	2,000	1 Nov 1875	Justice of the Peace (Petaluma Township)	Elected 20 Oct 1875	1	169
Chandler, Josiah	Speers, William B.; Lamb, H.	2,000	1 Oct 1862	Justice of the Peace (Petaluma Township)	Elected 3 Sep 1862, witness D. D. Carder, includes oath of office dated 1 Oct 1862	B	291
Chandler, Josiah	Hunt, Manassah; Parker, Freeman	2,000	25 Sep 1861	Justice of the Peace [Petaluma Township]	Elected 4 Sep 1861, witness L. C. Reyburn	B	209
Chandler, Josiah	Hunt, Manasah; Doyle, M.	2,000	3 Dec 1867	Justice of the Peace (Petaluma Township)	Elected 16 Oct 1867, witness J. Cavanagh	B	598
Chapman, A. P.	Carson, Lindsey; Slusser, Levi S. B.	2,000	27 Nov 1852	Constable (Russian River Township)	Elected 2 Nov 1852, includes oath of office dated 27 Nov 1852	A	73-74
Charles, E. R.	Chapman, T. M.; Higgins, A.	2,000	13 Jul 1880	Road Overseer (Vallejo Road District South)	Appointed 10 Jul 1880 [by the Board of Supervisors]		

28

Principal Name	Sureties	Amount ($)	Date	Office	Notes	Book	Page(s)
Charles, J. M.	Charles, E. R.; Hasbrouck, H. B.; Fritsch, John; Wiswell, J. A.; Veale, W. R.; Green, G. D.	10,000	17 Sep 1877	Supervisor (District No. 2)	Elected 5 Sep 1877	1	317-318
Cheney, J. M.	Clewe, F.; Weyl, Henry	1,000	29 Nov 1890	Justice of the Peace (Sonoma Township)	Elected 4 Nov 1890	4	143
Cheney, J. M.	Clewe, F.; Weyl, H.	1,000	3 Dec 1888	Justice of the Peace (Sonoma Township)	Elected 6 Nov 1888	4	13
Cheney, J. M.*	Weyl, H.; Clewe, F.	1,000	5 Dec 1892	Justice of the Peace (Sonoma Township)	Elected 8 Nov 1892	4	227
Chenoweth, J. J. H.	Craig, D. N.; Chenoweth, John H.	1,000	1 Dec 1888	Constable (Bodega Township)	Elected 6 Nov 1888	3	297-298
Churchman, William	Peugh, James A.; Downs, Vernon; Meacham, Alonzo; Gray, James W.; Heisel, Paul	5,000	16 Mar 1872		Appointed 8 Mar 1872 by the Governor of California, includes oath of office dated 20 Mar 1872 and a petition dated 12 Sep 1872 by A. Meacham and P. Heisel to A. P. Overton, County Judge, requesting to be released from this bond because of William Churchman's "addiction to dissolute habits"	C	164-168
Churchman, William	Bassett, H.; Zartman, William; Reed, J. F.; Harris, G.; Hunt, Charles	5,000	2 May 1855	Notary Public	Appointed and commissioned 28 Apr 1855 by the Governor of California, witness E. F. Martin, includes oath of office dated 2 May 1855	A	98
Churchman, William	Smith, H. H.; Bassett, H.; Zartman, William	5,000	29 Sep 1854	Justice of the Peace (Petaluma Township)	Elected 6 Sep 1854, witness William Tibbetts	A	16
Clark, J. W.	Bloom, D.; Meyer, S.; Rosenberg, W.; Bell, J. S.	2,000	6 Oct 1871	Constable (Mendocino Township)	Elected 6 Sep 1871	C	82
Clark, John W.	Bloom, David; Poor, F. G.	1,000	26 Sep 1865	Constable (Mendocino Township)	Elected 6 Sep 1865, witness A. L. Boggs	B	474
Clark, John W.	Haigh, John B.; Miller, Thomas B.; Barnes, E. H.; Clark, Benjamin	5,000	3 Aug 1874	Assessor (Healdsburg & Pine Flat Road District)	Appointed & commissioned 27 Jul 1874 by Newton Booth, Governor of California	1	57-59
Clanton, D. C.	Lueberke, Henry; Leopold, Henry	1,000	30 Nov 1886	Constable (Russian River Township)	Elected 2 Nov 1886	3	64-65
Clanton, D. C.	Laughlin, L.; Bonnel, B. F.	1,000	5 Feb 1885	Pound Master (Pound District No. 4)	Appointed 2 Feb 1885 [by the Board of Supervisors]		
Clanton, David C.	Bruner, Phillip; McCulough, Michial	1,000	22 Nov 1884	Constable (Russian River Township)	Elected 4 Nov 1884, witness T. J. Jones	2	423-425
Clark, A. N.	Black, W. A.; Parker, Isaac	1,000	6 Dec 1890	Road Overseer (Skaggs Springs Road District, Mendocino Township)	Elected 4 Nov 1890	4	158
Clark, Benjamin	Berber, W. H.; Brooks, William; Barth, Adam H.	1,000	17 Jan 1885	Road Overseer (Russian River Road District)	Appointed 13 Jan 1885 [by the Board of Supervisors]	2	451-452
Clark, Benjamin	Story, S. C.; Laughlin, James H.; Gray, J. W.; Brown, Harry C.; Brown, Fred T.; Kennedy, A. E.; Lindsay, J. J.; Bell, Henry; Cunningham, Z. H.	15,000	5 Dec 1888	Supervisor (District No. 3)	Elected 6 Nov 1888	4	14

Principal Name	Sureties	Amount ($)	Date	Office	Notes	Book	Page(s)
Clark, Cardwell	Laymance, L. C.; Skaggs, A.	1,000	15 Sep 1862	Justice of the Peace [Mendocino Township]	Elected 3 Sep 1862	B	278
Clark, Cardwell	Bice, Cornelius; Laymance, J. C.	1,000	26 Sep 1861	Justice of the Peace [Mendocino Township]	Elected 4 Sep 1861	B	218
Clark, James P.	Marks, B.; Adams, John; Grant, John D.; Manion, William; Smyth, Thomas U.; Arnold, G. W.; Wise, M.; Taylor, John S.; Goldfish, B.; Hahman, F. G.; Wright, Joseph; Holmes, C. H.; Hendley, John; Lawton, John W.; Boyce, J. F.; Matthews, C. W.; Farmer, E. T.; March, W. I.; May, J. J.; Bedwell, J. C.; Pool, Henry J.; Aull, A. B.; McManus, J. G.; Hassett, J. D.; Forrister, A. J.; Barnes, E. H.; Hudspeth, J. M.; Wright, Winfield S. M.; Wise, Henry; Ellis, John J.; Hunt, Charles; Commins, Edward	25,000	[?] Jan 1864	Sheriff	Elected 2 Sep 1863	B	424-426
Clark, James P.	Marks, B.; Adams, John; Grant, John D.; Manion, William; Smyth, Thomas U.; Arnold, G. W.; Wise, M.; Taylor, John S.; Goldfish, B.; Hahman, F. G.; Wright, Joseph; Holmes, C. H.; Hendley, John; Lawton, John W.; Boyce, J. F.; Matthews, C. W.; Farmer, E. T.; March, W. I.; May, J. J.; Bedwell, J. C.; Pool, Henry J.; McManus, J. G.; Hassett, J. D.; Forrister, A. J.; Barnes, E. H.; Hudspeth, J. M.; Wright, Winfield S. M.; Wise, Henry; Ellis, John J.; Hunt, Charles; Aull, A. B.	25,000	[?] Jan 1864	Tax Collector	Elected 2 Sep 1863	B	427-429
Clark, James P.	Hendley, John; Taylor, John S.; Farmer, E. T.; Wise, Henry; Lawton, John W.; Marks, B.; Morris, A.; Brown, Daniel; Towne, Smith D.; Doyle, M.; Huie, J. T.; Conrad, S.; Cowen, Philip; Hopper, Thomas; Edwards, Thomas; Tempel, C.; Hardin, James A.; McPherson, C. P.; Ellis, John J.; Potter, Samuel; Wright, W. S. M.; Hudson, Martin; Thompson, Thomas L.; Weiss, M.	25,000	[7 Feb 1866]	Sheriff	Elected 6 Sep 1865	B	532-533
Clark, James P.	Hendley, John; Taylor, John S.; Farmer, E. T.; Wise, Henry; Lawton, John W.; Marks, B.; Morris, A.; Brown, Daniel; Towne, Smith D.; Doyle, M.; Huie, J. T.; Conrad, S.; Cowen, Philip; Hopper, Thomas; Edwards, Thomas; Tempel, C.; Hardin, James A.; McPherson, C. P.; Ellis, John J.; Potter, Samuel; Wright, W. S. M.; Hudson, Martin; Thompson, Thomas L.; Weiss, M.	25,000	[7 Feb 1866]	Sheriff & ex officio Tax Collector	Elected 6 Sep 1865	B	534-535
Clark, James P.	Linville, H. H.; Barnes, Mike	200	7 Nov 1862	Road Master (District No. 2, Santa Rosa Township)	Appointed 7 Nov 1862 by the Board of Supervisors, includes oath of office dated 7 Nov 1862	B	325

Principal Name	Sureties	Amount ($)	Date	Office	Notes	Book	Page(s)
Clark, James P.	Barnes, M.; Pyatt, Thomas H.	500	9 Apr 1862	Road Overseer (Road District No. 2, Santa Rosa Township)	Appointed		
Clark, William S.	Steadman, Amos; McIntire, Horatio	200	30 Nov 1861	Road Overseer (District No. 2, Russian River Township)	Appointed, includes oath of office dated 2 Dec 1861	B	246
Clark, William S.	Kennedy, James; Merideth, Elihu	200	7 Nov 1862	Road Master (District No. 2, Russian River Township)	Appointed, includes oath of office dated 7 Nov 1862	B	327
Clarke, Asahel	Pettus, James E.; McClure, William A.	10,000	[4 Oct 1853]	District Attorney (Sonoma County)	Elected, witness R. W. Pettus	A	38
Clarke, James	Tighe, Kelly; Little, James; Wiers, James; O'Reilly, Martin	4,000	22 Nov 1880	Road Overseer (District No. 2, Vallejo Township)	Elected 2 Nov 1880	2	61-62
Clarke, James	Lynch, John; Dunnigan, George J.	1,000	23 Feb 1876	Road Overseer (Vallejo Township, northern portion)	Appointed 11 Feb 1876 by the Board of Supervisors	1	206-207
Claypool, Jeremiah	Carter, L.; Davis, E. L.; Lane, J. J.	1,500	2 Oct 1865	Road Master (Road District No. 2, Santa Rosa Township)	Elected 6 Sep 1865	B	478
Claypool, Jeremiah*	Farmer, E. T.; Carter, L.	[?]	29 Nov 1864	Road Master (District No. 2, Santa Rosa Township)	Elected 8 Nov 1864, includes oath of office dated 29 Nov 1864	B	468-469
Cleveland, F. S.	Herbert, Alexander; Burns, Charles F.	1,000	8 Dec 1888	Justice of the Peace (Ocean Township)	Elected 6 Nov 1888	4	26
Clover, M.	Heald, Thomas T.; Murphy, Rufus	2,000	3 Dec 1875	Justice of the Peace (Redwood Township)	Elected 20 Oct 1875	1	174
Clover, Milton	Bagley, J. W.; Beaver, Henry	2,000	7 Jan 1874	Justice of the Peace (Redwood Township)	Elected 15 Oct 1873	B	761-763
Clyman, James	Boggs, L. W.; Hendley, John	5,000	14 Sep 1851	Assessor	Elected 3 Sep 1851	A	72
Cobb, O. O.*	Joost, Jacob; Wescott, O.	1,000	4 Oct 1892	Justice of the Peace (Redwood Township)	Appointed 4 Oct 1892 by the Board of Supervisors, vice H. L. Bagley, resigned	4	205
Cochran, A. E.	Barnes, E. H.; Warfield, R. H.	5,000	15 Jan 1886	Notary Public	Appointed 12 Jan 1886 [by George Stoneman, Governor of California], witness W. B. Reynolds	2	518-520
Cochran, A. E.	Brown, H. K.; Barnes, E. H.	5,000	17 Jan 1884	Notary Public	Appointed & commissioned 11 Jan 1884 by George Stoneman, Governor of California	2	316-317
Cochran, Warren W.	Beardin, Lewis M.; Beeson, William S.	1,000	5 Dec 1860	Constable (Washington Township)	Elected 6 Nov 1860	B	123
Cockrill, B. T.	McGregor, F. D.; Carroll, Patrick	1,000	8 Dec 1890	Justice of the Peace (Analy Township)	Elected 4 Nov 1890	4	157

Principal Name	Sureties	Amount ($)	Date	Office	Notes	Book	Page(s)
Cockrill, Bruce T.	McGregor, F. D.; Shelton, A. C.	1,000	12 Dec 1888	Justice of the Peace (Analy Township)	Elected 6 Nov 1888	4	24
Cockrill, Bruce T.	Carroll, Patrick; Cannon, L. L.	1,000	4 Dec 1886	Justice of the Peace (Analy Township)	Elected 2 Nov 1886	3	96-97
Cockrill, Bruce T.	Parks, D. H.; Carroll, Patrick	1,000	8 Dec 1888	Justice of the Peace (Analy Township)	Elected 6 Nov 1888	4	21
Cockrill, Bruce T.*	Carroll, P.; Parks, D. H.	5,000	[?] May 1888	Notary Public	Appointed 30 Apr 1888 by R. W. Waterman, Governor of California	3	241-243
Cockrill, Bruce T.*	Parks, D. H.; Carroll, P.	5,000	27 Jun 1890	Notary Public	Appointed 21 Jun 1890	4	90
Cockrill, Bruce T.*	Carroll, P.; Easman, Peter	1,000	8 Dec 1892	Justice of the Peace (Analy Township)	Elected 8 Nov 1892	4	258
Cockrill, Harrison	Moore, A. C.; Beaver, Henry; Boyce, J. F.; Crane, James E.	1,000	25 Sep 1855	Constable (Santa Rosa Township)	Elected 5 Sep 1855	A	145
Cockrill, Harrison	Gregg, G. T., Beaver, Henry, Cockrill, A., Ward, N.	1,000	29 Nov 1856	Constable (Santa Rosa Township)	Elected 4 Nov 1856	A	169
Cockrill, L. D.	Hoag, Jared C.; Pyatt, Thomas H.; Farmer, C. C.; Farmer, E. T.	5,000	17 Mar 1866	Coroner	Elected 6 Sep 1865	B	543
Cockrill, L. D.	Loucks, A. H.; McReynolds, James	1,000	18 Jul 1885	Justice of the Peace (Analy Township)	Appointed 9 Jul 1885 [by the Board of Supervisors, vice John H. Burnett, resigned]	2	482-483
Cockrill, L. D.	Hall, Charles T.; Lefebvre, O. M.; Hanratty, Patrick; Smith, William A.	2,000	26 Nov 1873	Justice of the Peace (Analy Township)	Elected 15 Oct 1873	B	754-755
Cockrill, L. D.	McReynolds, Jacob; Knapp, A. H.	1,000	26 Sep 1879	Justice of the Peace (Analy Township)	Elected 3 Sep 1879	1	
Cockrill, L. D.	Hall, William P.; Lefebvre, O. M.	1,000	27 Oct 1877	Justice of the Peace (Analy Township)	Elected 17 Oct 1877	1	361-363
Cockrill, L. D.	Lefebvre, O. M.; Knapp, G. W.	1,000	28 Nov 1882	Justice of the Peace (Analy Township)	Elected 7 Nov 1882	2	245-246
Cockrill, L. D.	Bradshaw, Isaac A.; Green, E. L.	1,000	3 Oct 1859	Justice of the Peace (Analy Township)	Elected 7 Sep 1859 for the term of one year	B	33
Cockrill, L. D.	Stewart, Charles; Lefebvre, O. M.; Oliver, John S.	2,000	30 Oct 1875	Justice of the Peace (Analy Township)	Elected 20 Oct 1875	1	161-162
Cockrill, L. D.	Williamson, William M.; Hood, Thomas B.	1,000	4 Oct 1858	Justice of the Peace (Annally Township)	Elected 1 Sep 1858	A	328
Cockrill, Larkin D.	Crane, G. L.; Green, C. C.	1,000	3 Dec 1860	Justice of the Peace (Analy Township)	Elected 6 Nov 1860	B	127
Cockrill, Larkin D.	Singley, James; Hagans, W. B.; Bledsoe, A. C.; Hoen, B.; Hendley, John; Williamson, Thomas D.; Ross, William; McReynolds, William	5,000	5 Oct 1857	Justice of the Peace (Annally Township)	Elected 2 Sep 1857, accepted by W. B. Hagans, Chairman of the Board of Supervisors	A	280-281
Coffman, J. T.	Samuels, James; Rosenberg, W.; Truitt, R. K.	5,000	24 Mar 1887	Notary Public	Appointed & commissioned 11 Mar 1887 by Washington Bartlett, Governor of California	3	142-143

32

Principal Name	Sureties	Amount ($)	Date	Office	Notes	Book	Page(s)
Coffman, J. T.	Cox, N. H.; Prince, J. B.	1,000	25 Nov 1890	Justice of the Peace (Mendocino Township)	Elected 4 Nov 1890	4	115
Coffman, J. T.	Mead, James A.; Cunningham, F. Z.	1,000	28 Nov 1888	Justice of the Peace (Mendocino Township)	Elected 6 Nov 1888	3	289-291
Coffman, J. T.	Fox, Henry; Willson, H. M.	1,000	7 Sep 1887	Justice of the Peace (Mendocino Township)	Appointed 6 Sep 1887 by the Board of Supervisors	3	194-195
Coffman, J. T.*	Rosenberg, W.; Haig, George W.	5,000	11 Mar 1889	Notary Public	Appointed & commissioned 9 Mar 1889 by R. W. Waterman, Governor of California	4	41
Coffman, J. T.*	Wilson, J. W.; Raymond, Charles F.	1,000	30 Nov 1892	Justice of the Peace (Mendocino Township)	Elected 8 Nov 1892	4	237
Cohn, Richard	Cohn, J. H.; Mannheim, Henry	5,000	29 May 1867	Auctioneer	Witness John Cavanagh	B	605
Coleman, James	Barnes, Aaron, Sr.; Walker, John	1,000	12 Jan 1891	Justice of the Peace (Analy Township)	Appointed 12 Jan 1891 by the Board of Supervisors, vice L. G. Culver, failed to qualify	4	182
Coleman, James	Walker, John; Allen, S. I.	1,000	13 Jun 1890	Justice of the Peace (Analy Township)	Appointed 7 Jun 1890 by the Board of Supervisors	4	88
Colgan, Edward P.	Noonan, George P.; Overton, A. P.; Marshall, James; Davis, E. W.; Brush, J. H.; Byington, H. W.; Guerne, George E.; Shea, Con.; Taylor, O. A.; Murphy, Rufus; Noonan, P. H.; Davis, George W.; Strong, John; Underhill, W. H.; Burris, L. W.; Ware, A. B.	50,000	15 Nov 1886	Tax Collector	Elected 2 Nov 1886, witness F. G. Nagle	3	108-112
Colgan, Edward P.	Hopper, Thomas; Laughlin, James H.; Taylor, John S.; McConnell, William E.; Noonan, George P.; Overton, A. P.; Roney, James M.; Austin, James; Carithers, D. N.; Seegelken, E. A.; Philips, Walter; Ross, Losson; Davis, E. W.; Brush, J. H.; DeTurk, Isaac; Finlaw, W.; McFadyen, A.; Towey, Peter	60,000	15 Nov 1886	Sheriff	Elected 2 Nov 1886, witness F. G. Nagle	3	112-116
Colgan, Edward P.	Marshall, James; Noonan, George P.; Overton, A. P.; Byington, H. W.; Shea, Con; Seegelken, E. A.; Laughlin, James H.; McFadyen, Allan; DeTurk, Isaac; Guerne, George E.; Murphy, Rufus; Noonan, P. H.	50,000	24 Nov 1888	Tax Collector	Elected 6 Nov 1888	3	332-334
Colgan, Edward P.	Marshall, James; Noonan, George P.; Overton, A. P.; Shea, Con; Davis, George W.; Seegelken, E. A.; McConnell, William E.; Laughlin, James H.; McFadyen, Allan; DeTurk, Isaac; Finlaw, W.; Murphy, Rufus; Austin, James; Towey, Peter; Hopper, Thomas; Philips, Walter	60,000	24 Nov 1888	Sheriff	Elected 6 Nov 1888, witness F. G. Nagle	3	328-331
Collins, F. M.	Gale, D.; Wilsey, H.	2,000	13 Jan 1879	Road Master (Road District No. 2, Petaluma Township)	Appointed [?] Jan 1879 [by the Board of Supervisors]		

33

Principal Name	Sureties	Amount ($)	Date	Office	Notes	Book	Page(s)
Collins, F. M.	Merritt, John; Wilsey, Henry	2,000	15 Jan 1880	Road Overseer (Petaluma Road District No. 3)	Appointed 7 Jan 1880 [by the Board of Supervisors]		
Collins, F. M.	Hill, William; Mecham, H.; Tempel, C.; Gossage, J. B.	8,000	18 Nov 1880	Road Overseer (Petaluma Township)	Elected 2 Nov 1880	2	63-64
Collins, F. M.	Lougee, F. W.; Hill, William	5,000	25 Nov 1882	Road Overseer (Petaluma Township)	Elected 7 Nov 1882	2	231-232
Collins, F. M.	Wilsey, H.; Merritt, John	1,000	7 Feb 1878	Road Overseer [[Road] District No. 2, Petaluma Township)	Appointed 7 Feb 1878 [by the Board of Supervisors]	1	387-388
Collister, Oscar	Howard, William; Drago, Nelson; Chenoweth, John H.; Perry, Ira C.; Meeker, M. C.; Meeker, A. P.	5,000	30 May 1879	Notary Public	Commissioned 5 May 1879	1	458-459
Colton, F. D.	Cavanagh, John; Speers, William B.; Williams, George B.; Brown, S. C.	5,000	12 May 1862	Notary Public	Appointed & commissioned 1 May 1862 by Leland Stanford, Governor of California, for the term of two years, witness J. Chandler	B	260
Colton, F. D.	Speers, William B.; Derby, A. B.; Cavanagh, John; Thompson, A. W.; Hemenway, D. D.	5,000	5 May 1864	Notary Public	Appointed 2 May 1864, witness W. D. Bliss, includes oath of office dated 5 May 1864	B	451
Colvin, James	Thompson, J. D.; Yates, J. W.	1,000	25 Sep 1861	Constable (Russian River Township)	Elected 4 Sep 1861	B	175
Colvin, James A.	Powell, R.; Throp, John	1,000	23 Sep 1862	Constable (Russian River Township)	Elected 3 Sep 1862	B	312
Colvin, James A.	Gentry, W. O.; Esmond, C. H.	1,000	23 Sep 1867	Constable [Russian River Township]	Elected [4 Sep 1867], witness G. W. Petray	B	582
Colvin, James A.	Hembree, A. T.; Prewett, John	1,000	28 Sep 1863	Constable (Russian River Township)	Elected 2 Sep 1863	B	367
Colvin, James A.	Hembree, A. J.; Esmond, Cornwell	1,000	29 Sep 1865	Constable (Russian River Township)	Elected 6 Sep 1865	B	497
Connell, C. H.	Lafferty, H. C.; Lynch, John; Joyce, M.	1,000	3 Dec 1880	Constable (Vallejo Township)	Elected 2 Nov 1880	2	37-38
Connell, C. H.*	Shearer, John; Walsh, M.	1,000	23 Nov 1882	Constable (Vallejo Township)	Elected 7 Nov 1882	2	166-167
Connell, Charles H.	Walsh, Michael; Murry, Denis	1,000	24 Nov 1884	Constable (Vallejo Township)	Elected 4 Nov 1884	2	363-364
Connell, Charles H.*	O'Hara, John; Kahn, M.	1,000	20 Jul 1892	Constable (Petaluma Township)	Appointed 8 Jan 1892 by the Board of Supervisors	4	196
Connell, Charles*	O'Hara, John; Kahn, Moise	1,000	30 Nov 1892	Constable (Petaluma Township)	Elected 8 Nov 1892	4	213
Conner, F. P.	Brush, William T.; Coomes, A. M.	1,000	13 May 1892	Justice of the Peace (Cloverdale Township)	Appointed 3 May 1892 by the Board of Supervisors, vice Isidore Abraham, resigned	4	200
Conner, Fred. P.*	Brush, W. T.; Coomes, A. M.	1,000	1 Dec 1892	Justice of the Peace (Cloverdale Township)	Elected 8 Nov 1892	4	220

34

Principal Name	Sureties	Amount ($)	Date	Office	Notes	Book	Page(s)
Connolly, John D.	Overton, A. P.; Doyle, M.	15,000	29 Sep 1885	Supervisor (District No. 5)	Appointed 28 Sep 1885 [by George Stoneman, Governor of California], vice [S. R.] Houser, removed	2	493-494
Converse, Allen A.*	Weyl, Henry; Aguillon, Camille; Wegner, Edward; Clark, George W.; Howe, Robert	5,000	21 Nov 1890	Notary Public	Appointed & commissioned 26 Nov 1890 by R. W. Waterman, Governor of California	4	177
Cook, Charles	Bentley, A.; Schäfer, Ignatz	1,000	[?] Feb 1889	Justice of the Peace (Cloverdale Township)	Appointed 7 Feb 1889 by the Board of Supervisors	4	38
Cook, Charles	Woods, W. M.; Goetzelman, John; Linville, J. A.; Gropp, Charles; Muntz, Jacob; Davis, B. J.	2,000	22 Sep 1874	Constable [Cloverdale Township]	Appointed 8 Sep 1874 by the Board of Supervisors, witness D. C. Brush	1	63-64
Cook, Charles	Sissengood, John; Goetzelman, John	1,000	22 Sep 1879	Constable (Cloverdale Township)	Elected 3 Sep 1879	1	504
Cook, Charles	Hoadley, James F., Sr.; Reger, Vital	1,000	24 Nov 1884	Constable (Cloverdale Township)	Elected 4 Nov 1884, witness D. B. Morgan	2	378-379
Cook, Charles	Rains, J. K. Polk; Schäfer, Ignatz; Davis, G. V.; Smith, C. W.	1,000	24 Oct 1879	Constable (Cloverdale Township)	Appointed 9 Oct 1879 by the Board of Supervisors	1	551-552
Cook, Charles*	Goetzelman, John; Schäfer, Ignatz; Brush, W. T.; Reger, Vital	5,000	[?] Feb 1888	Notary Public	Appointed & commissioned 17 Feb 1888 by R. W. Waterman, Governor of California	3	227-229
Cook, Charles*	Menihan, M.; Schaefer, Ignatz; Reger, Vital; Brush, William T.	5,000	10 Oct 1890	Notary Public	Appointed & commissioned 8 Oct 1890 by R. W. Waterman, Governor of California	4	173
Cook, Charles*	DeHay, A.; Schaeffer, Ignatz	1,000	24 Nov 1882	Constable (Cloverdale Township)	Elected 7 Nov 1882	2	220-221
Cook, Charles*	Armstrong, J. B.; Goetzelman, John; Schaefer, Ignatz; Reger, Vital	5,000	26 Mar 1890	Notary Public	Appointed 20 Mar 1890 by R. W. Waterman, Governor of California	4	77
Cook, David	McCracken, J. C.; Lyon, A. G.; Snoddy, B. A.; Long, Ive. D.	5,000	13 Feb 1856	Justice of the Peace (Sonoma Township)	Appointed 28 Dec 1855 by the Board of Supervisors to fill unexpired term of James A. Reynolds, Esq., who resigned	A	151-152
Cook, I. F.	Wise, Henry; Hopper, Thomas	1,000	15 Jan 1879	Road Overseer (Santa Rosa Road District No. 4)	Appointed [?] Jan 1879 [by the Board of Supervisors]		
Cook, I. F.	Prindle, William; Gray, J. W.	1,000	7 Feb 1880	Road Overseer (Santa Rosa Road District No. 4)	Appointed 3 Feb 1880 [by the Board of Supervisors]		
Cooke, Martin E.	Hendley, John; Brockman, Israel	5,000	14 Jun 1852	Notary Public		A	31
Cooke, Martin E.	Pierpont, Robert R.; Campbell, Peter	5,000	14 May 1850	Notary Public	Appointed and commissioned	A	71
Cooke, Martin E.	Ross, William; Hendley, John	5,000	4 Feb 1856	Notary Public	Commissioned		
Cooke, Martin E.	Vallejo, Mariano G.; Ellis, John J.	20,000	6 Jun 1853	Notary Public	Commissioned 1 Jun 1853		
Coolbroth, S. W.	Schwartz, C.; Patterson, A. S.	2,000	20 Oct 1855	Constable (Bodega Township)	Includes oath of office dated 20 Oct 1855	A	146
Cooley, Charles H.	Shaw, I. E.; Brush, William T.	1,000	10 Dec 1888	Justice of the Peace (Cloverdale Township)	Elected 6 Nov 1888	4	23
Cooley, Charles H.	Kleiser, James A.; Knowles, Stephen W.	1,000	25 Nov 1884	Justice of the Peace (Cloverdale Township)	Elected 4 Nov 1884, witness D. B. Morgan	2	374-375
Cooley, Charles H.	Shaw, I. E.; Brush, William T.	1,000	26 Nov 1886	Justice of the Peace (Cloverdale Township)	Elected 2 Nov 1886	3	40-41

Principal Name	Sureties	Amount ($)	Date	Office	Notes	Book	Page(s)
Cooley, Charles H.	Sink, William D.; Shaw, I. E.	5,000	3 May 1886	Notary Public	Appointed 30 Apr 1886 [by George Stoneman, Governor of California, to fill the vacancy caused by the death of Captain Morgan], witness William Caldwell	2	534-535
Cooley, Charles H.*	Shaw, Isaac E.; Brush, William T.	5,000	1 May 1888	Notary Public	Appointed 28 Apr 1888	3	239-241
Cooley, John B.	Brush, William T.; Spencer, Frank	1,000	26 Nov 1890	Road Overseer (Cloverdale Road District)	Elected 4 Nov 1890	4	104
Cooper, J. D.	Pool, H. J.; Philpott, B. F.	1,000	5 Dec 1890	Justice of the Peace (Russian River Township)	Elected 4 Nov 1890	4	152
Cooper, S. E.	McCoy, James; Willis, T. N.; Powers, David P.; Hughes, H. M.; Miller, L. W.	5,000	27 Jul 1875	Auctioneer		1	109-110
Cooper, Samuel E.	Browne, Daniel; Hunt, Charles	5,000	20 Jun 1868	Auctioneer		B	616
Copeland, William L.	Beasly, Jesse; Leavenworth, T. M.	1,000	1 Oct 1858	Constable (Sonoma Township)	Elected 1 Sep 1858	A	341
Copeland, William L.	McCracken, J. C.; Hooker, Joseph	1,000	30 Sep 1857	Constable (Sonoma Township)	Elected 2 Sep 1857, accepted by W. B. Hagans, Chairman of the Board of Supervisors	A	289-290
Cornwall, William A.	Hartman, J. William; Leguine, Bront	5,000	6 Dec 1855	Notary Public	Appointed	A	111
Coulter, C. A.*	Smith, R. Press; Coulter, S. T.; Ross, Robert	5,000	7 Jan 1891	Notary Public	Appointed & commissioned 5 Jan 1891 by R. W. Waterman, Governor of California	3	355-356
Coulter, S. T.	Fulkerson, Richard; Peugh, James A.	4,000	16 May 1860	Road Overseer (Santa Rosa District)	Appointed 10 May 1860 by the Board of Supervisors for the term of one year	B	78
Coulter, S. T.	Farmer, E. T.; Overton, A. P.	15,000	2 Jan 1885	Supervisor (District No. 3)	Elected 4 Nov 1884	2	441-442
Coulter, Sterling T.	Smith, Robert E.; Myers, D. D.	5,000	1 Dec 1856	Justice of the Peace (Santa Rosa Township)	Elected 4 Nov 1856	A	160
Coulter, Sterling T.	Beaver, Henry; Boyce, John F.	5,000	1 Oct 1855	Justice of the Peace (Santa Rosa Township)	Elected 5 Sep 1855	A	148-149
Coulter, Sterling T.	Wright, Charles H.; Crane, James E.	5,000	26 Sep 1854	Justice of the Peace (Santa Rosa Township)	Elected 6 Sep 1854	A	15
Coulter, Sterling T.	Treadway, R. M.; Treadway, Griffin; Carrillo, Julio; Bledsoe, A. C.; Hoen, Berthold; Beaver, Henry; Hendley, John	5,000	3 Oct 1857	Justice of the Peace (Santa Rosa Township)	Elected 2 Sep 1857, accepted by W. B. Hagans, Chairman of the Board of Supervisors	A	222-226
Cowan, S. Finley	Smith, C. D.; Grayson, Daniel	1,000	4 Oct 1858	Justice of the Peace (Sonoma Township)	Elected 1 Sep 1858, witness Frederick Rohrer	A	350
Cox, Arthur L.	Cox, Charles B.; Neblett, E.; Murphy, Wyman	5,000	14 Sep 1877	Surveyor	Elected 5 Sep 1877	1	286-287
Cox, Arthur L.	Mills, E. T.; Cox, C. B.	5,000	17 Sep 1879	Surveyor	Elected 3 Sep 1879	1	468-469
Cox, C. B.	Armstrong, J. B.; Smith, John K.	2,000	24 Oct 1877	Justice of the Peace (Santa Rosa Township)	Elected 17 Oct 1877	1	363-364

36

Principal Name	Sureties	Amount ($)	Date	Office	Notes	Book	Page(s)
Cox, N. H.	Barnes, W. H.; Ferguson, H. O.	1,000	25 Nov 1890	Road Overseer (Healdsburg Road District)	Elected 4 Nov 1890	4	98
Cralle, L. J.	Berger, M.; Davis, W. K.	2,000	18 Mar 1872	Justice of the Peace (Vallejo Township)	Appointed [6 Feb 1872 by the Board of Supervisors, vice John Powell, resigned], witness F. W. Shattuck	C	163-164
Cralle, L. J.	Humphries, Charles; Munday, B. B.	1,000	30 May 1868	Justice of the Peace (Vallejo Township)	Appointed 8 May 1868 by the Board of Supervisors, witness F. W. Shattuck	B	618
Cramer, Thomas	McPeak, M. A.; Lunsford, R. B.	1,000	22 Sep 1879	Justice of the Peace (Redwood Township)	Elected 3 Sep 1879	1	501-502
Cramp, William	Oakes, Anthony G.; Pauli, G. T.	1,000	2 Oct 1858	Constable (Sonoma Township)	Elected 1 Sep 1858, witness Frederick Rohrer	A	346
Crane, E. T.	Allen, Samuel I.; Noonan, George P.; Ludwig, Thomas J.; Roney, J. M.; Carithers, D. N.; Keser, Louis, Jr.	5,000	26 Dec 1883	Notary Public	Appointed 24 Dec 1883, witness Fred. G. Nagle	2	307-308
Crane, R.	Payran, Stephen; Crane, Richard H.	1,000	30 Sep 1862	Justice of the Peace (Vallejo Township)	Elected 3 Sep 1862, witnesses John Cavanagh & L. C. Reyburn	B	289
Crane, Robert	Copeland, Alexander; Powell, John	100	[18 Jun 1858]	Road Overseer (Road District No. 14 in Vallejo Township)	Appointed by the Board of Supervisors	A	312
Crane, Robert	Martin, H. B.; Williamson, J. R.	100	1 Mar 1859	Road Overseer (Road District No. 14, Vallejo Township)	Appointed	A	370
Crane, Robert	Patton, Charles; Crane, Joel	1,000	1 Oct 1855	Constable (Vallejo Township)	Elected 5 Sep 1855	A	136
Crane, Robert	Latapie, Edward; Wright, W. S. M.; Fulkerson, T. S.; Fulkerson, Richard; Kohle, A.; Hopper, Thomas	10,000	11 Sep 1878	Supervisor (District No. 3)	Elected 4 Sep 1878	1	441-442
Crane, Robert	Mitchell, R. T.; Fulkerson, Richard; Peterson, A.; Hopper, Thomas; Latapie, E.; McClelland, J. J.; Underhill, J. G.; McMinn, John	10,000	20 Sep 1879	Supervisor (District No. 3)	Elected 3 Sep 1879	1	486-488
Crane, Robert	Copeland, A.; Smith, Robert E.	1,000	4 Oct 1854	Constable (Vallejo Township)	Elected	A	27-28
Cravens, T. A.	Markle, R. B.; Henderson, J. W.	200	[?] Feb 1863	Road Master (Cloverdale Township)	Appointed	B	338
Cravens, T. A.	Markle, R. B.; Caldwell, William	1,000	5 Oct 1863	Constable (Cloverdale Township)	Elected [2 Sep 1863], witness J. Ramey	B	370
Crigler, A. P.	Crigler, William E.; Black, George H.	1,000	13 Apr 1885	Constable (Cloverdale Township)	Appointed 13 Apr 1885	2	473-474
Crigler, A. P.	Crigler, William E.; Mitchell, C. E.	1,000	30 Nov 1886	Constable (Cloverdale Township)	Elected 2 Nov 1886	3	66-67
Crigler, Lloyd A. *	Crigler, William E.; Field, John	1,000	29 Nov 1882	Constable (Cloverdale Township)	Elected 7 Nov 1882	2	207-208

37

Principal Name	Sureties	Amount ($)	Date	Office	Notes	Book	Page(s)
Crigler, William E.	Shores, Leander; Sissengood, John	1,500	7 Jan 1873	Road Master (Cloverdale Road District)	Appointed 7 Jan 1873 by the Board of Supervisors		
Crispin, Nathan W.	Antrim, Adin; Alexander, Cyrus	300	24 Sep 1862	Road Master (District No. 1, Washington Township)	Elected [3 Sep 1862]	B	329
Critchfield, George W.	Barnes, Edwin H.; Miller, Samuel E.	1,000	23 Sep 1862	Justice of the Peace (Russian River Township)	Elected 3 Sep 1862	B	313
Crocker, H.	Teaby, W. H.; Harris, W. F.	1,000	28 Nov 1890	Justice of the Peace (Washington Township)	Elected 4 Nov 1890	4	142
Crocker, H.	Teaby, W. H.; Goodrich, C. B.	1,000	5 Dec 1888	Justice of the Peace (Washington Township)	Elected 6 Nov 1888	3	315-316
Crocker, H.*	Teaby, W. H.; Crowell, A.	1,000	9 Dec 1892	Justice of the Peace (Washington Township)	Elected 8 Nov 1892	4	253
Crocker, Henry*	Wood, J. J.; Skaggs, J. (Mrs.); Perry, E. G.; Harris, W. F.; Burr, Frank	5,000	3 Apr 1889	Notary Public	Appointed 28 Mar 1889	4	49
Crofoot, Charles H.	Borman, C. O.; Gibson, John	1,000	9 May 1889	Constable (Sonoma Township)	Appointed 7 May 1889 by the Board of Supervisors, vice J. J. Law, resigned	4	58
Crowe, Charles Williams	Millen, George B.; Lafranky, John	1,000	4 Dec 1888	Constable (Ocean Township)	Elected 6 Nov 1888	3	327-328
Crowell, William H.	Crane, James E.; Hartman, J. W.	5,000	21 Nov 1856	Justice of the Peace (Santa Rosa Township)	Elected 4 Nov 1856	A	163
Crowell, William H.*	Fitch, William; Fitch, Fred R.; Tate, Thomas H.; Rudesill, J. A.; Johnson, Fred; Towne, Smith D.; Delahanty, John	6,000	26 Sep 1857	Clerk	Elected 2 Sep 1857	A	79-82
Cryder, Daniel W.	Wilkinson, R.; Mock, Wesley	1,000	12 Feb 1877	Road Overseer (Santa Rosa Township No. 1)	Appointed 9 Feb 1877 [by the Board of Supervisors]	1	233-234
Cummings, Eli	Hamilton, Emmor; Cummings, James M.	1,000	15 Jan 1876	Road Overseer (Washington Township)	Appointed 8 Jan 1876 by the Board of Supervisors	1	194-195
Cummings, Eli	Cummings, James M.; Wisecarver, Joseph R.	1,000	20 Feb 1877	Road Overseer (Washington Township)	Appointed 9 Feb 1877 by the Board of Supervisors	1	249-251
Cummons, Eli R.	Dickinson, H. W.; McDarment, Richard	1,000	5 Oct 1863	Constable (Washington Township)	Elected 2 Sep 1863	B	368
Cunninghame, W. J.	McCaughey, James; Taylor, Despard; Fitzpatrick, Andrew	2,000	18 Nov 1880	Road Overseer (Bodega Township)	Elected 2 Nov 1880	2	68-69
Cunninghame, William J.	Taylor, Despard; Wilkinson, Jeremiah	1,000	13 Jan 1879	[Road Overseer (Bodega Road District No. 3)]	[Appointed 8 Jan 1879 by the Board of Supervisors], sworn 13 Jan 1879 at Bodega Corners		
Cunninghame, William J.	Cunningham, John; McCaughey, James	1,000	15 Jul 1879	Road Overseer (Bodega Township [Road] District No. 1)	Appointed 15 Jul 1879 [by the Board of Supervisors, vice Wiley Frazier, resigned]	1	463-464

38

Principal Name	Sureties	Amount ($)	Date	Office	Notes	Book	Page(s)
Cunninghame, William J.	McCaughey, James; Cunningham, John	1,000	20 Jan 1880	Road Overseer (Bodega Township)	Appointed 7 Jan 1880 [by the Board of Supervisors]		
Cunninghame, William J.	McCaughey, James; Caseres, Cereo F.	1,000	22 Apr 1890	Justice of the Peace (Bodega Township)	Appointed 11 Apr 1890 by the Board of Supervisors, vice F. G. Blume, deceased	4	82
Cunninghame, William J.	Clark, James; Goodman, L. S.; McCaughey, James	3,500	23 Nov 1882	Road Overseer (Bodega Township)	Elected 7 Nov 1882	2	244-245
Cunninghame, William J.	McCaughey, James; Goodman, L. S.	1,000	24 Jan 1885	Road Overseer (Bodega Road District)	Appointed 13 Jan 1885 [by the Board of Supervisors], witness Joseph Keniston	2	457-458
Cunninghame, William J.	Clark, James; Goodman, L. S.	1,000	28 Nov 1890	Justice of the Peace (Bodega Township)	Elected 4 Nov 1890	4	144
Cunninghame, William J.*	Clark, James; Fitzpatrick, Andrew	1,000	6 Dec 1892	Justice of the Peace (Bodega Township)	Elected 8 Nov 1892	4	248
Currin, George W.	Helmke, F.; Miller, William R.	1,000	17 Oct 1863	Constable (Salt Point Township)	Elected 2 Sep 1863	B	395
Curtis, James H.	Clark, J. P.	200	[7 May 1863]	Road Overseer (Road District No. 2, Bodega Township)	Appointed	B	345
Dana, M. V. B.*	Feldmeyer, B. W.; Gater, F. I.	1,000	7 Dec 1892	Constable (Washington Township)	Elected 8 Nov 1892	4	221
Darrow, John O.	Norton, L. A.; Warren, Fenno V.; White, T. H.	5,000	1 Jul 1864	Notary Public	Commissioned 23 Jun 1864 by Frederick F. Low, Governor of California, includes oath of office dated 2 Jul 1864	B	457
Darrow, John O.	Bloom, D.; Norton, L. A.; Fike, N.; Proctor C. B.; Curtis, J. H.; Ley, H. D.; Grant, J. D.	5,000	6 Jul 1866	Notary Public	Commissioned 25 Jun 1866 by F. F. Low, Governor of California, includes oath of office dated 19 Jul 1866	B	550-551
Dashiell, Benjamin	Dashiell, Thaddeus W.	100	6 Feb 1858	Road Overseer (Russian River Township)	Appointed February Session 1858 by the Board of Supervisors		
Davis, Delos D.*	Pressley, John G.; Noonan, George P.	5,000	23 Nov 1891	Notary Public	Appointed & commissioned 19 Nov 1891 for the term of 4 years	4	193
Davis, E. L.	Taylor, John S.; White, John M.	1,000	11 Feb 1878	Road Overseer (Santa Rosa [Road District] No. 4)	[Appointed] 7 Feb 1878 [by the Board of Supervisors]	1	393-394
Davis, E. L.	Wright, W. S. M.; Latapie, E.	1,000	12 Feb 1877	Road Master (Santa Rosa Road District No. 4)	Appointed 9 Feb 1877 [by the Board of Supervisors]	1	234-235
Davis, E. L.	Noonan, George P.; Thomas, A.; Boyce, J. F.	3,000	19 Sep 1868	Road Commissioner	Appointed 18 Sep 1868 by the Board of Supervisors	B	623
Davis, E. W.	Hood, T. B.; Boyce, J. F.; Davis, George W.	3,000	14 Sep 1877	Superintendent of Public Schools	Elected 5 Sep 1877	1	282-283
Davis, G. V.	Menihan, M.; Shaw, I. E.; Brush, William T.; Caldwell, William; Field, John	15,000	26 Nov 1886	Supervisor (District No. 4)	Elected 2 Nov 1886	3	52-53
Davis, J. V.	Prows, Daniel; Prows, Sylvester; Lambert, Henry F.	5,000	4 Apr 1859	Auctioneer		A	373

39

Principal Name	Sureties	Amount ($)	Date	Office	Notes	Book	Page(s)
Davis, Levi	Jackson, Zadok	500	19 Jun 1861	Road Overseer (Petaluma Road District No. 2)	Appointed, includes oath of office dated 19 Jun 1861	B	157
Davis, Moses	McClellan, M. T.; Wilson, W. H.	500	4 Nov 1862	Justice of the Peace (Salt Point Township)	Appointed 4 Nov 1862 by the Board of Supervisors, includes oath of office dated 4 Nov 1862	B	315
Davis, P. R.	Hopper, Thomas; Hardin, James A.; Brooke, T. J.; Overton, A. P.	10,000	26 Nov 1886	Surveyor	Elected 2 Nov 1886, witness J. F. Mulgrew	3	31-32
Davis, P. R.	Roney, J. M.; Campbell, J. T.; Ware, A. B.; McGee, J. H.; Brooke, T. J.	10,000	30 Nov 1888	Surveyor	Elected 6 Nov 1888	3	278-280
Davis, Preston R.	Davis, Josias; Taylor, John S.; Armstrong, J. B.; Hahman, F. G.	10,000	22 Nov 1882	Surveyor	Elected 7 Nov 1882	2	156-158
Davis, Preston R.*	Taylor John S.; Woodward, E. F.; McPike, A. J.; Doran, W. M.; Doyle, M.; Murphy, Rufus; Nagle, F. G.; Noonan, George P.	10,000	1 Dec 1892	Surveyor	Elected 8 Nov 1892	4	218
Davis, Walter S.	Montgomery, William; Allen, S. I.; Palmer, S. G.; Roney, J. M.; Hoag, O. H.	5,000	6 May 1882	Notary Public	Appointed 6 May 1882 by George C. Perkins, Governor of California, witness R. A. Thompson	2	131-133
Davisson, D. D.	Wright, W. S. M.; Smith, John K.; Gale, Otis	5,000	29 Jan 1878	Notary Public	Appointed & commissioned 22 Jan 1878	1	380-381
Davisson, D. D.	Cox, C. B.; Overton, A. P.	5,000	29 Jan 1880	Notary Public	Appointed & commissioned 22 Jan 1880	1	565-566
Davisson, D. D.*	Wright, W. S. M.; Walker, John	5,000	15 Dec 1875	Notary Public	Commissioned 10 Dec 1875	1	178
Davisson, Jesse		5,000	24 Sep 1853	Justice of the Peace (Sonoma Township)	Elected 7 Sep 1853		
Dayton, John J.	Duncan, Samuel M., Jr.; Moore, T. B.	1,000	20 Jan 1881	Constable (Ocean Township)	Appointed 7 Jan 1881 [by the Board of Supervisors, vice Alex. Duncan who failed to qualify]	2	55-56
Denman, Ezekiel	Lewis, Lewis C.; Wood, William B.	5,000	2 Oct 1854	Justice of the Peace (Petaluma Township)	Elected 6 Sep 1854, witness Thomas McMurray	A	86
Denman, Frank H.	Lougee, F. W.; Denman, E.	5,000	10 Dec 1881	Surveyor	Appointed 5 Dec 1881 [by the Board of Supervisors, vice A. L. Cox, resigned]	2	110-112
Denman, Frank H.	Denman, E.; Mecham, H.	10,000	20 Nov 1884	Surveyor	Elected 4 Nov 1884	2	352-353
Denman, Frank H.*	Denman, E.; Lougee, F. W.	5,000	2 Mar 1888	Notary Public	Appointed & commissioned 27 Feb 1888 by R. W. Waterman, Governor of California	3	230-232
Denman, Frank H.*	Lougee, F. W.; Putnam, T. C.	5,000	27 Feb 1890	Notary Public	Appointed & commissioned 24 Feb 1890 by R. W. Waterman, Governor of California, includes oath of office dated 27 Feb 1890	3	341-344
Derieux, J. L.	Caldwell, William; Shores, Leander	1,000	27 Nov 1869	Justice of the Peace [Cloverdale Township]	Elected 20 Oct 1869	C	11
Diamond, James C.	Cary, Bartley; Putnam, T. C.	1,000	10 Feb 1888	Pound Master (Vallejo Township)	Appointed 6 Feb 1888 by the Board of Supervisors	3	223-224
Dickey, Sebastian R.	Rathbun, J. S.; Oman, George W.	1,000	1 Oct 1855	Constable (Vallejo Township)	Elected 5 Sep 1855	A	115

40

Principal Name	Sureties	Amount ($)	Date	Office	Notes	Book	Page(s)
Dinwiddie, J. L.	Laughlin, John M.	30,000	12 Mar 1881	Sheriff & ex officio Tax Collector	Elected 3 Sep 1879, a supplemental bond substituting John M. Laughlin for W. Y. Wilson (removed from California) as surety on J. L. Dinwiddie's original bond dated 23 Sep 1879, includes several Superior Court documents relating to this matter	1	584-586
Dinwiddie, J. L.	DeTurk, I.; Fulkerson, Richard	30,000	14 Jun 1881	Sheriff & ex officio Tax Collector	Elected 3 Sep 1879, a supplemental bond substituting I. DeTurk & Richard Fulkerson for W. R. Roberts (died) as sureties on J. L. Dinwiddie's original bond dated 23 Sep 1879, includes several Superior Court documents relating to this matter	1	590-594
Dinwiddie, J. L.	Whitney, A. P.; Fairbanks, H. T.	5,000	16 Jun 1883	Auctioneer		1	
Dinwiddie, J. L.	Fairbanks, H. T.; Whitney, A. P.; Poehlmann, Conrad; Zartman, William; Fritsch, John; Jewell, J. R.	25,000	21 Sep 1877	Sheriff	Elected 5 Sep 1877	1	307-309
Dinwiddie, J. L.	Fairbanks, H. T.; Hill, William; Denman, E.; Roberts, W. R.	30,000	21 Sep 1877	Sheriff & ex officio Tax Collector	Elected 5 Sep 1877	1	306-307
Dinwiddie, J. L.	Hill, William; Fritsch, John; Zartman, William; Whitney, A. P.; Denman, E.	25,000	23 Sep 1879	Sheriff	Elected 3 Sep 1879	1	510-512
Dinwiddie, J. L.	Fairbanks, H. T.; Byington, H. W.; Adams, James; Roberts, William R.; Laughlin, James H.; Farmer, E. T.; Wilson, William Y.	30,000	23 Sep 1879	Sheriff & ex officio Tax Collector	Elected 3 Sep 1879	1	508-510
Dittemore, Theodore	Willson, H. M.; Hall, L. J.	1,000	13 Feb 1877	Road Overseer (Mendocino District)	Appointed 9 Feb 1877 by the Board of Supervisors, witness W. W. Moreland	1	239-240
Dittemore, Theodore	Hall, L. J.; Sondheimer, E.	200	27 Oct 1863	Road Master (District No. 2, Washington Township)	Elected [2 Sep 1863]	B	376
Dobyns, W. H.*	Lemmon, Allen B.; Smith, James F.	5,000	29 Jul 1890	Notary Public	Appointed 16 Jul 1890 for the term of 4 years	4	93
Dodge, Edward	Forsythe, B. F.; Wright, Berry	300	22 Nov 1858	Road Overseer (Road District No. 21 in Mendocino County)	Appointed November Term 1858 by the Board of Supervisors	A	362
Dooley, Elijah	Hood, Thomas B.; Smith, William R.	100	9 Mar 1860	Road Overseer (Road District No. 7, Santa Rosa Township)	Appointed [?] Feb 1860 by the Board of Supervisors	B	69
Dormann, William	Larsen, Olef; Pauli, G. T.	1,000	29 Sep 1863	Constable (Sonoma Township)	Elected 2 Sep 1863	B	362
Dougherty, John W.	Bell, Benjamin C.	500	5 May 1862	Road Master (Bodega Road District No. 2)	Appointed by the Board of Supervisors, includes oath of office dated 5 May 1862	B	266
Dow, Charles S.	Potter, Samuel, Jr.; Smith, Jeremiah	1,000	4 Oct 1853	Constable (Bodega Township)	Elected 7 Sep 1853, witness Charles Schwarz	A	49-50
Dow, J. G.	Bledsoe, A. C.; March, William J.; Bloom, David	4,000	17 May 1860	Road Overseer (Mendocino District)	Appointed 10 May 1860 by the Board of Supervisors for the term of one year	B	80-81

Principal Name	Sureties	Amount ($)	Date	Office	Notes	Book	Page(s)
Dow, J. G.	Engel, H. S.; Truitt, J. H.	100	22 Dec 1859	Road Overseer (Road District No. 5, Mendocino Township)	Appointed November Term 1859 by the Board of Supervisors	B	65
Dow, J. G.	Stearns, M. S.; Edgerton, George O.	100	8 May 1858	Road Overseer (Road District No. 5 of Mendocino County)	Appointed		
Dow, Joseph G.	Green, E. L.; Rosenberg, M.	1,000	10 Nov 1855	Constable (Mendocino Township)	Appointed 9 Nov 1855 by the Board of Supervisors, includes oath of office dated 10 Nov 1855	A	134
Dow, William B.	Storey, George; Dow, J. G.	200	19 Sep 1861	Road Overseer (District No. 2, Mendocino Township)	Elected 4 Sep 1861	B	233
Dow, William B.	Stearns, Marshall S.; Dow, Joseph G.	100	8 May 1858	Road Overseer (Sotoyome Road District No. 4)	Appointed		
Drake, George*	Mitchell, R. T.; Hembree, A. J.	1,000	26 Dec 1892	Pound Master (Russian River Pound District)	Appointed 8 Dec 1892 by the Board of Supervisors	4	262
Drake, George*	Cooper, J. D.; Luebberke, H.	1,000	6 Dec 1892	Constable (Russian River Township)	Elected 8 Nov 1892	4	231
Dumars, William	Clark, Charles; Pool, Henry J.	1,000	5 Oct 1859	Constable (Russian River Township)	Elected 7 Sep 1859, witness George C. McFadden	B	35
Dumars, William	Runyan, Henry L.; Kidd, P.	2,000	7 Jun 1864	Justice of the Peace (Russian River Township)	Appointed 6 May 1864 by the Board of Supervisors, vice J. C. Sacry, resigned, includes oath of office certification dated 7 Jun 1864	B	456
Dunlap, Hiram C.	McDonald, Donald; Dow, C. S.	5,000	[?] Dec 1854	Constable (Bodega Township)	Elected 6 Sep 1854	A	17-18
Dupont, Alfred	Litchfield, Martin; Wightman, C.; Hayden, E. W.; Gannon, James P.; Morris, Joseph H. P.; Gossage, H. S.; Huntly, G. W.; McChristian, Owen	1,000	13 Apr 1889	Pound Master (Sebastopol Pound District)	Appointed 10 Apr 1889 by the Board of Supervisors, witness L. W. Juilliard	4	50
Durand, Victor	Luttringer, Joseph; Knipp, -; Stengel, -	1,000	15 Jan 1886	Road Overseer (Salt Point Township)	Appointed 6 Jan 1886 [by the Board of Supervisors, vice Peter Eckert, resigned]	2	525-527
Durand, Victor	Stockhoff, John H.; Luttringer, Joseph	1,000	29 Nov 1890	Road Master (Fort Ross [Road] District, Salt Point Township)	Elected 4 Nov 1890	4	141
Dyer, James R.	Winkle, Henry; McMackin, James	1,000	2 Feb 1885	Pound Master (Sonoma Pound District)	Appointed 10 Jan 1885 [by the Board of Supervisors, vice G. W. Sparks, resigned]	2	462-463
Dyson, J. H.	Ragsdale, J. W.; French, J. H.; Brush, J. H.; Tupper, George A.; Ludwig, T. J.; McCumiskey, J.	5,000	7 Apr 1887	Notary Public	Appointed & commissioned 1 Apr 1887 by Washington Bartlett, Governor of California	3	155-157
Eagan, John S.	Barnes, Thomas L.; McCune, James N.	1,000	1 Oct 1859	Justice of the Peace (Vallejo Township)	Elected 7 Sep 1859	B	42
Eardley, W. J.*	Noonan, George P.; Overton, John P.; Allen, Samuel I.; Talmadge, Samuel	5,000	3 Mar 1888	Notary Public	Appointed & commissioned 27 Feb 1888 by [R. W. Waterman], Governor of California	3	232-234

42

Principal Name	Sureties	Amount ($)	Date	Office	Notes	Book	Page(s)
Eardley, W. J.*	Talmadge, Samuel; Hardin, James A.; Roney, J. M.; Overton, John P.	5,000	5 Mar 1890	Notary Public	Appointed & commissioned 24 Feb 1890	4	78
Eckert, Peter	Piezzi, Victor; Tupper, George A.	1,000	13 Jan 1885	Road Overseer (Salt Point Road District)	Appointed 13 Jan 1885 [by the Board of Supervisors]	2	448-449
Eckert, Peter	Luttringer, Joseph; Warren, Benjamin F.	1,000	23 Jan 1880	Road Overseer ([Ridge Road District])	Appointed 8 Jan 1880 [by the Board of Supervisors]		
Eckert, Peter	Luttringer, Joseph; Tomassini, Julian	1,500	3 Dec 1880	Road Overseer (Salt Point Township)	Elected 2 Nov 1880	2	74-75
Eckert, Peter	Marshall, Hugh; Luttringer, Joseph	1,500	4 Dec 1882	Road Overseer [Salt Point Township]	Elected 7 Nov 1882	2	270-271
Eikenbary, J. S.	Bell, J. S.; Giles, L. R.; Lewis, R. E.; Hassett, Aaron	5,000	1 Jun 1878	Auctioneer	Appointed [?] Jun 1878	1	428-429
Eikenbary, J. S.	Bell, J. S.; Vaughan, W. J.; Hassett, A.	2,000	24 Sep 1875	Constable [Mendocino Township]	Elected 1 Sep 1875	1	146-147
Eikenbery, J. S.	Hassett, J. D.; Sargent, H.; Young, John; Wright. A.; Jordan, Leslie A.	2,000	21 Sep 1877	Constable (Mendocino Township)	Elected 5 Sep 1877	1	318-320
Ellis, John J.	Barnes, M.; Martin, H. B.; Thompson, Thomas L; Holman, John H.; Clark, James P.	5,000	[?] [?] 1861	Sheriff & ex officio Tax Collector	Authorized [1 Apr 1861] as Sheriff and ex officio Tax Collector to continue the collection of State and County taxes until the first Monday of Jun 1861 [3 Jun 1861]	B	151
Ellis, John J.	Holmes, Henderson P.; Warner, Philemon; Green, C. C.	3,000	[?] Feb 1860	Sheriff & ex officio Tax Collector	John J. Ellis as Sheriff and ex officio Tax Collector authorized to continue to collect State and County taxes until the first Monday in March 1860 [5 Mar 1860]	B	68
Ellis, John J.	Rochford, Thomas; Overton, A. P.; Matthews, O. B.; Rohrer, Calvin; Sroufe, John; Richardson, John H.; Edwards, Uriah; Sloan, Bernard; Huie, J. Thompson; Cross, J. D.; McGuire, A.; Rodgers, A. W.; Brown, Daniel; Alberding, Frederick H.; Farley, Francis H.; Cavanagh, John; Hunt, Charles; Doyle, M.; Thompson, A. W.; Ordway, William; Hill, William	25,000	22 Sep 1859	Sheriff	Elected 7 Sep 1859	B	28-29
Ellis, L. G.	Ellis, W. C.; Stites, A. H.; Morrill, C. A.; Hassett, J. D.; Cohn, S.	15,000	29 Nov 1884	Supervisor (District No. 4)	Elected 4 Nov 1884	2	385-386 & 433-434
Ellis, Leander G.	Remmel, Charles; Stites, A. H.; Steward, M.; Ellis, W. C.; Cummings, J. M.; Leigh, A. G.; Cohn, Samuel	15,000	27 Nov 1882	Supervisor (District No. 6)	Elected 7 Nov 1882	2	248-250
Ellis, Thomas	Fisk, J. C.; Morris, John C.	1,000	28 Dec 1870	Justice of the Peace (Salt Point Township)	Appointed [10 Nov 1870 by the Board of Supervisors]	C	67
Ellis, Thomas	Allison, William; Helmke, F.	1,000	9 Nov 1867	Justice of the Peace (Salt Point Township)	Elected 16 Oct 1867	B	573
Ellis, William	Dyer, Claborn; Litzius, Louis; Oettl, F.; Linnehan, Jerry	2,000	1 Dec 1869	Justice of the Peace (Sonoma Township)	Elected 20 Oct 1869	C	12

43

Principal Name	Sureties	Amount ($)	Date	Office	Notes	Book	Page(s)
Ellis, William	Pauli, G. T.; Wilson, W. L.	1,000	1 Oct 1858	Justice of the Peace (Sonoma Township)	Elected 1 Sep 1858	A	340
Ellis, William	McConnell, Georg M.; Thompson, John B.	1,000	21 Sep 1861	Justice of the Peace (Sonoma Township)	Elected 4 Sep 1861, witness W. M. Boggs	B	207
Ellis, William	Pauli, G. T.; Cook, David	1,000	24 Sep 1859	Justice of the Peace (Sonoma Township)	Elected 7 Sep 1859, witness G. L. Wratten	B	23
Ellis, William	Brockman, Israel; Brunner, Christian	5,000	26 Nov 1856	Constable (Sonoma Township)	Elected 4 Nov 1856	A	170
Ellis, William	Ellis, John J.; Barnes, M.	1,000	3 Dec 1860	Justice of the Peace (Sonoma Township)	Elected 6 Nov 1860	B	128
Ellis, William	Munday, B. B.; Bates, H. F.	2,000	31 Oct 1863	Justice of the Peace (Sonoma Township)	Elected 21 Oct 1863	B	389
Ellis, William	Vaslit, Frank S.; Oettl, Franz; Dyer, Clayburn; Lennehen, Jerry	2,000	5 Nov 1867	Justice of the Peace (Sonoma Township)	Elected [16 Oct 1867], witness L. W. Worth	B	604
Ellis, William	Pauli, G. T.; Lutgens, John	2,000	9 Nov 1865	Justice of the Peace (Sonoma Township)	Elected 18 Oct 1865	B	487
Ellison, L. M.	Lunsford, R. B.; Yarbrough, Crockett D.	1,000	22 Sep 1879	Constable (Redwood Township)	Elected 3 Sep 1879	1	499-500
Ellison, L. M.	Lowery, G. W.; Henckell, George; Vanderlieth, John	1,000	27 Sep 1861	Constable (Bodega Township)	Elected 4 Sep 1861	B	196
Elmore, Orvis	Whitney, A. L.; Scott, J. C.	1,000	29 Nov 1890	Road Overseer (Penns Grove Road District, Vallejo Township)	Elected 4 Nov 1890	4	140
Ely, Elisha	Estes, J. B.; Cook, Rudolph D.	100	8 Feb 1859	Road Overseer (Road District No. 3)	Appointed, witness William H. Crowell	A	364
Emerson, J. P.	Hassett, John D.; Brown, H. K.	1,000	17 Nov 1880	Justice of the Peace (Mendocino Township)	Elected 2 Nov 1880	2	10-11
Emerson, J. P.	King, John; Samuels, James	1,000	25 Nov 1884	Justice of the Peace (Mendocino Township)	Elected 4 Nov 1884	2	392-393
Emerson, John P.	Mead, James A.; Lannan, Patrick; Rosenberg, W.; Ferguson, H. O.	5,000	15 Feb 1883	Notary Public	Commissioned 9 Feb 1883, witness W. B. Reynolds, includes oath of office dated 15 Feb 1883	2	284-286
Emerson, John P.	Clack, John W.; Brown, H. K.; Carruthers, T. C.	5,000	15 Jun 1876	Auctioneer		1	218
Emerson, John P.	Brown, H. K.; Rupe, Sam H.	2,000	22 Sep 1875	Constable (Mendocino Township)	Elected 1 Sep 1875	1	149-150
Emerson, John P.	Bailhache, John N.; Powell, R.	1,000	23 Sep 1879	Justice of the Peace (Mendocino Township)	Elected 3 Sep 1879	1	527-528
Emerson, John P.	Brown, H. K.; Gaines, W. C.	1,000	27 Nov 1882	Justice of the Peace (Mendocino Township)	Elected 7 Nov 1882	2	221-223
English, C. H.	McGee, H. P.; O'Naell, J. P.	1,000	14 Oct 1858	Constable (Ukiah Township)	Elected 1 Sep 1858	A	352

Principal Name	Sureties	Amount ($)	Date	Office	Notes	Book	Page(s)
Ensign, J. C.*	Stites, A. H.; Cummings, E.	2,000	11 Dec 1875	Constable (Washington Township)	Appointed 8 Dec 1875 by the Board of Supervisors	1	179
Eproson, J.	Stites, A. H.; Ellis, L. G.	1,000	5 Dec 1888	Constable (Washington Township)	Elected 6 Nov 1888	4	3
Eproson, J.*	Stites, A. H.; Ellis, L. G.	1,000	28 Nov 1890	Constable (Washington Township)	Elected 4 Nov 1890	4	139
Esmond, G. H.	Forsythe, Charles; Barnes, E. H.	1,000	26 Feb 1870	Constable (Russian River Township)	Appointed 1 Feb 1870 by the Board of Supervisors	C	39
Esmond, James A.	Fewell, Henry; Wilkerson, William C.	1,000	20 Jul 1883	Pound Master (Russian River Township, District No. 4)	Appointed 11 Jul 1883 [by the Board of Supervisors, Columbus Sawtelle having refused to qualify]		
Fair, James G.	Reynolds, James A.; Thompson, Phillip R.	1,000	[?] Oct 1853	Constable (Vallejo Township)	Elected 7 Sep 1853	A	69
Fair, James G.	Thompson, Phillip R.; Hine, James B.	1,000	2 [Oct] 1854	Constable (Vallejo Township)	Elected 6 Sep 1854	A	19-20
Fairbanks, D. B.	Poehlmann, Conrad; Fairbanks, H. T.	5,000	19 Oct 1887	Notary Public	Appointed & commissioned 13 Oct 1887 by R. W. Waterman, Governor of California	3	202-203
Fairbanks, D. B.	Fairbanks, H. T.; Maynard, F. T.	5,000	21 Oct 1885	Notary Public	Appointed & commissioned 15 Oct 1885 by George Stoneman, Governor of California, witness J. P. Rodgers	2	499-500
Fairbanks, D. B.*	Fairbanks, H. T.; Haskell, William B.	5,000	24 Oct 1889	Notary Public	Appointed & commissioned 21 Oct 1889 by R. W. Waterman, Governor of California	3	337-339
Fairclo, Charles	Walker, John; Berry, S. B.	1,000	1 Dec 1888	Road Overseer (Sebastopol Road District)	Elected 6 Nov 1888	3	291-292
Fairclo, Charles	Walker, John; Barnes, Aaron, Sr.	1,000	28 Nov 1890	Road Overseer (Sebastopol Road District, Analy Township)	Elected 4 Nov 1890	4	138
Fannin, Robert C.	Thompson, John D.; Bell, J. S.	1,000	28 Nov 1856	Constable (Russian River Township)	Elected 4 Nov 1856	A	168
Farmer, Elijah T.	Cocke, William E.; Wright, W. S. M.; Black, Houston; Lane, J. J.; Smith, J. T.; Taylor, John S.; Smith, Jacob; Smyth, T. U.; Powell, Ransom; Marks, B.; Davidson, J. E.; McPherson, C. P.; Hopper, Thomas; McReynolds, James; Hoen, B.; Forsyth, Robert; Noonan, George P.; Wise, Henry; Roney, J. M.; Manion, William; Farmer, William; Cook, J. B.; Tempel, C.; Wilson, H.; Wilkinson, R.; Bostwick, A. W.; Clark, J. P.; McGee, H. W.; Farmer, C. C.; Carithers, D. N.; Hendley, John; Martin, R. M.; Boyce, J. F.; Forsyth, B.; Holman, J. H.; Davis, E. L.; Mizer, Henry C.; Ames, C. G.	70,000	[27 Dec 1867]	Treasurer	Elected 4 Sep 1867	B	610-611

Principal Name	Sureties	Amount ($)	Date	Office	Notes	Book	Page(s)
	Cocke, William E.; Farmer, William; Hendley, John; Taylor, John S.; McGee, Henry W.; Lawrence, J. A.; Lane, John J.; Linville, Hiram H.; Noonan, George P.; Forsyth, Robert; Vaughn, Daniel; Farmer, W. H.; Fulkerson, Richard; Smyth, T. U.; Smith, J. P.; Davis, E. L.; McClelland, J. J.; Smith, Jacob; Wilkinson, Reason; Forsyth, Briant; Hoen, Berthold; Moore, John; Boyce, John F.; Griggs, J. H.; Lewis, Joshua; Marks, B.; Hewett, H. T.; Wright, W. S. M.; Underhill, J. G.; Drennan, T. J.; Wilson, Henderson; Davisson, Daniel D.; Haraszthy, A.; Pauli, G. T.; Agnew, S. J.; Davidson, J. E.; Leigh, Barton; Lutgens, John; Holmes, H. P.; Hudson, Martin; Howard, A. S.; Ferguson, W. W.; Lawton, John W.; Wise, H.; Pyatt, Thomas H.; Williams, James M.; Hood, T. B.; Bostwick, N. W.; Gray, J. W.; Edwards, Thomas; Bowles, J. M.; Towne, Smith D.; Hardin, James A.; Tuttle, B. F.; Ellsworth, L.; Huie, George W.; Berger, M.; Hopper, Thomas; Hunt, Charles; Overton, A. P.; Brown, Daniel; Gill, George; Payran, Stephen; Humphries, Charles; Munday, B. B.; Edwards, Uriah; Huie, J. Thompson; Veal, Richard R.; Martin, S. M.; Ellis, John J.; Newburgh, Edward; Smith, John K.; Clark, James P.; Thompson, Thomas L.						
Farmer, Elijah T.		100,000	11 Dec 1865	Treasurer	Elected 6 Sep 1865	B	524-529
Farmer, John H.	Clark, James P.; Holman, John H.	1,000	20 Sep 1867	Constable (Santa Rosa Township)	Elected 4 Sep 1867	B	560
Farmer, John H.	Farmer, E. T.; Hendley, John	1,000	29 Sep 1865	Constable (Santa Rosa Township)	Elected 6 Sep 1865	B	479
Farmer, John H.*	Clark, J. P.; Boyce, J. F.	1,000	21 Sep 1863	Constable (Santa Rosa Township)	Elected 2 Sep 1863	B	356
Farnsworth, C. C.	Oliver, J. S.; Knapp, G. W.; Metcalf, C. E.; Lefebvre, O. M.; Carroll, Patrick	5,000	10 Aug 1884	Notary Public	Appointed & commissioned 1 Aug 1884	2	331-332
Farnsworth, C. C.	Carroll, Patrick; Gaver, A. P.; Lefebvre, O. M.; McReynolds, Jacob	2,000	10 May 1878	Constable (Analy Township)	Appointed 6 May 1878 [by the Board of Supervisors to fill the vacancy occasioned by the refusal of G. W. Anderson to serve]	1	440-441
Farnsworth, C. C.	Knapp, G. W.; Oliver, J. S.; Lefebvre, O. M.; Eastman, Peter; Doss, J. W.	5,000	23 Nov 1882	Notary Public	Appointed 29 Jun 1882	2	163-164
Farnsworth, C. C.	Parks, D. H.; Percival, W. C.; Knapp, A. H.; Lefebvre, O. M.	5,000	25 Mar 1876	Notary Public	Appointed 6 Mar 1876	1	207-208
Farnsworth, C. C.	Carroll, Patrick; Burns, Owen; Hanratty, Patrick; Parks, D. H.; Mullally, Patrick	5,000	25 May 1880	Notary Public	Appointed 3 May 1880	1	575-576
Farnsworth, C. C.	Percival, W. C.; Oliver, J. S.; Mooney, T.; Hatton, William; Lefebvre, O. M.	5,000	26 May 1878	Notary Public	Appointed 3 May 1878	1	436-437

46

Principal Name	Sureties	Amount ($)	Date	Office	Notes	Book	Page(s)
Farquar, C. S.	Whitney, A. P.; Wiswell, J. A.	5,000	31 Jan 1880	Notary Public	Appointed & commissioned 29 Jan 1880 by George C. Perkins, Governor of California, includes oath of office dated 31 Jan 1880	2	1-3
Farquar, C. S.	Whitney, A. P; Wiswell, J. A.	5,000	4 Feb 1882	Notary Public	Appointed & commissioned 2 Feb 1882 by George C. Perkins, Governor of California	2	123-124
Farquar, C. S.*	Allen, S. I.; Ragsdale, J. W.; Davis, W. S.; Nagle, F. G.	5,000	18 Jul 1888	Notary Public	Appointed & commissioned 14 Jul 1888 by R. W. Waterman, Governor of California	3	252-253
Farquar, C. S.*	Brown, H. C.; Tupper, G. A.	5,000	22 Sep 1890	Notary Public	Appointed 15 Sep 1890 for the term of 4 years	4	172
Farwell, E. P.	Hoag, Jared C.; Bailey, R.; Jones, William	1,000	[?] Oct 1855	Constable (Annally Township)	Elected 5 Sep 1855	A	119
Faught, Willis	Barney, M. W.; Foster, Joseph	2,000	12 Jan 1874	Justice of the Peace (Russian River Township)	Elected 15 Oct 1873	B	760-761
Fenno, James E.	Barnes, Edwin H.; Powell, Ransom; Hassett, Aaron; Miller, George T.	5,000	11 Apr 1887	Notary Public	Appointed & commissioned 1 Apr 1887 by Washington Bartlett, Governor of California	3	183-184
Fenno, James E.	Barnes, Edwin Harrison; Powell, Ransom	1,000	30 Nov 1886	Justice of the Peace (Mendocino Township)	Elected 2 Nov 1886	3	70-71
Fenno, James E.	Heald, J. G.; Hooper, V. C. W.	1,000	6 Oct 1858	Constable (Mendocino Township)	Elected 1 Sep 1858	A	348
Ferguson, H. O.	Porterfield, J. W.; Crigler, W. E.	2,000	18 Sep 1875	Constable (Cloverdale Township)	Elected 1 Sep 1875	1	125-126
Ferguson, Henry O.	Walker, Silas; Trimble, W. H.	1,000	3 Oct 1863	Constable (Washington Township)	Elected [2 Sep 1863], witness David Odell	B	369
Ferguson, John	Rochford, Thomas; Palmer, William	5,000	13 Jan 1873	Road Master (Petaluma Road District)	Appointed 7 Jan 1873 by the Board of Supervisors		
Ferril, William N.	Steward, Charles; Lamb, Horace	2,000	18 Sep 1862	Constable (Petaluma Township)	Elected 3 Sep 1862	B	309
Ferrill, William N.	Steward, Charles; Berger, M.	2,000	25 Sep 1861	Constable (Petaluma Township)	Elected 4 Sep 1861	B	178
Ferry, John	Scott, Sylvester; Menihan, Michael	1,000	17 Nov 1880	Justice of the Peace (Cloverdale Township)	Elected 2 Nov 1880	2	12-13
Fewel, Henry	Hembree, A. J.; Pool, H. J.; Graham, J. W.; Clark, Benjamin	2,000	26 Feb 1881	Deputy Assessor	Appointed 26 Feb 1881 by George W. Lewis, Assessor	2	89-90
Field, J. S.	Zartman, William; Bassett, Heman	1,000	2 Oct 1855	Constable (Petaluma Township)	Elected 5 Sep 1855, witness William Churchman	A	112
Field, J. S.	Lewis, M. G.; Smith, H. H.; Freeman, John M.	2,000	4 Nov 1852	Constable (Petaluma Township)	Elected	A	28
Field, J. Sewell	Hunt, Charles; Reed, J. F.	5,000	28 Nov 1856	Constable (Petaluma Township)	Elected 4 Nov 1856	A	158

Principal Name	Sureties	Amount ($)	Date	Office	Notes	Book	Page(s)
Field, John	Cooper, John; Crigler, W. E.; Gerkhardt, H. F.; Likins, Levi	10,000	[?] Sep 1877	Supervisor (District No. 5)	Elected 5 Sep 1877	1	287-288
Field, John	Crigler, W. E.; Crigler, L. A.	2,000	11 Feb 1876	Road Master (Cloverdale Road District)	Appointed [7 Jan 1876] by the Board of Supervisors	1	205-206
Field, John	Gerkhardt, H. F.; Kier, H.; Scott, S.; McCray, W. H.; Porterfield, J. W.	10,000	20 Sep 1879	Supervisor (District No. 5)	Elected 3 Sep 1879	1	481-482
Field, John	Ontis, John; Doyle, M.	1,000	3 Feb 1874	Road Master (Cloverdale Township)	Appointed 2 Feb 1874 by the Board of Supervisors, witness Thomas M. Crigler		
Field, John	Ethridge, D.; Larison, S.; Howard, S. D.; Shaw, Isaac E.; King, M. W.; Crigler, L. A.; Rickard, Leroy	5,000	31 Jan 1879	Notary Public	Appointed 22 Jan 1879 by William Irwin, Governor of California, witnesses D. B. Morgan & F. B. Fish	1	454-456
Field, John	Abraham, Casper; Davis, G. V.; Waite, W. N.; Carrie, Joseph A.; Davis, B. J.; Ontis, John	5,000	4 Jan 1877	Notary Public	Commissioned 18 Dec 1876 by William Irwin, Governor of California	1	227-229
Field, John*	McCray, William H.; Goetzelman, John	1,000	21 Jan 1875	Road Master (Cloverdale Road District)	Appointed 7 Jan 1875 by the Board of Supervisors	1	89-90
Fields, J. W.	Mitchell, C. E.; Field, John	1,000	2 Oct 1865	Constable (Cloverdale Township)	Elected 6 Sep 1865	B	493
Fine, Emsley	Merritt, John; Gale, Otis	1,000	13 Jan 1885	Road Overseer (Vallejo Road District)	Appointed 10 Jan 1885 [by the Board of Supervisors]	2	445-446
Finley, John	McReynolds, James; Hoag, O. H.	1,000	14 Feb 1877	Road Master (Bodega [Road] District No. 1)	Appointed 9 Feb 1877 [by the Board of Supervisors]	1	238-239
Finley, S. J.	Piggott, A. K.; Ellison, L. M.	200	8 Oct 1862	Road Master (District No. 2, Bodega Township)	Elected 3 Sep 1862, includes oath of office dated 8 Oct 1862	B	323
Finley, Samuel J.	Barnes, J. D.; Fitzpatrick, Andrew	1,000	[?] Dec 1860	Constable (Bodega Township)	Elected, witnesses J. L. Springer & D. H. Brown	B	124-125
Firebaugh, H. C.	Canan, W. S.; Clack, John W.; Meyer, Sam; Powell, Ransom	5,000	5 Mar 1872	Notary Public	Appointed & commissioned 1 Mar 1872 by Newton Booth, Governor of California	C	158-160
Firebaugh, H. C.	Powell, Ransom; Meyer, Sam	5,000	5 Mar 1874	Notary Public	Appointed & commissioned 3 Mar 1874 by Newton Booth, Governor of California	1	15-16
Fisher, Edward	Williams, John S.; Hoen, Berthold; Richardson, Achilles	5,000	10 Mar 1855	Justice of the Peace (Santa Rosa Township)	Elected 17 Feb 1855 in place of Henry Beaver who resigned, witness Israel Brockman	A	97
Fisher, Edward	Ormsby, J. S.; Moore, William; Carrillo, Julio; Hendley, John	5,000	26 Nov 1856	Superintendent of Public Instruction	Elected 4 Nov 1856	A	167
Florence, Marshall	Schloss, S.; Guerne, George E.	1,000	1 Dec 1884	Justice of the Peace (Redwood Township)	Elected 4 Nov 1884	2	389-390
Florence, Marshall	Willits, W. H.; Schloss, S.	1,000	14 Dec 1882	Justice of the Peace (Redwood Township)	Elected 7 Nov 1882	2	264-265
Florence, Marshall	Torrance, S. H.; Coon, R. W.	1,000	29 Nov 1886	Justice of the Peace (Redwood Township)	Elected 2 Nov 1886	3	50-51
Florence, Marshall	Coon, R. W.; Wescott, O.	1,000	30 Nov 1888	Justice of the Peace (Redwood Township)	Elected 6 Nov 1888	3	288-289

48

Principal Name	Sureties	Amount ($)	Date	Office	Notes	Book	Page(s)
Flournoy, R. C.	Towne, Smith D.; Cavanagh, John; Barnes, Thomas L.; Haydon, S. C.; Robinson, C. I.; Bliss, William D.; Lovell, H. L.; Huie, J. Thompson; Overton, A. P.; Gill, George; Matthews, O. B.; Edwards, Uriah	10,000	21 Sep 1859	District Attorney	Elected 7 Sep 1859 for the term of two years	B	9-10
Forsee, Peter A.	Green, Edward L.; Molleson, H. P.	5,000	1 Oct 1855	Justice of the Peace (Mendocino Township)	Elected 5 Sep 1855	A	110
Fortson, John T.	Overton, A. P.; Hunt, Charles	2,000	[?] Nov 1860	Justice of the Peace (Petaluma Township)	Elected 6 Nov 1860	B	95
Fortson, John T.	Walker, John; Foster, Joseph; Hitchcock, Hollis; Gale, Otis; Hopper, Thomas; Wilkinson, Reason; Hewitt, H. T.; McReynolds, John; Ducker, William; Badger, J. J.; Staley, Theodore; Harris, Jacob; Phinney, R.; Labell, H.; Wise, Henry	15,000	12 Sep 1873	Clerk	Elected [3 Sep 1873]	B	690-692
Fortson, John T.	Bowles, J. M.; Alberding, Fredric H.; Overton, A. P.; Towne, Smith D.	5,000	13 Jul 1861	Notary Public	Commissioned 10 Jul 1861 by John G. Downey, Governor of California; includes oath of office dated 13 Jul 1861	B	160-161
Fortson, John T.	Hunt, Charles; Lewis, Samuel; Edwards, Uriah; Barnes, Thomas L.	5,000	29 Jun 1859	Notary Public	Appointed, includes certification of oath of office dated 28 Jun 1859	B	2-3
Fortson, John T.*	Roberts, Charles; Newburgh, E.; Temple, C.; Bliss, William D.; Lewis, William A.; Boyce, J. F.; Pauli, G. T.; Hewitt, H. T.; Taylor, John S.; McCoy, James; Roney, J. M.	15,000	17 Sep 1875	Clerk	Elected 1 Sep 1875	1	120-122
Foss, Clark	Holmes, C. H.; McDonald, F.	1,000	16 Jan 1879	[Road Overseer (Knight's Valley Road District]	[Appointed 8 Jan 1879 by the Board of Supervisors]		
Foss, Clark	Holmes, C. H.; McDonald, Frank	1,000	2 Mar 1878	Road Overseer (Knight's Valley Road District)	Appointed 7 Feb 1878 [by the Board of Supervisors]	1	421-422
Foster, D. A.*	Ward, W. H.; Dibble, N. P.	1,000	14 Jan 1891	Pound Master (Forrestville District)	Appointed 12 Jan 1891 by the Board of Supervisors	3	356-358
Fouts, Jacob	Hendley, John; Cockrill, L. D.	1,000	4 Oct 1858	Constable (Annally Township)	Elected 1 Sep 1858	A	338
Fowler, John H.	French, John H.; Coon, R. W.	1,000	2 Dec 1884	Justice of the Peace (Redwood Township)	Elected 4 Nov 1884	2	399-400
Fowler, John H.	Fowler, James E.; Fowler, Benjamin	1,000	23 May 1873	Justice of the Peace (Bodega Township)	Appointed 10 May 1873	1	2-3
Fowler, John H.	Fowler, James E.; Smith, Thomas; Rien, John W.	5,000	28 Apr 1873	Notary Public	Appointed & commissioned 19 Apr 1873 by Newton Booth, Governor of California	1	1-2
Fowler, John H.	Smith, Thomas; Percival, W. C.	5,000	30 Apr 1875	Notary Public	Appointed & commissioned 19 Apr 1875 by Romualdo Pacheco, Governor of California; includes oath of office dated 30 Apr 1875; Bond & oath of office written on the back of commission	1	102-104
Fowler, John H.	Smith, Thomas; Duncan, Alexander	5,000	9 May 1877	Notary Public	Appointed & commissioned 19 Apr 1877 by William Irwin, Governor of California, witness Albert H. Heffron	1	268-269

Principal Name	Sureties	Amount ($)	Date	Office	Notes	Book	Page(s)
Fowler, Robert F.	Munday, B. B.; Pauli, G. T.	200	20 Sep 1862	Road Master (Sonoma Township)	Elected 3 Sep 1862	B	319
Fowler, Robert F.	Pauli, G. T.; Wilson, W. L.; Reynolds, W. J.; Ellis, William; Thornley, Henry	4,000	22 May 1860	Road Overseer (Sonoma District comprising Sonoma Township)	Appointed 10 May 1860 by the Board of Supervisors for the term of one year, witness G. L. Wratten	B	85-86
Fowler, Robert F.	Davisson, Daniel D.; Rupe, Sam H.; Hendley, John	100	7 Jan 1860	Road Overseer (Road District No. 15)	Appointed 7 Jan 1860 by the Board of Supervisors	B	73
Fowler, Whitehead	Fowler, James E.; Arthur, Charles R.	1,000	15 Oct 1861	Constable [Analy Township]	Elected 4 Sep 1861	B	223
Frame, R. A.	Mills, E. T.; Stone, N. J.; DeTurk, I.; Chamberlain, D.; Ludwig, T. J.; Murphy, Wyman	5,000	17 Dec 1881	Notary Public	Appointed & commissioned 13 Dec 1881 [by the Governor of California] for the term of two years, vice J. T. Campbell, term expired	2	112-113
Frazier, Wiley	Gallagher, John; Estes, H.	1,000	14 Jan 1879	Road Overseer (Bodega Road District No. 1)	Appointed 10 Jan 1879 [by the Board of Supervisors]	1	396-397
Frazier, Wiley	McCaughey, James; Goodman, L. S.	1,000	8 Feb 1878	Road Master (Bodega Road District)	Appointed 8 Feb 1878 [by the Board of Supervisors]	B	318
Freeman, John M.	McCune, Alexander; Hahman, F. G.	200	13 Sep 1862	Road Master (Road District No. 2, Petaluma Township)	Elected 3 Sep 1862	3	48-49
French, George W.	Hollings, Nicholas; Torrance, S. H.	1,000	27 Nov 1886	Constable (Redwood Township)	Elected 2 Nov 1886	B	403
Frick, G. W.	Show, D.; Jackson, L.	2,000	12 Dec 1863	Justice of the Peace (Vallejo Township)	Elected 21 Oct 1863, witness F. D. Colton	A	51
Frisbie, John B.	Vallejo, Mariano G.; Brockman, Israel	5,000	7 Apr 1852	Notary Public	Appointed	B	298
Fulton, James	Fulton, Thomas; Lewis, Joshua	2,000	16 Sep 1862	Constable (Santa Rosa Township)	Elected 3 Sep 1862	B	352
Fulton, Thomas	Wall, Thomas; Carter, L.	1,000	[21 Sep 1863]	Constable (Santa Rosa Township)	Elected 2 Sep 1863	4	10
Furlong, Thomas	Goodman, L. S.; Furlong, James	1,000	[7 Dec 1888]	Road Overseer (Bodega Road District)	Elected 6 Nov 1888	2	544-545
Furlong, Thomas	Keefe, Nathaniel; Goodman, L. S.	1,000	19 Jun 1886	Road Overseer (Bodega Township)	Appointed 11 Jun 1886 by the Board of Supervisors, [vice W. J. Cunninghame, resigned]	3	176-177
Furlong, Thomas	Goodman, L. S.; Vanderlieth, John	1,000	20 Jan 1887	Road Overseer (Bodega Road District comprising all of Bodega Township)	Appointed 5 Jan 1887	C	123-124
Gaines, R. C.	Esmond, Cornwall; Graham, J. W.; Kennedy, C. W.; Williams, G. F.	2,000	13 Dec 1871	Justice of the Peace (Russian River Township)	Elected 18 Oct 1871	C	114-116
Gaines, W. C.	Barnes, E. H.; Pool, H. J.; Petray, R. A.	5,000	4 Nov 1871	Assessor	Elected 6 Sep 1871		

Principal Name	Sureties	Amount ($)	Date	Office	Notes	Book	Page(s)
Gale, D. R.	Geary, T. J.; McConnell, William E.; Murphy, Rufus; Pearce, George; Reed, W. C.	5,000	23 Mar 1887	Notary Public	Appointed & commissioned 14 Mar 1887	3	140-141
Gale, D. R. *	Noonan, George P.; Gale, Otis	5,000	14 Mar 1889	Notary Public	Appointed & commissioned 12 Mar 1889	4	42
Gale, D. R. *	Mailer, J. C.; Neblett, E.; Prindle, William; Eveleth, J. A.	5,000	27 Feb 1891	Notary Public	Appointed & commissioned 25 Feb 1891 by H. H. Markham, Governor of California	4	184
Gallagher, Jacob M.	Hendley, John; Hoen, Berthold	1,000	24 Sep 1858	Constable (Santa Rosa Township)	Elected 1 Sep 1858	A	315
Gammon, George P.	Phariss, P. H.; Lennox, James W.; Glynn, M.; Martin, James; Leavenworth, T. M.; Lyon, R. B.	2,000	15 Sep 1877	Constable (Sonoma Township)	Elected 5 Sep 1877	1	288-290
Gannon, James	Allen, Otis; Ragle, George J.; McChristian, Patrick	15,000	27 Nov 1882	Supervisor (District No. 4)	Elected 7 Nov 1882	2	190-192
Gannon, James	Orr, John; Sheridan, Flan; Walker, John; Allen, Otis	2,000	28 Oct 1871	Constable (Analy Township)	Elected 6 Sep 1871	C	98
Garrison, William W.	Shoemake, Omer; Coon, R. W.	1,000	6 Jan 1887	Road Overseer (Redwood Township)	Appointed 5 Jan 1887	3	161-162
Gearing, Charles	Mead, James A.; Gladden, W. N.	1,000	19 Feb 1884	Pound Master (part of Mendocino Township, Pound District No. 6)	[Appointed] 5 Feb 1884 [by the Board of Supervisors]		
Geary, Thomas J.	Bliss, William D.; Franklin, D. B.	5,000	17 Oct 1879	Notary Public	Appointed & commissioned 13 Oct 1879 by William Irwin, Governor of California, includes oath of office dated 20 Oct 1879	1	544-546
Geary, Thomas J.	Merritt, John; Tempel, Conrad; Lawrence, H. E.; Hess, Fred; O'Hara, John; Brown, Daniel; McNamara, M.	15,000	18 Nov 1882	District Attorney	Elected 7 Nov 1882	2	144-146
Geary, Thomas J.	Franklin, D. B.; Cavanagh, John	5,000	21 Sep 1877	Notary Public	Appointed 17 Sep 1877 by William Irwin, Governor of California, witness E. S. Lippitt, includes oath of office dated 21 Sep 1877	1	311-312
Gibbens, A. H.	Koch, N. R. S.; Spencer, Frank	1,000	23 Jul 1888	Constable (Cloverdale Township)	Appointed 7 Jul 1888 by the Board of Supervisors	3	255-257
Gibbens, A. H.	Crigler, W. E.; Coomes, A. M.	1,000	4 Dec 1888	Constable (Cloverdale Township)	Elected 6 Nov 1888	3	321-322
Gibbens, A. H. *	Koch, N. R. S.; Yordi, F.	1,000	28 Nov 1890	Constable (Cloverdale Township)	Elected 4 Nov 1890	4	135
Giberson, Charles M.	Hitchcock, Hollis; Loucks, A. H.	1,000	15 Jun 1883	Pound Master (Petaluma Township, Petaluma Pound District)	Appointed 6 Jun 1883 [by the Board of Supervisors]	2	295-296
Gibson, C. S.	Putnam, T. C.; Charles, E. R.	1,000	17 Jan 1889	Pound Master (Vallejo Pound District)	Appointed 18 Jan 1889 by the Board of Supervisors	4	35
Gibson, C. S.	Stewart, David; Hill, William	1,000	19 Apr 1884	Pound Master (Vallejo Township)	Appointed 8 Apr 1884 [by the Board of Supervisors]		

Principal Name	Sureties	Amount ($)	Date	Office	Notes	Book	Page(s)
Gibson, J. W.	Gibson, John; Weise, C.	1,000	25 Nov 1884	Constable (Sonoma Township)	Elected 4 Nov 1884	2	369-370
Gibson, James W.	Drummond, J. H.; Poppe, Charles J.	1,000	25 Feb 1886	Pound Master (Sonoma Pound District)	Appointed 3 Feb 1886 [by the Board of Supervisors, vice James R. Dyer, left the county]	2	533-534
Gilham, W. W.	White, William H.; Kuffel, Isaac	1,000	2 May 1864	Constable (Analy Township)	Appointed 2 May 1864 by the Board of Supervisors, vice J. W. Borton, resigned, includes oath of office dated 7 May 1864	B	452
Gilham, W. W.	McReynolds, Jacob; Patterson, A. S.	500	23 May 1862	Constable (Analy Township)	Appointed 21 May 1862 by the Board of Supervisors, witness W. G. Lee	B	268
Gillan, E.	Weyl, Henry; Schocken, S.	1,000	19 Jan 1885	Road Overseer (Sonoma Road District)	Appointed 13 Jan 1885 [by the Board of Supervisors]	2	490-491
Gillan, E.	Tivnen, John; McDonell, Angus; Akers, S.; Hill, William McPherson	2,000	22 Sep 1875	Constable (Sonoma Township)	Elected 1 Sep 1875, witness G. L. Wratten	1	152-153
Gillan, E.	Weyl, Henry; Schocken, S.	5,000	23 Nov 1882	Road Overseer (Sonoma Township)	Elected 7 Nov 1882	2	234-235
Gillan, E.	Pauli, G. T.; Tivnen, John	1,000	8 Mar 1877	Road Overseer (Sonoma Township)	Appointed 9 Feb 1877 [by the Board of Supervisors]	1	262-263
Gillan, Ed	Edwards, A. S.; Pauli, G. T.	2,000	6 Jan 1875	Road Overseer (Sonoma Township)	Appointed 6 Jan 1875 by the Board of Supervisors	1	73-74
Gillan, Edward	Pauli, G. T.; Tivnen, John	2,000	18 Sep 1877	Constable (Sonoma Township)	Elected 5 Sep 1877	1	309-310
Gillan, Edward	Hill, William McPherson; Pauli, G. T.	1,000	20 Sep 1879	Constable (Sonoma Township)	Elected 3 Sep 1879	1	493-494
Gillan, Edward	Brockman, Israel; Shipley, R. J.	5,000	26 Nov 1856	Constable (Sonoma Township)	Elected 4 Nov 1856	A	180
Gillan, Edward	Edwards, A. S.; Pauli, G. T.	2,000	29 Apr 1876	Road Overseer (Sonoma Road District)	Appointed 3 Jan 1876 [by the Board of Supervisors]	1	215-216
Gillan, Edward	Schetter, Otto; Carriger, David W.	1,000	4 Mar 1881	Deputy Assessor	Appointed [?] [?] 1881 by George W. Lewis, Assessor	2	87-88
Gillan, Edward	Carriger, N.; Pauli, G. T.	2,500	7 Jan 1873	Road Master (Sonoma Road District)	Appointed 7 Jan 1873 by the Board of Supervisors		
Gilliland, John M.	Horne, Amos A.; Ray, John G.; Warden, Robert; Renick, A. B.	2,000	28 Nov 1852	Constable (Sonoma Township)	Elected 2 Nov 1852, includes oath of office dated 30 Nov 1852	A	84
Ginther, Jacob B.	Allen, Samuel I.; Palmer, S. G.; Hoag, O. H.; Montgomery, William; Roney, J. M.	5,000	12 Apr 1882	Notary Public	Appointed 12 Apr 1882 by George C. Perkins, Governor of California	2	130-131
Gird, Henry S.	Bedwell, John C.; Bedwell, Franklin	5,000	[4 Oct 1855]	Justice of the Peace (Washington Township)	Elected 5 Sep 1855	A	150
Gird, Henry S.	Brown, Asher M.; Bedwell, Thomas J.	5,000	1 Dec 1856	Justice of the Peace (Washington Township)	Elected 4 Nov 1856	A	175
Glenn, T. P.	Stevenson, David; Carlton, Columbus	1,000	18 Nov 1865	Justice of the Peace (Bodega Township)	Elected 18 Oct 1865	B	513

52

Principal Name	Sureties	Amount ($)	Date	Office	Notes	Book	Page(s)
Godwin, A. C.	Singley, R. R.; Smith, G. Canning; Bell, William	5,000	1 Oct 1855	Justice of the Peace (Washington Township)	Elected 5 Sep 1855, insufficient sureties		
Godwin, A. C.		5,000	3 Oct 1853	Justice of the Peace (Washington Township)	Elected 7 Sep 1853	A	62
Goodman, W. C.	Tivnen, John; Pauli, G. T.	1,500	16 Jan 1879	Road Overseer (Sonoma Township South)	Appointed 8 Jan 1879 [by the Board of Supervisors]		
Goodman, W. C.	Wegner, Edward; Carriger, David W.	1,000	16 Jan 1880	Road Overseer (Sonoma Road District South)	Appointed 7 Jan 1880 [by the Board of Supervisors]		
Goodman, W. C.	Haraszthy, A. F.; Wegner, Edward; Schocken, Solomon; Martin, James	5,000	18 Nov 1880	Road Overseer (Sonoma Township)	Elected 2 Nov 1880	2	71-72
Goodman, Willis C.	Burris, David; Tivnen, John	1,000	9 Mar 1878	Road Overseer (Sonoma Road District, Southern Division)	Appointed 5 Mar 1878 [by the Board of Supervisors]	1	418-419
Goodwin, Frank	Miller, William R.; Allison, William	1,000	24 Sep 1867	Constable (Salt Point Township)	[Elected 4 Sep 1867]	B	584
Gordon, A. J.	Clack, John W.; Bloom, David	200	[16 Sep 1863]	Road Overseer (District No. 1, Mendocino Township)	Elected 2 Sep 1863	B	357
Gordon, A. J.	McManus, John G.; Bloom, Joseph; Norton, L. A.	6,000	29 Oct 1869	Assessor	Elected 1 Sep 1869	B	636
Gordon, Andrew J.	Hudson, Thomas W.; Hopper, Thomas; Norton, L. A.	5,000	11 Nov 1867	Assessor	Elected 4 Sep 1867	B	593
Gordon, E.	Crigler, W. E.; Porterfield, J. W.; Davis, B. J.	2,000	[20 Sep 1873]	Constable (Cloverdale Township)	Elected 3 Sep 1873	1	5-6
Gordon, W. H.	Hassett, John D.; Warner, A. L.	1,000	10 Jan 1880	Road Master (Road District No. 2, Mendocino Township)	Appointed 7 Jan 1880 [by the Board of Supervisors], includes W. H. Gordon's letter to the Board of Supervisors dated 1 Oct 1880 requesting that he be released from his bond because he had left or was leaving Sonoma County		
Gordon, W. H.	Hendricks, J. M.; Bryant, J. J.	1,000	11 Jan 1879	Road Overseer (Mendocino Road District No. 2)	[Appointed] 7 Jan 1879 [by the Board of Supervisors]		
Gordon, William G.	McManus, John G.; Powell, R.; Ormsby, J. S.; Gordon, A. J.; Bamford, William; Bledsoe, A. C.; Wilkerson, William C.; Carson, Lindsey; Barnes, Edwin H.; Campbell, J. A.; Thompson, J. D.	10,000	25 Sep 1857	District Attorney (Sonoma & Mendocino Counties)	Elected 2 Sep 1857, accepted by W. B. Hagans, Chairman of the Board of Supervisors	A	258-262
Goss, John*	Shea, Con; Muther, Frank; Murphy, Rufus; Davidson, S. E.	5,000	3 Dec 1889	Notary Public	Appointed 27 Nov 1889	4	69
Gossage, Joseph	Dinwiddie, J. L.; Bryant, C. G.	1,000	2 Dec 1890	Road Overseer (Petaluma Road District)	Elected 4 Nov 1890	4	137
Gould, T. J.	King, William; Brown, Richard	1,000	29 Nov 1890	Road Overseer (Ocean Township)	Elected 4 Nov 1890	4	136

Principal Name	Sureties	Amount ($)	Date	Office	Notes	Book	Page(s)
Graeff, John U.	Walker, John; Wightman, Chancy	1,000	29 Nov 1884	Constable (Analy Township)	Elected 4 Nov 1884	2	438-439
Graeff, John U.	Solomon, Charles; Glynn, F. B.	1,000	4 Dec 1886	Constable (Analy Township)	Elected 2 Nov 1886, witness A. D. Laughlin	3	92-93
Gray, Nicholas	Calhoun, John W.; Clark, J. P.; Lawton, John W.; Ballou, V. J.; Hudspeth, James M.	5,000	2 Nov 1863	Surveyor	Elected 2 Sep 1863 for the term of two years from 1 Oct 1863	B	437
Grayson, Daniel	Berggren, John Fr.; Leavenworth, Thaddeus M.; Tate, T. H.	5,000	8 Oct 1857	Justice of the Peace (Sonoma Township)	Elected 2 Sep 1857, oath of office administered 13 Oct 1857 by G. L. Wratten, Notary Public	A	277-279
Green, A. M.	Laymance, I. C.; Miller, George	200	15 Sep 1863	Road Master (District No. 3, Mendocino Township)	Elected [2 Sep 1863]	B	358
Green, Edward L.	Todd, S. S.; Nalley, A. B.; Treadway, Griffin; Hoen, Berthold; Ormsby, J. S.; Young, John; Harris, Jacob; Bledsoe, A. C.; Beaver, Henry; Holloway, J. B.; Gallagher, Jacob M.; Hill, James M.; Hahman, F. G.; Thompson, J. D.; McCollough, S. G.; Barnes, Edwin H.; McClish, Thomas; Rickman, David H.; Brown, J. H.; March, William J.; Miller, Valentine; Storey, George; Wilkerson, William C.; Page, H. F.; Francis, A. J.; Allen, William T.; Gordon, A. J.; Brumfield, George P.; Cavanagh, John; Smith, J. P.; Espey, John; Ellis, John J.; Russell, A. W.; Rudesill, J. A.	25,000	[?] [?] 1857	Sheriff	Elected 30 Sep 1857 at a special election by order of the Board of Supervisors	A	192-198
Green, Edward L.	Chapman, A. P.; Espey, John; Slusser, L. S. B.; Smith, J. P.; Smyth, Thomas W.; White, Henry M.; Jones, W. L.; Allen, William T.; Story, George; Barnes, Edwin H.; Cook, David W.	12,000	[?] May 1856	Under Sheriff	Appointed by A. C. Bledsoe, Sheriff		
Green, Edward L.	Storey, George; Molleson, H. P.; Laymance, J. B.; Allen, William T.; Capell, C. W.; Snuffin, Amos; Barnes, Edwin H.; Prewett, James; Cook, David W.; Armes, Charles W.; Slusser, Levi S. B.; Smith, Isaac P.; Smith, A. H.; Smyth, Thomas W.	12,000	27 Sep 1855	Deputy Sheriff	Appointed by A. C. Bledsoe, Sheriff		
Greenwell, S. T.*	Hardin, W. J.; Williams, C. A.	1,000	5 Jul 1892	Constable (Cloverdale Township)	Appointed 7 Jun 1892 by the Board of Supervisors	4	202
Greenwell, Stephen T.*	Williams, C. A.; Hardin, W. J.	1,000	2 Dec 1892	Constable (Cloverdale Township)	Elected 8 Nov 1892	4	243
Greenwood, George J.	Ormsby, John S.; Thurgood, William S.	100	21 May 1859	Road Overseer (Road District No. 29)	Appointed	A	381
Griffin, T. A.*	Wehrspon, Aug; McPeak, M. A.	1,000	6 Dec 1890	Constable (Redwood Township)	Elected 4 Nov 1890	4	159
Griffin, George W.	Torrance, Shebal H.; Murphy, Rufus	1,000	21 Dec 1883	Justice of the Peace (Redwood Township)	Appointed 4 Dec 1883 [by the Board of Supervisors, J. M. Miller having removed]	2	306-307

Principal Name	Sureties	Amount ($)	Date	Office	Notes	Book	Page(s)
Griggs, Joseph H.	Linville, H. H.; Cook, J. G.	100	[?] Mar 1860	Road Overseer (Road District No. 9, Santa Rosa Township)	Appointed [?] Feb 1860 by the Board of Supervisors	B	70
Griggs, Joseph H.	Lawton, John W.; Smith, I. P.; Linville, H. H.; Holmes, H. P.; Smyth, Thomas U.	2,000	3 Oct 1863	Justice of the Peace (Santa Rosa Township)	Elected [21 Oct 1863]	B	417
Griggs, William B.	Griggs, J. H.; Caldwell, F. M.; Smith, R. Press, Jr.	1,000	10 Aug 1877	Road Master (Santa Rosa [Road] District No. 1)	Appointed 8 Aug 1877 [by the Board of Supervisors]	1	272-273
Griggs, William B.	Smith, R. Press; Griggs, J. H.; Caldwell, F. M.	1,000	8 Feb 1878	Road Overseer (Santa Rosa [Road] District No. 1)	Appointed 7 Feb 1878 [by the Board of Supervisors]	1	389-390
Grove, W. H.	Lindsay, J. J.; Mackinder, George	1,000	23 Nov 1880	Constable (Russian River Township)	Elected 2 Nov 1880	2	26-27
Grove, W. H.*	Bell, Henry; Barth, A. H.	1,000	27 Nov 1882	Constable (Russian River Township)	Elected 7 Nov 1882	2	217-218
Grove, W. Henry	Wilson, M. A.; Laughlin, L.	1,000	24 Oct 1879	Constable (Russian River Township)	Appointed 9 Oct 1879 [by the Board of Supervisors] to fill the unexpired term of A. H. Barth, [resigned]	1	547-548
Grove, William Henry	Gaines, W. C.; Clark, W. S.	1,000	20 Sep 1879	Constable (Russian River Township)	Elected 3 Sep 1879	1	521-522
Gschwend, John	Lamar, J. B.; Kirry, Oswald; Sondheimer, E.	100	12 May 1858	Road Overseer (Public road leading from the Barnes Rancho to the mouth of the Albion River in Mendocino County)	Appointed May Term 1858 by the Board of Supervisors	A	311
Haehl, Henry	Kier, Harry; Haehl, Conrad	1,000	12 Nov 1879	Justice of Peace (Cloverdale Township)	Appointed 5 Nov 1879 [by the Board of Supervisors] to fill the vacancy occasioned by the death of D. C. Brush	1	554-555
Hahman, F. G.	Holmes, H. P.; Atterbury, William B.; Meacham, Alonzo; Holman, John H.; Taylor, John S.; Hannath, Charles John; Hood, William; Bernhard, Isaac; Rexford, E. A.; Towne, Smith D.; Brown, S. C.; Payran, Stephen; Schmitt, George; Baylis, T. F.; Starke, August	25,000	13 Sep 1861	Treasurer	Elected 4 Sep 1861	B	185-188
Hahman, Feodore G.	Carrillo, Julio; Hoen, Berthold; Payran, Steven; Newman, B.; Long, M. A.; Brockman, Israel; Kamp, Harold Lud.; Bruns, Hermann; Cooper, E. B.; Bernhard, Isaac; Rudesill, J. A.; Fulkerson, Richard; Wright, W. S. M.; Akers, Stephen; Baylis, Thomas F.; Ellis, John J.; Baldwin, O. T.; Weil, M.; Schmitt, George; McVicar, C. M. C.; Holmes, H. P.; Hartman, J. W.	30,000	24 Sep 1857	Public Administrator	Elected 2 Sep 1857, accepted by W. B. Hagans, Chairman of the Board of Supervisors	A	240-248
Hall, Gil P.*	Harris, Richard; Tomasini, L.; Lawrence, H. E.; Zimmerman, George	10,000	1 Dec 1890	Recorder	Elected 4 Nov 1890	4	150

Principal Name	Sureties	Amount ($)	Date	Office	Notes	Book	Page(s)
Hall, Gil P.*	Brown, Daniel; Lewis, W. A.; McNamara, M.; Bowles, J. M.; Scott, John C.; Poehlman, C.	20,000	1 Dec 1890	Auditor	Elected 4 Nov 1890	4	149
Hall, Gilbert P.*	Show, A. J.; Bowles, J. M.; Cowen, Philip; Poehlmann, Conrad;	10,000	5 Dec 1892	Recorder	Elected 8 Nov 1892	4	226
Hall, Gilbert P.*	Lewis, W. A.; Brown, Daniel; McNamara, M.	20,000	5 Dec 1892	Auditor	Elected 8 Nov 1892	4	223
Hall, J. W.	Britten, R. H.; Forsyth, W. H.	1,000	10 Jan 1880	Road Overseer (Santa Rosa Road District No. 5)	Appointed 9 Jan 1880 [by the Board of Supervisors]		
Hall, James W.	Peterson, A.; Smith, J. K.; Ames, C. G.; Carithers, D. N.; Pfister, C.; Hughes, John; Gauldin, W. W.; Clark, D.; Brittan, R. H.	9,000	20 Nov 1880	Road Overseer (Santa Rosa Township)	Elected 2 Nov 1880	2	66-67
Hall, James W.	Forsyth, B.; Britten, R. H.	1,000	24 Jan 1879	Road Overseer (Santa Rosa Road District No. 5)	Appointed 9 Jan 1879 [by the Board of Supervisors]		
Hall, James W.	Carithers, D. N.; Clark, David; Forsyth, W. H.; Gauldin, W. W.; Forsyth, Robert A.	5,000	25 Nov 1882	Road Overseer (Santa Rosa Township)	Elected 7 Nov 1882	2	236-237
Hall, James W.*	Hopper, Thomas; Forsyth, B.; Forsyth, Robert A.	15,000	30 Nov 1892	Supervisor (District No. 3)	Elected 8 Nov 1892, witness L. W. Juilliard	4	211
Hall, L. B.	Mapes, Ira C.; Davis, E. L.; Clark, David; Neblett, E.; McMinn, John; Mizer, Henry C.; Lewis, Joshua; McReynolds, William	15,000	24 Jan 1872	Public Administrator	Elected 6 Sep 1871	C	148-150
Hamilton, Archibald	Allison, Robert; Oliver, William	1,000	25 Sep 1858	Justice of the Peace (Big River Township)	Elected 1 Sep 1858	A	318
Hanratty, Patrick	Carroll, Patrick; Hoag. O. H.	1,000	4 Jan 1876	Road Master (Analy Township, District No. 1)	Appointed 4 Jan 1876 by the Board of Supervisors	1	192-193
Harbach, Daniel L.	Stengel, Christion; Helke, F.; Fisk, A. J.; Vance, E. H.	2,000	2 Dec 1873	Justice of the Peace (Salt Point Township)	Elected 15 Oct 1873	B	770-772
Harback, D. L.	Stengel, Christion; Herritage, John	1,000	11 Nov 1871	Justice of the Peace (Salt Point Township)	Elected 18 Oct 1871	C	102
Harback, Daniel L.	Knipp, Adam; Stengel, Christion	2,000	8 Nov 1875	Justice of the Peace (Salt Point Township)	Elected 20 Oct 1875	1	189-190
Hardin, George M.	Gossage, H. S.; Wilton, T. G.; Ayer, H. George; Walker, Ed. L.	1,000	8 Apr 1890	Constable (Analy Township)	Appointed 8 Apr 1890 by the Board of Supervisors	4	80
Hardin, James T.*	Thomas, A.; Willis, T. N.; Farmer, E. T.; Cocke, W. E.; Clark, J. P.	5,000	24 Dec 1868	Notary Public	Appointed & commissioned 15 Dec 1868 for the term of two years, includes oath of office dated 24 Dec 1868	B	622
Hardy, William J.	Anderson, William L.; Roney, J. M.; Beam, J.; Hayward, D. L.	5,000	23 Jan 1874	Notary Public	Appointed 19 Jan 1874	B	780-781
Harmon, Luther N.	Ordway, William	200	25 Sep 1861	Road Master & Overseer (District No. 1, Petaluma Township)	Elected 4 Sep 1861, witness J. Chandler	B	243
Harper, Theo.	Shores, L.; Ontis, John; Wood, W. M.; Goetzelman, John	2,000	20 Sep 1873	Constable (Cloverdale Township)	Elected 3 Sep 1873	1	8-9

56

Principal Name	Sureties	Amount ($)	Date	Office	Notes	Book	Page(s)
Harris, Arthur L.*	Ragsdale, J. W.; Brown, H. C.; Kier, H.	5,000	24 Feb 1890	Notary Public	Appointed 17 Feb 1890 for the term of 4 years, witness F. G. Nagle	4	76
Harris, E. D.	Hardin, A. H.; McReynolds, John; Morris, Joseph H. P.; Hughes, Rowland	6,000	21 Jun 1860	Superintendent of Common Schools	Appointed 19 Jun 1860 by the Board of Supervisors until next general election	B	90
Harris, E. D.	McReynolds, John; Ross, Losson; Cocke, William E.	12,000	21 Nov 1860	Superintendent of Public Schools	Elected 6 Nov 1860	B	121
Harris, E. D.	Hardin, Henry; Hardin, James A.; Rogers, William H.	5,000	5 Oct 1857	Justice of the Peace (Anally Township)	Elected 2 Sep 1857, accepted by W. B. Hagans, Chairman of the Board of Supervisors, includes oath of office dated [?] Oct 1857	A	275-276
Harris, Ephraim D.	Miller, J. M.; Dougherty, John; Manning, John	5,000	24 Nov 1856	Justice of the Peace (Annally Township)	Elected 4 Nov 1856	A	165
Harris, Jacob	Willis, T. N.; Taylor, John S.	1,000	10 Feb 1877	Road Master (Santa Rosa Road District No. 2)	Appointed 9 Feb 1877 [by the Board of Supervisors]	1	232-233
Harris, Jacob	Taylor, John S.; Mills, A. J.	1,000	7 Feb 1878	Road Overseer (Santa Rosa [Road] District No. 2)	[Appointed] 7 Feb 1878 [by the Board of Supervisors]	1	383-384
Harris, Jacob	Willis, T. N.; Boyce, J. F.	5,000	7 Jan 1873	Road Master (Santa Rosa Road District)	Appointed 7 Jan 1873 by the Board of Supervisors		
Harris, Jacob	Boyce, John F.; Willis, T. N.	5,000	8 Jan 1876	Road Master (Santa Rosa Township)	Appointed 7 Jan 1876 by the Board of Supervisors	1	191-192
Harris, Jacob	Murphy, R.; Wright, Joseph	1,000	8 Jan 1879	Road Overseer (Santa Rosa Road District [No. 2])	Appointed 8 Jan 1879 [by the Board of Supervisors]		
Harris, Thomas M.	Burger, C. H.; Bostwick, W. H.; Fulkerson, S. T.; Fulkerson, Richard	2,000	22 Sep 1879	Constable (Santa Rosa Township)	Elected 3 Sep 1879	1	496-497
Harris, Thomas M.	Loucks, A. H.; Fulkerson, John	2,000	24 Nov 1884	Constable (Santa Rosa Township)	Elected 4 Nov 1884	2	425-426
Harris, W. F.	Meyer, C.; Cummings, J. M.	1,000	[?] Jan 1887	Road Overseer (Washington Road District comprising all of Washington Township)	Appointed 5 Jan 1887	3	165-166
Harris, W. F.	Hamilton, E.; Carver, H. E.	1,000	10 Dec 1885	Road Overseer (Washington Road District)	Appointed 13 Jan 1885 by the Board of Supervisors	2	509-510
Harris, W. F.	Hamilton, Emmor; Remmel, Charles	1,000	13 Feb 1878	Road Overseer (Washington Road District)	Appointed 7 Feb 1878 [by the Board of Supervisors]	1	403-404
Harris, W. F.	Cummings, James M.; Odell, S. G.	1,000	15 Jan 1880	Road Overseer (Washington Township)	Appointed 7 Jan 1880 [by the Board of Supervisors]		

Principal Name	Sureties	Amount ($)	Date	Office	Notes	Book	Page(s)
Harris, W. F.	Meyer, C.; Remmel, Charles	1,000	17 Jan 1885	Road Overseer (Washington Road District)	Appointed 13 Jan 1885 [by the Board of Supervisors]	2	456-457
Harris, W. F.	Sylvester, D. W.; Hamilton, E.	1,500	17 Nov 1880	Road Overseer (Washington Township)	Elected 2 Nov 1880	2	77-78
Harris, W. F.	Ellis, L. G.; Cummings, J. M.	1,000	26 Nov 1890	Road Overseer (Washington Township)	Elected 4 Nov 1890	4	106
Harris, W. F.	Ellis, L. G.; Meyer, C.	1,000	5 Dec 1888	Road Overseer (Washington Road District)	Elected 6 Nov 1888	3	324-325
Harris, Wilbur F.	Wood, J.J.; Remmel, Charles	1,500	23 Nov 1882	Road Overseer (Washington Township)	Elected 7 Nov 1882	2	241-242
Harris, Wilbur F.	Remmel, Charles; McPherson, L.	1,000	7 Jan 1879	Road Overseer (Washington [Road] District)	Appointed 7 Jan 1879 [by the Board of Supervisors]		
Hasbrouck, H. B.	Unckless, Thomas T.; Button, Joseph	1,000	11 Jan 1875	Road Master (part of Petaluma Township)	Appointed [?] Jan 1875 by the Board of Supervisors, witness D. D. Carder	1	78-79
Hasbrouck, H. B.	Hinshaw, E. C.; Hinman, M.	200	6 Nov 1863	Road Master (District No. 2, Petaluma Township)	Appointed, witness William L. Anderson, includes oath of office dated 6 Nov 1863	B	383-384
Haskell, William B.	Fairbanks, H. T.; Maynard, F. T.	5,000	19 Oct 1886	Notary Public	Appointed & commissioned 14 Oct 1886 by George Stoneman, Governor of California, includes oath of office dated 19 Oct 1886	2	557-558
Haskell, William B.	Fritsch, John; Fairbanks, H. T.	5,000	21 Oct 1884	Notary Public	Appointed & commissioned 14 Oct 1884 by George Stoneman, Governor of California, includes oath of office dated 21 Oct 1884	2	336-337
Haskell, William B.	Poehlmann, Conrad; Fairbanks, H. T.	5,000	26 Oct 1882	Notary Public	Appointed & commissioned 19 Oct 1882 by George C. Perkins, Governor of California, for the term of two years, includes commission dated 19 Oct 1882	2	140-141
Haskell, William B.*	Fairbanks, H. T.; Maynard, F. T.	5,000	13 Oct 1888	Notary Public	Appointed & commissioned 11 Oct 1888 by R. W. Waterman, Governor of California	3	259-260
Haskell, William B.*	Poehlman, Conrad; Fairbanks, H. T.	5,000	23 Oct 1890	Notary Public	Appointed & commissioned 21 Oct 1890 by R. W. Waterman, Governor of California	4	175
Hassett, John D.	Powell, Ransom; Bailhache, John N.	10,000	7 Sep 1874	Supervisor [District No. 5]	Elected 2 Sep 1874 at a special election [held in and for the Townships of Mendocino, Cloverdale, Washington, and Redwood], witnesses A. Hassett & J. B. Beeson	1	59-60
Haydon, William	Haydon, Stephen C.; Payran, Stephen	2,000	24 Sep 1859	Justice of the Peace (Petaluma Township)	Elected 7 Sep 1859 for the term of one year	B	17
Hays, S. M.	McManus, John G.; Clack, John W.; Hassett, John D.; Willson, H. M.	2,000	22 Dec 1869	Justice of the Peace (Mendocino Township)	Elected 20 Oct 1869	C	26

Principal Name	Sureties	Amount ($)	Date	Office	Notes	Book	Page(s)
Hays, Samuel M.	Hassett, Aaron; Hays, Mat.; Mead, James A.; Powell, R.; McManus, J. G.	5,000	5 Mar 1870	Notary Public	Appointed 25 Feb 1870, includes certificate of oath of office dated 4 Mar 1870	C	48-50
Head, Robertson	Pool, Henry J.; Barnes, E. H.	3,000	23 Nov 1871	Road Commissioner	Elected 6 Sep 1871	C	104
Head, Robertson	Barnes, Edwin H.; Pool, Henry J.; Metcalf, L. T.; Graham, J. W.	3,000	29 Nov 1869	Road Commissioner	Elected 1 Sep 1869	C	8
Head, Robinson	Knox, John T.; Willis, T. N.; Gentry, William O.; Mathews, John	2,000	13 Sep 1873	Constable (Santa Rosa Township)	Elected 3 Sep 1873	B	701-702
Heald, Jacob G.	Hudson, T. W.; Alexander, Charles	500	20 Dec 1855	Road Overseer (Russian River District No. 9)	Appointed by the Board of Supervisors		
Hedges, N. M.	Charles, J. M.; Carpenter, L. F.; Fritsch, John; Maynard, F. T.	2,000	10 Mar 1881	Constable (Petaluma Township)	Appointed 7 Mar 1881 [by the Board of Supervisors], vice W. M. Brown, resigned	2	84-85
Hedges, N. M.	Doyle, M.; Tempel, C.	1,000	11 Apr 1883	Constable (Petaluma Township)	Appointed 4 Apr 1883 by the Board of Supervisors, [vice William J. Jordan, resigned]	2	291-292
Hedges, N. M.	Lawrence, Henry; Maynard, F. T.	2,000	17 Jan 1885	Constable (Petaluma Township)	Appointed 10 Jan 1885 [by the Board of Supervisors]	2	454-455
Hedges, W. H.	Tempel, C.; Roberts, Charles	2,000	25 Nov 1884	Constable (Petaluma Township)	Elected 4 Nov 1884	2	371-372
Hedges, W. H.	Tempel, C.; Lawrence, H. E.	2,000	27 Nov 1886	Constable (Petaluma Township)	Elected 2 Nov 1886	3	42-43
Hedges, W. H.*	Lawrence, H. E.; Temple, C.	2,000	26 Nov 1890	Constable (Petaluma Township)	Elected 4 Nov 1890	4	107
Hedges, William H.	Ellsworth, L.; Berger, M.; Van der Noot, John; Knowles, James H.	2,000	17 Sep 1875	Constable (Petaluma Township)	Elected 1 Sep 1875, witness Frank W. Shattuck	1	130-132
Hedges, William H.	Bowles, Joseph M.; Ellsworth, Legrand; Lawrence, Henry E.; Dalton, William H.	2,000	18 Sep 1877	Constable (Petaluma Township)	Elected 5 Sep 1877	1	320-321
Hedges, William H.	Bowles, J. M.; Lawrence, Henry E.; Doyle, M.	2,000	18 Sep 1879	Constable (Petaluma Township)	Elected 3 Sep 1879	1	488-489
Hedges, William H.	Ellsworth, L.; Bernhard, Isaac; Van der Noot, Joseph; Berger, M.	2,000	2 Jan 1874	Deputy Constable (Petaluma Township)	Appointed 2 Jan 1874 by James H. Knowles, Constable (Petaluma Township), witness Frank W. Shattuck		
Hedges, William H.	Tempel, C.; Lawrence, Henry E.	2,000	3 Dec 1888	Constable (Petaluma Township)	Elected 6 Nov 1888	3	309-310
Hedges, William H.	Tempel, C.; Ellsworth, L.	2,000	6 Oct 1871	Constable (Petaluma Township)	Elected 6 Sep 1871, witness Frank W. Shattuck	C	83
Hedges, William H.	Tempel, Conrad; Pearce, George; McCune, Alexander; Bowles, J. M.; Derby, A. B.; Cavanagh, John; Lodge, J. D.; Tighe, Kelly; Bliss, William D.; Towne, Smith D.; Schmitt, George; Skillman, Theodore; Seavey, Robert; Knowles, James H.; Matthies, Heinrich; Meyer, Anton	20,000	9 May 1874	Collector (Petaluma Road District)	Elected 25 Apr 1874 at an election held in Petaluma Road District		
Hedges, William H.*	Doyle, M.; Bowles, J. M.; Lawrence, H. E.	2,000	22 Nov 1882	Constable (Petaluma Township)	Elected 7 Nov 1882	2	186-187

Principal Name	Sureties	Amount ($)	Date	Office	Notes	Book	Page(s)
Heffron, A. H.	Duncan, S. M., Jr.; Duncan, A.	1,000	[10 Sep 1878]	Justice of the Peace (Ocean Township)	Elected 17 Oct 1877	1	443-444
Heffron, Albert H.	Beacom, Thomas; Goodman, L. S.	2,000	6 Nov 1875	Justice of the Peace (Ocean Township)	Elected 20 Oct 1875	1	167
Helmke, F.	Miller, W. R.; Dixon, James	1,000	5 Jan 1874	Road Overseer (Salt Point Road District)	Appointed 5 Jan 1874 by the Board of Supervisors		
Helmke, Fred	Call, G. W.; Shone, Robert	1,000	28 Feb 1878	Road Overseer (Salt Point Road District No. 2)	Appointed 7 Feb 1878 [by the Board of Supervisors]	1	419-420
Helmke, Fred	Beacom, Thomas; Stengel, Christion	2,000	5 May 1873	Road Overseer (Salt Point Township)	Appointed 5 May 1873 by the Board of Supervisors		
Hembree, A. J.	Yates, J. W.; Maddux, L. D.	1,000	29 Nov 1890	Road Overseer (Russian River Road District, Russian River Township)	Elected 4 Nov 1890	4	131
Hembree, A. J.	Pool, H. J.; Gaines, W. C.	1,000	29 Sep 1879	Constable (Russian River Township)	Elected 3 Sep 1879	1	539-540
Hembree, Andrew J.	Meyers, D. P.; Grove, W. H.; Brooks, William; Graham, James W.	2,000	27 Nov 1882	Road Overseer (Russian River Township)	Elected 7 Nov 1882	2	228-229
Hembree, Andrew J.	Jones, Thomas J.; Tebbs, Q. C.	2,000	9 Oct 1877	Constable (Russian River Township)	Elected 5 Sep 1877	1	349-350
Henckell, G.	O'Farrell, John; Wilson, William H.	2,000	26 Jan 1864	Justice of the Peace (Bodega Township)	Elected 21 Oct 1863, includes oath of office dated 26 Jan 1864	B	440
Henckell, George	Caseres, Francisco; Kohle, August	1,000	2 Jan 1866	Justice of the Peace (Bodega Township)	Elected 18 Oct 1865	B	518
Henckell, George	Vanderlieth, John; Ellison, L. M.	1,000	2 Oct 1861	Justice of the Peace (Bodega Township)	Elected 4 Sep 1861	B	203
Henckell, George	Kohle, August; Purrine, A. S.	2,000	6 Jan 1868	Justice of the Peace (Bodega Township)	Elected 16 Oct 1867	B	566
Henckell, George	Sherman, Caleb; Carrillo, Julio	1,000	6 Oct 1862	Justice of the Peace (Bodega Township)	Elected 3 Sep 1862, witness William L. Anderson, includes oath of office dated 6 Oct 1862	B	292
Hendley, John	Brockman, Israel; Boggs, William M.	5,000	15 Dec 1850	County Clerk	Elected at a special election 30 Nov 1850 to fill a vacancy caused by the resignation of R. B. Butler, includes oath of office dated [?] Dec 1850	A	70
Hendley, John	Carrillo, Julio; Atterbury, William B.; Wright, W. S. M.; Griggs, Joseph H.; Hudson, Martin; Green, C. C.; Hoen, Berthold; Smyth, Thomas U.; McManus, J. G.; Holmes, C. H.; Smith, J. P.; Hall, L. B., Cameron, Daniel E.; Campbell, J. A.	25,000	21 Sep 1859	Treasurer	Elected 7 Sep 1859	B	12-16
Hendley, John	McDonald, A. C.; Brockman, Israel	5,000	25 Feb 1851	Justice of the Peace (Sonoma County)	Elected at a special election 22 Feb 1851	A	77-78

60

Principal Name	Sureties	Amount ($)	Date	Office	Notes	Book	Page(s)
Hendley, John	Carrillo, Julio; Bledsoe, A. C.; Hudson, Martin; Griggs, Joseph H.; Atterbury, William B.; Long, M. A.; Wright, W. S. M.; Gordon, A. J.; Campbell, J. A.; Cock, W. H.; Smith, I. P.; Hoen, Berthold; Carson, Lindsey; Barnes, Edwin H.; Thompson, John D.; Calhoon, J. W.; Drum, B. H.; Brockman, Joseph E.; Beaver, Henry; Ormsby, J. S.; Copeland, A.; Holman, F. M.; Payran, S.; Elliot, Emsley A.	25,000	26 Sep 1857	Treasurer	Elected 2 Sep 1857, accepted by W. B. Hagans, Chairman of the Board of Supervisors	A	227-235
Hendley, John	Atterbury, William B.; Beaver, Henry; Hoen, B.; Carrillo, Julio; Smith, Jacob; Fisher, Ed.; Maupin, R. A.	20,000	6 Feb 1857	Treasurer	Appointed 6 Feb 1857 by the Board of Supervisors to fill the vacancy after the resignation of William A. Buster	A	185-186
Hendrix, Lewis	Staley, Theodore; Jacobs, Eli	1,000	9 Jan 1879	Road Overseer [Santa Rosa [Road] District No. 1)	Appointed 9 Jan 1879 [by the Board of Supervisors]		
Henley, Barclay	Doyle, M.; Boyce, J. F.	10,000	18 Sep 1875	District Attorney	Elected 1 Sep 1875	1	122-123
Henley, Barclay	Brown, John; McCullough, William	5,000	2 Jan 1872	District Attorney	Appointed 20 Nov 1871 by the Board of Supervisors [to fill the vacancy occasioned by the resignation of A. P. Overton, who will assume the duties of County Judge; The appointment to take effect 1 Jan 1872]	C	138-140
Henley, Barclay	Pyatt, Thomas H.; Farmer, Elijah T.	5,000	28 May 1868	Notary Public	Commissioned 2 May 1868 by H. H. Haight, Governor of California; includes oath of office dated 28 May 1868	B	619
Henry, James	Liebig, Fred; Luttringer, Joseph	1,000	17 Oct 1881	Justice of the Peace (Salt Point Township)	Appointed 5 Oct 1881 [by the Board of Supervisors, vice M. W. Plumley, resigned]	2	103-104
Herbert, Alick	Burns, C. F.; Brown, R.	1,000	13 Oct 1888	Road Overseer (Ocean Road District)	Appointed 9 Oct 1888 by the Board of Supervisors		
Herrick, Alfred F.	Smith, Stephen, 2nd; Gifford, Thomas; Thurston, J. M.	1,000	1 Oct 1855	Constable (Bodega Township)	Elected 5 Sep 1855	A	136-137
Hickey, Maurice	Merritt, John; Erwin, N.	1,000	14 May 1885	Pound Master (Petaluma Pound District)	Appointed 4 May 1885 [by the Board of Supervisors]	2	479-480
Hickey, Maurice	Merritt, John; Naughton, Hubert	2,000	15 Jan 1880	Road Overseer (Petaluma Road District No. 2)	Appointed 7 Jan 1880 [by the Board of Supervisors]		
Hicks, George M.	Richardson, H. A.; Clark, John	1,000	12 Dec 1890	Road Overseer (Stewarts Point Road District, Salt Point Township)	Elected 4 Nov 1890	4	165
Higgins, A.	Campbell, George; Stewart, David	1,000	15 Feb 1876	Road Overseer (Vallejo Road District, southern portion)	Appointed 12 Feb 1876 by the Board of Supervisors	1	197-198
Higgins, A.	Pierce, H. L.; White, William	2,000	18 Jan 1879	Road Overseer (Vallejo Road District [No. 2])	Appointed 8 Jan 1879 [by the Board of Supervisors]		

61

Principal Name	Sureties	Amount ($)	Date	Office	Notes	Book	Page(s)
Higgins, A.	Campbell, George; Charles, E. R.	1,000	2 Mar 1878	Road Overseer (Vallejo Road District, South)	Appointed 7 Feb 1878 [by the Board of Supervisors]	1	412–413
Higgins, Alfred	Perkins, A. T.; Jose, M. H.	100	18 Nov 1858	Road Overseer (District embracing all that section of County between Huttons at the forks of the road leading to Anderson Valley and Fehrl Valley and Edsill's ranch on the Ukiah Road)		A	367
Higgins, Silas G.	Cameron, John; Brockman, Israel; McDonald, A. C.; Vallejo, M. G.; Cooper, James	20,000	16 Oct 1850	Auctioneer	Appointed by Hon. H. A. Green, Sonoma County Judge, witnesses Charles P. Wilkins and Thomas Ollily, includes oath of office dated 19 Oct 1850	A	56–57
Highley, William	Call, George W.; Henry, James	1,000	2 Dec 1890	Justice of the Peace (Salt Point Township)	Elected 4 Nov 1890	4	134
Hill, A. B.*	Hill, William; Fairbanks, H. T.	5,000	26 Dec 1890	Notary Public	Appointed 26 Dec 1890, witness D. B. Fairbanks	4	180
Hill, Charles S.	Burns, J. A.; Heald, Thomas T.	1,000	5 Nov 1884	Constable (Redwood Township)	Elected 4 Nov 1884	2	440–441
Hoadley, J. F., Sr.	Field, John; Brush, William T.	1,000	1 Dec 1888	Justice of the Peace (Cloverdale Township)	Elected 6 Nov 1888	3	307–309
Hoadley, J. F., Sr.	Holloway, J. C.; Spencer, Frank	1,000	1 Dec 1890	Justice of the Peace (Cloverdale Township)	Elected 4 Nov 1890	4	133
Hoadley, J. F., Sr.*	Abraham, Casper; Davis, G. V.	5,000	27 Mar 1888	Notary Public	Appointed 23 Mar 1888 by R. W. Waterman, Governor of California	3	238–239
Hoadley, J. F., Sr.*	Ink, W. P.; Davis, G. V.	5,000	28 Mar 1890	Notary Public	Appointed 20 Mar 1890 by R. W. Waterman, Governor of California	4	79
Hoadley, J. F., Sr.*	Field, John; Brush, William T.	1,000	7 Feb 1888	Justice of the Peace (Cloverdale Township)	Appointed 6 Feb 1888 by the Board of Supervisors	3	220–221
Hoag, J. C.	Gilham, W.W.; McReynolds, Jacob	2,000	4 Nov 1863	Justice of the Peace (Annally Township)	Elected [21 Oct 1863]	B	386
Hoag, J. C.*	Walker, Alonzo; Fike, N.	1,000	5 Aug 1863	Justice of the Peace (Analy Township)	Appointed, includes oath of office dated 5 Aug 1863	B	350–351
Hoag, Jared C.	Hoag, S. Cushing; Wise, Henry	5,000	12 Mar 1872	Notary Public	Appointed 7 Mar 1872 for the term of two years, includes oath of office dated 16 Mar 1872	C	160–161
Hoag, Jared C.	Cockrill, L. D.; Fowler, John H.; Atterbury, William B.; Ames, C. G.; Clark, J. P.	5,000	17 Mar 1866	Notary Public	Appointed 27 Feb 1866, includes oath of office dated 17 Mar 1866	B	544
Hoag, Jared C.	Walker, Alonzo; Gordon, Joseph	2,000	3 Jan 1866	Justice of the Peace (Analy Township)	Elected 6 Sep 1865	B	517

Principal Name	Sureties	Amount ($)	Date	Office	Notes	Book	Page(s)
Hoag, Jared C.	Hoag, S. Cushing; Miller, L. W.	5,000	8 Mar 1864	Notary Public	Appointed & commissioned 27 Feb 1864 by Frederick F. Low, Governor of California, for the term of two years, includes oath of office dated 8 Mar 1864	B	441
Hoag, O. H.	Warner, James; Burger, C. H.; Ross, H. J.; Fisher, A. L.	5,000	1 Apr 1887	Notary Public	Appointed 23 Mar 1887	3	144-145
Hoag, O. H.	Henley, Barclay, Beam, J.; Franklin, D. B.; Loucks. A. H.; Heisel, Paul; Wright, Joseph	5,000	14 Apr 1880	Notary Public	Appointed 9 Apr 1880, witness John Tyler Campbell	1	577-578
Hoag, O. H.	Latapie, E.; Emerson, Henry; Peatross, W. W.; Phelps, Alma	5,000	20 Sep 1875	Recorder	Elected 1 Sep 1875	1	117-118
Hoag, O. H.	Latapie, E.; Emerson, Henry; Peatross, W. W.; Phelps, Alma; McReynolds, James; Thompson, Thomas L.	10,000	20 Sep 1875	Auditor	Elected 1 Sep 1875	1	119-120
Hoag, O. H.	White, William H.; Lefebvre, O. M.	1,000	21 Jan 1875	Road Master (Analy Township, District No. 1)	Appointed 6 Jan 1875 by the Board of Supervisors	1	90-91
Hoag, O. H.	Hoskins, T. D.; Loucks, A. H.; Roney, J. M.; Muther, Frank; Ross, H. J.	5,000	26 Mar 1885	Notary Public	Appointed 21 Mar 1885 [by George Stoneman, Governor of California], witness A. D. Laughlin	2	466-467
Hoag, O. H.	Brown, John; Taber, John S.; Kline, Jacob; Roney, James M.	5,000	28 Apr 1875	Notary Public	Appointed 23 Apr 1875 by the Governor of California	1	99-100
Hoag, O. H.	Roney, J. M.; Fick, J. F.; Kelly, J. W.; Loucks, A. H.; Muther, Frank; Hoskins, T. D.; Warner, James J.	5,000	4 Apr 1883	Notary Public	Appointed & commissioned 23 Mar 1883	2	289-291
Hoag, O. H.	Hoag, Jared C.; Miller, Lew W.; Wood, William B.; Lefebvre, O. M.	5,000	5 Mar 1868	Notary Public	Appointed 29 Feb 1868 by H. H. Haight, Governor of California, includes oath of office dated 5 Mar 1868	B	614
Hoag, O. H.	Hoag, Jared C.; Lefebvre, O. M.; Hall, Henry; Isom, H.	5,000	5 Mar 1870	Notary Public	Appointed & commissioned 1 Mar 1870 by H. H. Haight, Governor of California, includes certificate of oath of office dated 5 Mar 1870	C	50-51
Hoag, O. H.	Rogers, W. K.; Weatherington, Henry; Sparks, George W.; Carroll, Patrick; Wiley, J. W.	5,000	5 Mar 1878	Notary Public	Appointed 2 Mar 1878	1	416-418
Hoag, O. H.*	Warner, James; Murphy, Rufus; McReynolds, James; Doyle, M.	5,000	23 Mar 1889	Notary Public	Appointed 20 Mar 1889	4	43
Hoag, O. H.*	McReynolds, James; Doyle, M.; Bertoli, Paul; Ross, H. J.	5,000	23 Mar 1891	Notary Public	Appointed 19 Mar 1891 by H. H. Markham, Governor of California	3	364-365
Hoag, S. Cushing	Cockrill, L. D.; Ames, T. N.	5,000	1 Oct 1855	Justice of the Peace (Annally Township)	Elected 5 Sep 1855	A	123
Hoen, Berthold	Martin, H. B.; Boyce, J. F.; Smith, W. R.; Shane, Adam; Rosenberg, M.; Hahman, F. G.; Carrillo, Julio; Wright, Charles H.; Pearce, George; Richardson, A.; Hartman, J. William; Sanders, G. P.; Gallagher, Jacob M.; Fisher, Edward; Belden, Joseph W.; Hendley, John	20,000	10 Jul 1855	Treasurer	Appointed to fill the vacancy occasioned by the death of George W. Miller	A	104
Holland, Henry E.	Morris, Joseph H. P.; Taylor, Nelson	1,000	3 Jan 1855	Constable (Bodega Township)	Elected 30 Dec 1854	A	96
Hollaway, J. B.	Levy, Michel; Riley, A. P.	1,000	7 Oct 1859	Constable (Cloverdale Township)	Elected 7 Sep 1859, witness Eli Lester	B	58

Principal Name	Sureties	Amount ($)	Date	Office	Notes	Book	Page(s)
Hollaway, J. B.	Bledsoe, A. C.; Hooper, J. M.	1,000	8 Oct 1857	Constable (Washington Township)	Elected 2 Sep 1857, accepted by W. B. Hagans, Chairman of the Board of Supervisors	A	282-283
Hollaway, James B.	Levy, Michel; Taylor, Alex	1,000	[24] Nov [1860]	Constable (Cloverdale Township)	Elected 6 Nov 1860	B	105-106
Holman, John H.	Farmer, E. T.; Wise, Henry; Crane, G. L.	2,000	20 Sep 1873	Coroner	Elected 3 Sep 1873	**B**	721-722
Holman, John H.	Crane, Joel; Farmer, William	1,000	24 Sep 1858	Justice of the Peace (Santa Rosa Township)	Elected 1 Sep 1858	A	320
Holman, John H.	Williamson, William M.; Farmer, William; Carrillo, Julio; Manion, William; Nalley, A. B.; Crane, G. L.; Green, C. C.; Treadway, Griffin; Hendley, John; Cummons, M. B.; Sebring, Thomas; Barry, John; Bedwell, Franklin; Cattron, William C.; Kessing, John F.; Hewett, H. T.; Beaver, Henry; Day, Charles G.; Wood, John B.; Potter, Samuel, Jr.; Sackett, D. A.; Fine, Abraham; Johnson, Thomas J.; Runk, George A.; Lucas, James	30,000	30 Sep 1859	Public Administrator		B	51-55
Holmes, Henderson P.	Taylor, James M.; Campbell, James A.; Emerson, Henry; Espey, John; Ellis, John J.; Lane, J. J.; Barnes, E. H.; Grant, John D.; McPherson, Charles P.; Smith, Thomas U.; Arnold, G. W.; Goldfish, B.; Taylor, John S.; Weis, M.; Mizen, Henry C.; Holmes, C. H.; Forsyth, Robert; Wise, Henry; Marks, B.; Hendley, John; Hahman, F. G.; Boyce, J. F.; Matthews, C. W.; Farmer, E. T.; May, J. J.; Bedwell, J. C.; Pool, H. J.; Aull, A. B.; McManus, J. G.; Hassett, J. D.; Wright, Winfield S. M.; Warner, P.; Hardin, James A.; Commins, Edward; Hunt, Charles	30,000	[16 Jan 1864]	Treasurer	Elected 2 Sep 1863	B	420-423
Hood, James G.	Hood, George; Mailer, James	1,000	2 Feb 1880	Road Overseer (Knight's Valley Township)	Appointed 2 Feb 1880 [by the Board of Supervisors]		
Hooten, James J.*	Powell, R.; Jones, Charles	1,000	25 Nov 1890	Constable (Mendocino Township)	Elected 4 Nov 1890	4	132
Hopper, William	Hopper, Zachariah; Humes, David B.	200	[?] [?] 1863	Road Master (Cloverdale Township)	Elected [2 Sep 1863]	B	375
Houser, S. R.	Shea, Cornelius	15,000	13 Feb 1885	Supervisor (District No. 5)	Elected 4 Nov 1884, a supplemental bond was required because two of the sureties on his original bond dated 20 Nov 1884, James J. Warner & James McReynolds, were relieved of all liability on the bond	2	483-485
Houser, S. R.	McDonald, Mark L.	15,000	20 Jul 1885	Supervisor (District No. 5)	Elected 4 Nov 1884, a supplemental bond was required because one of the sureties on his original bond dated 20 Nov 1884, S. I. Allen, was released from all liability on the bond	2	485-487

Principal Name	Sureties	Amount ($)	Date	Office	Notes	Book	Page(s)
Houser, S. R.	Warner, James J.; Allen, S. I.; McReynolds, James; Glynn, F. B.; Murphy, Rufus; Walker, John	15,000	20 Nov 1884	Supervisor (District No. 5)	Elected 4 Nov 1884, witness A. D. Laughlin	2	359-360
Houser, S. R.	Luttringer, Joseph; Marshall, Hugh; Ruoff, John; Walk, A. J.; Waddell, John Hope	15,000	4 Dec 1882	Supervisor (District No. 7)	Elected 7 Nov 1882	2	254-255
Howe, E. A.	Maddux, John P.; Looney, William	2,000	17 Nov 1883	Justice of the Peace (Santa Rosa Township)	Appointed 8 Nov 1883 [by the Board of Supervisors, vice Judge Burckhalter, died]	2	303-304
Howe, E. A.	Potter, Samuel; Stevenson, David; Keniston, Joseph; Smith, Joseph; Thompson, Thomas L.; Kohle, August	3,000	20 Mar 1866	Commissioner of Highways	Appointed 19 Mar 1866 by the Board of Supervisors, witness T. P. Glenn	B	483
Howe, E. A.	Stump, James; Doran, W. M.	200	23 Jan 1865	Road Master (District No. 1, Bodega Township)	Elected 8 Nov 1864, witness G. Henckell, includes oath of office dated 23 Jan 1865	B	467
Howe, E. A.	Dwight, Lorenzo; Hendrix, Lewis	1,000	25 May 1889	Pound Master (Fulton Pound District)	Appointed 14 May 1889 by the Board of Supervisors	4	56
Howe, E. A.	O'Farrell, John; Vanderlieth, John	200	29 Sep 1863	Road Master (District No. 2, Bodega Township)	Elected 2 Sep 1863, includes oath of office dated 29 Sep 1863	B	378-379
Howell, B. F.*	McConnell, George M.; Davisson, D. D.; Tate, George S.	1,500	30 Sep 1865	Road Overseer (Sonoma Township)	Elected 6 Sep 1865	B	491
Howell, Benjamin F.*	McConnell, George M.; Tate, George S.	200	10 Feb 1865	Road Master (Sonoma Township)	Appointed, witness Philip Mahler	B	469
Hudson, David W.	Powell, Ransom; Gum, Isaac; Hudson, T. W.; Zane, Willis; Young, N. A.	5,000	29 Mar 1878	Notary Public	Appointed 23 Mar 1878	1	424-425
Hudson, S. N.	Burns, J. A.; Murphy, Rufus	1,000	17 Nov 1880	Justice of the Peace (Redwood Township)	Elected 2 Nov 1880	2	15-16
Hudson, Samuel N.	Murphy, Wyman; Willis, T. N.	2,000	18 Nov 1876	Justice of the Peace (Redwood Township)	Appointed 16 Nov 1876 [by the Board of Supervisors upon the death of Squire Clover]	1	276-277
Hudson, Thomas	Elliott, Emsley; Piner, Stephen	5,000	16 Sep 1851	Justice of the Peace (Santa Rosa Township)	Elected 3 Sep 1851	A	85
Hudson, Thomas W.	Heald, H. G.; Kinkead, William	1,000	[?] Oct 1853	Constable (Mendocino Township)	Elected 7 Sep 1853	A	63
Hudson, Thomas W.	Willson, H. M.; Prewett, James	1,000	2 Oct 1854	Constable (Mendocino Township)	Elected 6 Sep 1854	A	41
Hudson, Thomas W.	Clack, J. W.; Mead, James A.	2,000	6 Jan 1875	Road Master (Healdsburg & Pine Flat Road District)	Appointed 2 Oct 1874 by the Board of Supervisors	1	70-71
Hudspeth, Charles M.	Fine, A.	1,000	13 May 1850	Justice of the Peace (Sonoma County)	Elected 9 May 1850, witness Amon Butler	A	77
Hudspeth, Charles M.	Cooper, James	5,000	13 May 1850	Justice of the Peace (District of Bodega and Sonoma County)	Elected 13 May 1850, witness J. T. Terrill	A	70

Principal Name	Amount ($)	Date	Office	Notes	Sureties	Book	Page(s)
Hudspeth, Charles M.	5,000	14 Dec 1850	Assessor	Elected 30 Nov 1850, includes oath of office dated 14 Dec 1850	Fine, J. H.; Cooper, James; Cooke, Martin E.	A	38-39
Hudspeth, Charles M.	100	3 Nov 1858	Road Overseer (Road District No. 1, Ukiah Township (Cannon))	Appointed	Williamson, Thomas D.; Barnett, L.	A	366
Hudspeth, Charles M.	5,000	9 Apr 1850	Coroner	Elected 1 Apr 1850	Cooper, James; Hudspeth, James M.	A	46-47
Hughes, John	1,000	13 Feb 1877	Road Master (Santa Rosa Road District [No. 3])	Appointed 9 Feb 1877 by the Board of Supervisors	Bones, James C.; Wilks, George W.	1	235-236
Hughes, John	1,000	7 Feb 1878	Road Overseer (Santa Rosa [Road] District No. 3)	[Appointed] 7 Feb 1878 [by the Board of Supervisors]	Neblett, E.; Fisher, A. L.	1	382-383
Huie, George W.*	5,000	30 Sep 1865	Assessor	Elected 6 Sep 1865	Huie, J. Thompson; Towne, Smith D.; Payran, Stephen; Show, Daniel	B	498
Hull, John M.*	2,000	7 Sep 1872	Justice of the Peace [Salt Point Township]	Appointed 3 Sep 1872 by the Board of Supervisors, vice Albert Armstrong, resigned	Piver, Leroy; Struckmeyer, J. H.	B	529-530
Humphries, Charles	5,000	13 May 1874	Assessor (Petaluma Road District)	Elected 25 Apr 1874 at a Road election held at Petaluma	Harris, Richard; Hynes, James; Van der Noot, J.; Berger, M.; Bowles, J. M.		
Humphries, Charles	2,000	18 Mar 1881	Deputy Assessor	Appointed [?] [?] 1881 by George W. Lewis, Assessor	Cornwell, C. C.; Needham, Festus; Naughton, Hubert; Hardin, William Henry	2	86-87
Humphries, Charles	1,000	2 Nov 1867	Constable (Vallejo Township)	Elected 4 Sep 1867, witness John Cavanagh	Veal, Richard R.; Payran, Stephen	B	594
Humphries, Charles	200	21 Sep 1861	Road Overseer (Vallejo Township)	Elected 4 Sep 1861, witness S. Payran	Singley, James; Snow, Joshua	B	237
Humphries, Charles	200	22 Sep 1863	Road Overseer (District No. 2, Vallejo Township)	Elected 2 Sep 1863, witness J. Chandler	Whitesides, William H.; Payran, Stephen	B	380
Humphries, Charles	1,000	7 Mar 1866	Constable (Vallejo Township)	Appointed 16 Feb 1866 by the Board of Supervisors	Hunt, Charles; Huie, J. Thompson	B	540
Hunt, W. J.	2,000	17 Sep 1877	Constable (Analy Township)	Elected 5 Sep 1877	Sanborn, G. N.; Ragle, George J.; Allen, B. B.; Morris, Joseph H. P.	1	312-313
Hunt, W. J.	1,000	20 Sep 1879	Constable (Analy Township)	Elected 3 Sep 1879	Morris, Joseph H. P.; Ross, W. D.; Ragle, George J.; Seeley, David	1	473-474
Hunt, W. J.	2,000	23 Sep 1875	Constable (Analy Township)	Elected 1 Sep 1875	Ragle, George J.; Walker, John; Sanborn, George N.; Allen, B. B.	1	147-149
Hunter, Robert Eugene	1,000	18 Mar 1880	Justice of the Peace [Ocean Township]	Appointed 2 Mar 1880 [by the Board of Supervisors, vice Thomas Beacom, resigned]	Rien, Samuel; Thompson, Charles Huntington	1	571-572
Huntley, William*	5,000	21 Mar 1888	Notary Public	Commissioned 15 Mar 1888 by R. W. Waterman, Governor of California	Gobbi, Barnay; Daly, John; Steinbach, Fred; Powell, R.; Marshall, Robert	3	234-236
Hylton, Thomas A.	5,000	3 Oct 1855	Justice of the Peace (Petaluma Township)	Elected 5 Sep 1855	Cooper, Edward B.; Lusk, B.	A	133

66

Principal Name	Sureties	Amount ($)	Date	Office	Notes	Book	Page(s)
Hynes, James	Roach, Thomas; Erwin, Nicholas; Cavanagh, John	1,000	11 Jan 1875	Road Master (Petaluma Road District)	Appointed [?] Jan 1875 by the Board of Supervisors	1	79-80
Hynes, James	Erwin, Nicholas; Naughton, Hubert	2,000	15 Jan 1879	Road Master [Road District No. 1, Petaluma Township)	Appointed 10 Jan 1879 [by the Board of Supervisors]		
Hynes, James	Berger, M.; Roberts, Charles	1,000	23 Feb 1878	Road Overseer (Petaluma Road District No. 1)	Appointed 7 Feb 1878 [by the Board of Supervisors]	1	409-410
Hynes, James	Berger, M.; Tempel, C.	1,000	24 Feb 1877	Road Master (Petaluma Road District No. 1)	Appointed 9 Feb 1877 [by the Board of Supervisors]	1	257-258
Ingram, John	McHenry, James; Griggs, J. H.	1,000	[?] Sep 1861	Constable (Santa Rosa Township)	Elected 4 Sep 1861	B	193
Ingram, John	Carrillo, Julio; Richardson, Achilles	1,000	2 Oct 1854	Constable (Santa Rosa Township)	Elected 6 Sep 1854	A	39
Ingram, John	Fisher, Edward; Fisher, Fenwick; Cook, James G.; Moore, William H.; Crane, James E.	1,000	22 Nov 1856	Constable (Santa Rosa Township)	Elected 4 Nov 1856	A	166
Ingram, John	Griggs, Joseph H.; Holman, John H.	1,000	24 Nov 1860	Constable (Santa Rosa Township)	Elected 6 Nov 1860, witness James W. Shattuck	B	103
Ingram, John	Holmes, H. P.; Griggs, J. H.; Hahman, F. G.	3,000	28 Dec 1864	Steward for the County Hospital at Santa Rosa	Appointed by the Board of Supervisors for the term of one year from 1 Jan 1865 at a salary of $1,500 per annum, witness John T. Fortson	B	465
Ingram, John	Warner, Philemon; Long, M. A.	1,000	30 Sep 1857	Constable (Santa Rosa Township)	Elected 2 Sep 1857, accepted by W. B. Hagans, Chairman of the Board of Supervisors	A	216-217
Ingram, S. D.	Swett, Frank H.; Beam, J.	1,000	19 Jan 1885	Road Overseer (Ocean Road District)	Appointed 13 Jan 1885 [by the Board of Supervisors]	2	487-488
Ingram, Thomas W.	McHenry, James; Barnes, M.	200	[7 Nov 1861]	Road Overseer (District No. 1, Analy Township)	Appointed	B	240
Ireland, Johnston	Engel, H. S.; Espey, G. T.	1,000	1 Oct 1858	Justice of the Peace (Mendocino Township)	Elected 1 Sep 1858	A	329
Ireland, Johnston	Powell, R.; McManus, J. G.	1,000	20 Nov 1860	Justice of the Peace (Mendocino Township)	Elected 6 Nov 1860	B	93
Ireland, Johnston	Hooper, V. C. W.; Brown, J. H.; Hudson, T. W.; March, William J.; Bell, William T.; Raney, John B.; Lemons, Washington; Bagley, John W.	5,000	29 Sep 1857	Justice of the Peace (Mendocino Township)	Elected 2 Sep 1857, accepted by W. B. Hagans, Chairman of the Board of Supervisors	A	254-257
Ireland, Johnston	McCollough, S. G.; Power, S. T.	1,000	3 Oct 1859	Justice of the Peace (Mendocino Township)	Elected 7 Sep 1859	B	34
Jackson, Clem R.	Vasques, P. J.; Brockman, Israel	2,000	17 Sep 1851	Constable (Sonoma Township)	Elected 3 Sep 1851, includes oath of office dated 22 Sep 1851	A	67
Jackson, Henry	Benitz, William; Stevens, F. L.; Rogers, William; Blanchard, J. M.	1,000	26 Sep 1863	Constable (Salt Point Township)	Elected 2 Sep 1863	B	363

Principal Name	Sureties	Amount ($)	Date	Office	Notes	Book	Page(s)
Jackson, J. H.	Hiatt, Joel; Wheaton, John	1,000	8 Feb 1889	Pound Master (Dry Creek Pound District in Mendocino Township)	Appointed 7 Feb 1889 by the Board of Supervisors	4	39
Jackson, Zadok	Ricklifs, Peter H.; Roberts, W. R.	3,000	2 Dec 1867	Road Commissioner	Elected 4 Sep 1867	B	596
Jacobs, George*	Renick, A. B.; Hall, L. I.	1,000	16 Jan 1875	Road Overseer (Mendocino Township)	Appointed 7 Jan 1875 by the Board of Supervisors	1	86-87
Jacobs, J. B.	Cooper, J. D.; Rodgers, Silas	1,000	4 Mar 1878	Road Master (Pine Flat Road District)	Appointed 4 Mar 1878 [by the Board of Supervisors]	1	410-412
Jacobs, J. B.	Powell, R.; Jacobs, George H.	1,000	8 Jan 1880	Road Master/Overseer (Mendocino Road District No. 3)	Appointed 7 Jan 1880 [by the Board of Supervisors]		
Jacobs, James B.	Cooper, John D.; Byington, H. W.	1,000	8 Jan 1879	Road Overseer (Mendocino Road District No. 3)	Appointed 8 Jan 1879 [by the Board of Supervisors]		
James, John	Cuwell, Spencer	200	1 Oct 1861	Road Overseer (District No. 2, Bodega Township)	Elected 4 Sep 1861	B	244
Jannsen, F. A.*	Huntley, George W.; Allen, Sam I.	5,000	31 May 1890	Notary Public	Appointed 27 May 1890 by the Governor of California for the term of 4 years	4	85
Jarboe, W. S.	Lusk, Salmon B.; Richardson, John H.; Doyle, M.	1,000	27 Oct 1857	Judge of the Plains	Appointed 17 Oct 1857 by the Board of Supervisors		
Jewett, L. L.	Murphy, Rufus; French, John H.	1,000	30 Nov 1886	Justice of the Peace (Redwood Township)	Elected 2 Nov 1886	3	80-81
Jewett, L. L.	Turner, N. B., Jr.; Tomblinson, John	1,000	4 Dec 1888	Justice of the Peace (Redwood Township)	Elected 6 Nov 1888	3	312-313
Jewett, L. L.*	Wehrspon, H. W. Aug; Longley, R. G.; Turner, N. B., Jr.; Coon, R. W.	5,000	29 Nov 1889	Notary Public	Appointed 20 Nov 1889	4	70
Johnson, D. W.*	Ware, A. B.; Doyle, F. P.	5,000	26 Aug 1892	Notary Public	Appointed 24 Aug 1892 by H. H. Markham, Governor of California	4	204
Johnson, Gilbert	Buster, F. M.; Champlain, Erastus	1,000	[?] Sep 1867	Constable [Cloverdale Township]	Elected 4 Sep 1867	B	580
Johnson, Gilbert	Moore, Reuben; Shaw, Isaac E.; Shores, Leander	1,500	14 May 1875	Constable [Cloverdale Township]	Appointed 6 May 1875 by the Board of Supervisors [after the office was declared vacant]	1	105-107
Johnson, Gilbert	Shores, James M.; Field, John W.	1,000	15 Jul 1872	Constable (Cloverdale Township)	Appointed 11 Jul 1872 by the Board of Supervisors, [vice Phillip Bates, resigned]		
Johnson, J.J.	Henderson, J. W.; Whitman, J. H.	1,000	20 Sep 1862	Justice of the Peace (Cloverdale Township)	Elected [3 Sep 1862], witness J. Ramey	B	275
Johnson, J.J.	McClintick, S.; Birchett, J. M.	1,000	25 Sep 1861	Justice of the Peace (Cloverdale Township)	Elected [4 Sep 1861], witness James Ramey	B	205
Johnson, J.J.	Kowalsky, Harris; Carlton, Columbus	1,000	5 Nov 1867	Justice of the Peace (Bodega Township)	Elected 16 Oct 1867	B	589

Principal Name	Sureties	Amount ($)	Date	Office	Notes	Book	Page(s)
Johnson, John	Stillwell, V.; McReynolds, J.	1,000	1 Dec 1888	Road Overseer (Bloomfield Road District)	Elected 6 Nov 1888	3	296-297
Johnson, John	Stillwell, V.; Eastman, Peter	1,000	28 Nov 1890	Road Overseer (Bloomfield Road District, Analy Township)	Elected 4 Nov 1890	4	130
Johnson, Orrick	Hayes, William; Sears, G. C. P.	1,000	21 Jan 1876	Pound Master (Sonoma Township)	Appointed 7 Jan 1876 by the Board of Supervisors	1	199
Johnson, Sanborn	Tempel, Conrad; Bernhard, Isaac	2,000	7 Mar 1874	Road Overseer (Vallejo Road District)	Appointed 6 Feb 1874 by the Board of Supervisors		
Johnson, Thomas	Whitman, J. H.; Henderson, J. W.	1,000	14 May 1864	Justice of the Peace (Cloverdale Township)	Appointed 7 May 1864 by the Board of Supervisors, witness T. J. Gould, includes oath of office dated 14 May 1864	B	453
Johnson, Thomas	Wichelhausen, Louis; Taylor, Alexander	100	18 Nov 1858	Road Overseer (Road District No. 18, embracing all that ground between the residence of one Huttons at the forks of the road the one leading to Anderson Valley, the other to Fehrs Valley and Cloverdale including the village of Cloverdale)	Appointed November Term 1858 by the Board of Supervisors	A	363
Johnson, Thomas	Heald, J. G.; Gould, T. J.	1,000	24 Nov 1860	Justice of the Peace (Cloverdale Township)	Elected 6 Nov 1860	B	116
Jones, C. E.*	Moffet, John; Barnes, E. H.	1,000	28 Nov 1882	Constable (Mendocino Township)	Elected 7 Nov 1882	2	213-215
Jones, Charles*	Bell, G. K.; Smith, H. W.	1,000	5 Dec 1892	Constable (Mendocino Township)	Elected 8 Nov 1892	4	244
Jones, George W.	McReynolds, James; Wright, W. S. M.; Ragle, George J.; Laughlin, James H.; Smith, A. H.; Willis, T. N.	5,000	26 Feb 1872	Superintendent of Common Schools	Elected 6 Sep 1871		
Jones, George W.	McReynolds, James; Ragle, George J.; Gilliam, Mitchel	6,000	7 Mar 1870	Superintendent of Common Schools	Elected 1 Sep 1869	C	46-47
Jones, H. A.	Hanbrick, Peter; Grove, W. H.	1,000	4 Dec 1888	Justice of the Peace (Russian River Township)	Elected 6 Nov 1888	3	313-314
Jones, S. L.	Armstrong, Sheldon; Savage, G. N.	5,000	13 Nov 1879	Auctioneer	Witness William H. Bond		

Principal Name	Sureties	Amount ($)	Date	Office	Notes	Book	Page(s)
Jones, T. J.	Maddux, L. D.; Thomas, Henry H.	2,000	10 Dec 1873	Justice of the Peace (Russian River Township)	Elected 15 Oct 1873	B	753-754
Jones, Thomas J.	White, H. M.; Forsythe, Charles	1,000	12 Nov 1877	Justice of the Peace (Russian River Township)	Elected 17 Oct 1877	1	368-369
Jones, Thomas J.	Mackinder, George; Mitchell, R. T.; Clark, Benjamin; Hembree, A. J.	2,000	15 Nov 1881	Justice of the Peace (Russian River Township)	Appointed 7 Nov 1881 by the Board of Supervisors	2	109-110
Jones, Thomas J.	Clark, Charles; Mackinder, George	1,000	22 Nov 1882	Justice of the Peace [Russian River Township]	Elected 7 Nov 1882	2	171-172
Jones, Thomas J.	Hembree, A. J.; Bonnel, B. F.	1,000	22 Nov 1884	Justice of the Peace (Russian River Township)	Elected 4 Nov 1884	2	414-415
Jones, Thomas J.	Geer, Cyrus V.; Bell, Henry	1,000	27 Nov 1886	Justice of the Peace (Russian River Township)	Elected 2 Nov 1886	3	60-61
Jones, Thomas J.	McNeill, William H.; Barnes, E. H.	2,000	8 Nov 1875	Justice of the Peace (Russian River Township)	Elected 20 Oct 1875	1	168
Jones, W. Henry	Rathbun, Erskine; Fritsch, John	2,000	20 Nov 1865	Justice of the Peace (Petaluma Township)	Elected 18 Oct 1865	B	488
Jones, W. Henry	Ordway, William; Edwards, Uriah; Baylis, Thomas F.; Tustin, Columbus; Hedges, William H.; Ftritsch, John; Warner, Gustavus; Gill, George; Overton, A. P.; Hunt, Charles; Hendley, John; Pyatt, Thomas H.; Hudspeth, J. M.; Ellis, John J.	10,000	20 Sep 1861	District Attorney	Elected 4 Sep 1861	B	215-216
Jones, W. Henry	Swift, G. P.; Sears, Franklin; Maynard, F. T.; Bond, J. L.; Burnett, William; Stanley, A. J.; Cowen, Philip; Berger, M.; Runk, G. A.; Baylis, Thomas F.; Brown, S. C.; Hedges, N. M.	10,000	24 Dec 1861	District Attorney	Elected 4 Sep 1861	B	249-250
Jones, William	Gaver, A. P.; Parks, D. H.	3,500	[24 Nov 1880]	Road Overseer (Analy Township)	Elected 2 Nov 1880		
Jones, William M.	Taylor, Benjamin; McGuire, Cornelius	1,000	4 Oct 1858	Justice of the Peace (Annally Township)	Elected 1 Sep 1858, witness Thomas H. Pyatt	A	322
Joost, Jacob*	Armstrong, J. B.; Doyle, M.; Murphy, Rufus	15,000	1 Dec 1892	Supervisor (District No. 5)	Elected 8 Nov 1892	4	216
Jordan, William F.*	Derby, A. B.; Case, A. B.	2,000	28 Nov 1882	Constable (Petaluma Township)	Elected 7 Nov 1882	2	223-224

Principal Name	Sureties	Amount ($)	Date	Office	Notes	Book	Page(s)
Jose, M. H.	Hunt, Charles; Arthur, C. R.; Cross, J. D.; Baylis, T. F.	1,000	26 Sep 1857	Constable (Petaluma Township)	Elected 2 Sep 1857, accepted by W. B. Hagans, Chairman of the Board of Supervisors, witness Frank W. Shattuck	A	292-293
Juhl, Hans	King, Charles; Roberts, Charles	1,000	11 Mar 1884	Pound Master (Petaluma Township)	Appointed 4 Mar 1884 by the Board of Supervisors		
Juilliard, L. W.*	Burris, L. W.; Brooke, T. J.; Overton, A. P.; Walker, John; Wright, W. S. M.; Holmes, C. H.; Noonan, George P.; Ware, A. B.; McGee, James H.; Burger, C. H.; Dunbar, John; Carithers, D. N.	25,000	14 Nov 1888	Clerk	Elected 6 Nov 1888	3	260-263
Juilliard, L. W.*	Burger, C. H.; Dunbar, John; Maddux, J. P.; Burris, L. W.; Noonan, George P.; Overton, John P.; Roney, J. M.; Gauldin, W. W.; Brittain, R. H.; Ware, A. B.; Brooke, T. J.; Overton, A. P.	25,000	29 Nov 1890	Clerk	Elected 4 Nov 1890	4	168
Kavanaugh, Nicholas	Oakes, A. G.; Wilson, W. L.	1,000	24 Sep 1859	Constable (Sonoma Township)	Elected 7 Sep 1859, witness Ive D. Long	B	19
Kearney, J.	Grothaus, Ferdinand; Monahan, P.	1,000	1 Dec 1890	Road Overseer (Sonoma Road District)	Elected 4 Nov 1890	4	129
Keaton, John*	Torrance, S. H.; Burns, J. A.	1,000	26 Dec 1882	Constable (Redwood Township)	Elected 7 Nov 1882	2	275-276
Keenan, Alexander	Carpenter, L. F.; Meyerholtz, Henry	1,000	22 Dec 1880	Justice of the Peace (Vallejo Township)	Elected 2 Nov 1880	2	52-54
Keenan, Alexander	Peoples, Nathan; Carpenter, L. F.	1,000	27 Sep 1879	Justice of the Peace (Vallejo Township)	Elected 3 Sep 1879	1	526-527
Keenan, Alexander	Carpenter, L. F.; Meyerholtz, Henry	2,000	30 Dec 1884	Justice of the Peace (Vallejo Township)	Elected 4 Nov 1884	2	442-444
Keenan, Alexander	Carpenter, L. F.; Meyerholtz, H.	1,000	8 Jan 1883	Justice of the Peace (Vallejo Township)	Elected 7 Nov 1882	2	278-279
Keene, J. C.	Hanbrich, Peter; Brown, F. T.	1,000	18 Apr 1887	Justice of the Peace (Russian River Township)	Appointed 6 Apr 1887 by the Board of Supervisors	3	182-183
Keith, A. D.	Riley, Thomas; Stites, A. H.; Murrell, J. L.	1,000	20 Nov 1877	Justice of the Peace (Washington Township)	Elected 17 Oct 1877	1	374-375
Keith, A. D.	Metzger, J. E.; Riley, T. J.	1,000	29 Nov 1882	Justice of the Peace (Washington Township)	Elected 7 Nov 1882	2	215-216
Keith, A. D.	Remmel, Charles; McPherson, L.	1,000	4 Dec 1880	Justice of the Peace (Washington Township)	Elected 2 Nov 1880	2	43-44
Keith, Aylmer D.	Remmel, Charles; Fox, Henry	1,000	14 Oct 1879	Justice of the Peace (Washington Township)	Elected 3 Sep 1879	1	546-547
Keith, Aylmer D.	Stites, A. H.; Riley, Thomas	1,000	28 Feb 1877	Justice of the Peace (Washington Township)	Appointed 8 Feb 1877 [by the Board of Supervisors, vice W. H. Anderson, resigned]	1	260-261

71

Principal Name	Sureties	Amount ($)	Date	Office	Notes	Book	Page(s)
Kelley, Timothy	Foote, C. H.; Holmes, William F.	1,000	24 Feb 1888	Road Overseer (Knight's Valley Road District)	Appointed 5 Jan 1888 by the Board of Supervisors, includes J. H. Safley's withdrawl as surety on Timothy Kelley's original bond dated 7 Feb 1888		
Kelly, Charles	Tighe, Kelly; Toner, John	2,000	15 Jan 1880	Road Overseer (Vallejo Road District [South])	Appointed 7 Jan 1880 [by the Board of Supervisors]		
Kelly, D. M.	McReynolds, John; Walker, John; Gilliam, Mitchel; Schlake, Christian	1,000	23 Sep 1879	Constable (Analy Township)	Elected 3 Sep 1879	1	502-503
Kelly, T.	Holmes, William F.; Saffey, J. H.	1,000	12 Jan 1887	Road Overseer (Knight's Valley Road District)	Appointed 5 Jan 1887	3	170-171
Kelly, Timothy	Hopper, John William; Bennett, I. N.	1,000	29 Nov 1880	Road Overseer (Knight's Valley Township)	Elected 2 Nov 1880	2	72-73
Kelting, Joseph A.	Crigler, W. E.; Menihan, M.	1,000	13 Feb 1889	Constable (Cloverdale Township)	Appointed 5 Feb 1889 by the Board of Supervisors	4	40
Kelty, George	McCune, Alexander; Thompson, A. W.	5,000	8 Nov 1864	Auctioneer		B	461
Kendall, John	Thomas, Isaiah; Hotell, David	100	11 Feb 1858	Road Overseer (Road District No. 14, part of Vallejo Township north of the dry crossing of Petaluma Creek)	Appointed 8 Feb 1858 by the Board of Supervisors	A	302
Keniston, Joseph	Goodman, L. S.; McCaughey, James	1,000	29 Nov 1884	Justice of the Peace (Bodega Township)	Elected 4 Nov 1884	2	400-402
Kenny, Patrick	Miller, William R.; Dibble, William	1,000	15 Jan 1875	Road Master (Salt Point Township)	Appointed 4 Jan 1875 by the Board of Supervisors	1	82-83
Kern, Samuel F.	Doyle, M.	100	26 Feb 1859	Road Overseer (Road District No. 26, Vallejo Township)	Appointed by the Board of Supervisors	A	368
King, N.	Whitney, A. P.; Johnson, A. T.	5,000	16 Aug 1881	Notary Public	Appointed & commissioned 13 Aug 1881 by George C. Perkins, Governor of California, for the term of two years	1	598-599
King, N.	Carpenter, L. F.; Gibbs, H.	2,000	19 Nov 1880	Justice of the Peace (Petaluma Township)	Elected 2 Nov 1880	2	24-25
King, N.	Carpenter, L. F.; Gibbs, H.	2,000	22 Nov 1882	Justice of the Peace (Petaluma Township)	Elected 7 Nov 1882	2	155-156
King, N.	Hasbrouck, H. B.; Fritsch, John; Derby, A. B.; Loranger, John	2,000	24 Sep 1879	Justice of the Peace (Petaluma Township)	Elected 3 Sep 1879	1	513-514
King, N.*	Fairbanks, H. T.; Hill, A. B.; Lawrence, H. E.; Weston, H. L.	2,000	30 Nov 1892	Justice of the Peace (Petaluma Township)	Elected 8 Nov 1892	4	242
King, Nathaniel	Carpenter, L. F.; Williams, George B.	5,000	19 Nov 1884	Coroner	Elected 4 Nov 1884	2	354-355

Principal Name	Sureties	Amount ($)	Date	Office	Notes	Book	Page(s)
King, Nathaniel	Lougee, F. W.; Charles, J. M.; Wharff, David; Derby, A. B.; Hill, William; Mecham, H.; Denman, E.; Fritsch, John; Ayers, William; Gibbs, H.; Fairbanks, H. T.; Hasbrouck, H. B.	30,000	21 Nov 1884	Public Administrator	Elected 4 Nov 1884	2	355-357
Kinkead, William	Willson, Henry M.	5,000	3 Oct 1853	Justice of the Peace (Mendocino Township)	Elected 7 Sep 1853	A	76
Kirkpatrick, A. H.	Allison, George; Sargent, H.	500	14 May 1863	Constable [Mendocino Township]	Appointed by the Board of Supervisors	B	342
Kleiser, J. A.	Whitman, J. H.; Levy, Michel	2,000	21 May 1860	Road Overseer (Cloverdale District)	Appointed 9 May 1860 by the Board of Supervisors for the term of one year	B	79
Knapp, A. H.	McChristian, P.; Taylor, William	5,000	9 Aug 1886	Notary Public	Appointed 2 Aug 1886 by George Stoneman, Governor of California, witness J. F. Mulgrew	2	552-553
Knapp, C. H.	Knapp, G. W.; Oliver, John S.	1,000	15 Feb 1882	Justice of the Peace (Analy Township)	Appointed 7 Feb 1882 [by the Board of Supervisors, vice H. D. Carr, resigned]	2	124-125
Knapp, G. W.*	Hall, H. M.; Robinson, W. J.	1,000	[6 Dec 1892]	Constable (Analy Township)	Elected 8 Nov 1892	4	246
Knapp, G. W.*	Jones, William; Hinshaw, E. C.	1,000	3 Dec 1890	Constable (Analy Township)	Elected 4 Nov 1890	4	156
Knowles, D. C.	Morshead, Philip; Carithers, D. N.	1,000	9 May 1890	Road Overseer (Ocean Road District)	Appointed 8 May 1890 by the Board of Supervisors, vice Milton Watson, resigned	4	83
Knowles, J. H.	Poehlmann, Conrad; Matthies, H.	2,000	15 Sep 1873	Constable (Petaluma Township)	Elected 3 Sep 1873	B	708-709
Knowles, J. H.	Canfield, William D.; Hasbrouck, H. B.	1,000	21 Sep 1869	Constable (Petaluma Township)	Elected 1 Sep 1869	B	628
Knowles, James H.	Hill, William; Canfield, William D.	1,000	21 Sep 1867	Constable (Petaluma Township)	Elected 4 Sep 1867, witness A. W. Thompson, includes oath of office dated 21 Sep 1867	B	581
Knowles, James H.	Starke, August; Poehlmann, Conrad	2,000	27 Sep 1865	Constable (Petaluma Township)	Elected 6 Sep 1865, witnesses J. W. Owen & F. D. Colton	B	472
Knowles, James H.	McCune, Alex; Wiswell, J. A.	2,000	6 Oct 1871	Constable (Petaluma Township)	Elected 6 Sep 1871, includes oath of office dated 6 Oct 1871	C	84
Knowles, Joseph	Stumpf, Johann C.; Smith, Jacob	2,000	5 Nov 1863	Justice of the Peace (Bodega Township)	Elected [21 Oct 1863]	B	388
Lacost, William	Arthur, C. R.; Stewart, Charles	1,000	[?] Nov 1867	Constable (Analy Township)	Elected 4 Sep 1867, includes oath of office dated 27 Nov 1867	B	599
Lacost, William*	Hoag, Jared C.; Stewart, Charles	1,000	20 Oct 1865	Constable (Analy Township)	Elected 6 Sep 1865	B	499
Lafferty, H. H.	Laughlin, James; Barnes, E. H.; Clark, Charles	2,000	15 Oct 1873	Constable (Russian River Township)	Elected 3 Sep 1873	B	747-748
Lafferty, H. H.	Hopkins, Thomas J.; Forsythe, Charles	2,000	21 Sep 1875	Constable (Russian River Township)	Elected 1 Sep 1875	1	126-127

73

Principal Name	Sureties	Amount ($)	Date	Office	Notes	Book	Page(s)
Lambert, John W.	Underhill, Charles; Weatherington, R.	1,000	18 Jun 1887	Pound Master (Rincon Pound District)	Appointed 8 Jun 1887 by the Board of Supervisors	3	192-183
Lamkin, James L.	Ware, George W.; Mitchel, Charles E.; Bonham, B. B.	1,000	27 Sep 1859	Constable (Mendocino Township)	Elected 7 Sep 1859	B	20
Lane, John J.	Bills, Sherman; Cooper, John A.	200	22 Feb 1861	Road Overseer (Road District No. 2, Santa Rosa Township)	Appointed	B	143
Latapie, E.	Huie, J. Thompson; Barnes, Thomas L.	2,000	27 Sep 1859	Constable (Petaluma Township)	Elected 7 Sep 1859	B	18
Latapie, E.	Ellis, John J.; Huie, J. Thompson	2,000	7 Feb 1863	Constable (Petaluma Township)	Appointed to fill a vacancy occasioned by the resignation of W. N. Ferrill	B	332
Latapie, Edward	Huie, J. Thompson; Anderson, William L.; Bond, J. L.; Ellis, John J.; Barnes, M.; Lewis, Lewis C.	2,000	1 Oct 1858	Constable (Petaluma Township)	Elected 1 Sep 1858, witness D. D. Carder	A	324
Latapie, Edward	Wright, W. S. M.; Wright, Joseph; McReynolds, James; Farmer, E. T.; Clark, J. P.; Boyce, J. F.; Fulkerson, Richard; Dalton, William H.; Tuttle, B. F.; Roney, J. M.	25,000	11 Sep 1873	Sheriff	Elected 3 Sep 1873	B	692-694
Latapie, Edward	Wright, W. S. M.; Wright, Joseph; McReynolds, James; Farmer, E. T.; Clark, J. P.; Boyce, J. F.; Fulkerson, Richard; Dalton, William H.; Tuttle, B. F.; Roney, J. M.; Brown, John; Mason, M.; Hendley, John; Farrell, Martin	30,000	11 Sep 1873	Sheriff & ex officio Tax Collector	Elected 3 Sep 1873	B	694-696
Latapie, Edward	Bailhache, John N.; Thompson, Thomas L.; Munday, B. B.; McGuire, A.; Rochford, Thomas; Knowles, J. H.; Browne, Daniel; Pearce, George; Dalton, William H.; Bowles, J. M.	25,000	4 Oct 1871	Sheriff	Elected 6 Sep 1871	C	92-93
Latapie, Edward	Bailhache, John N.; Thompson, Thomas L.; Munday, B. B.; McGuire, A.; Rochford, Thomas; Knowles, J. H.; Browne, Daniel; Pearce, George; Dalton, William H.; Bond, J. L.; Bowles, J. M.; Doyle, M.	25,000	4 Oct 1871	Sheriff & ex officio Tax Collector	Elected 6 Sep 1871	C	94-95
Latimer, L. D.	Tupper, G. A.; Kessing, C.; Maxwell, J. G.; Martin, R. M.; Kessing, John F.; Roney, J. M.; Hood, T. B.; Williamson, James R.; Shane, Adam; Bostwick, N. W.; Heisel, Paul; Gray, William; Crane, G. L.	10,000	14 May 1864	Notary Public	Appointed 2 May 1864 for the term of two years, includes oath of office dated 14 May 1864	B	455-456
Latimer, L. D.	Hood, T. B.; Maxwell, J. G.; Tupper, G. A.; Hamilton, Thomas J.; Farmer, E. T.; Walker, Alonzo; Pyatt, Thomas H.; Atterbury, William B.	5,000	8 May 1866	Notary Public	Appointed 2 May 1866 for the term of two years, includes oath of office dated 8 May 1866	B	547
Laughlin, A. D.	Allen, S. I.; Fulkerson, Richard; Smith, J. K.; Hoag, O. H.	2,000	18 Nov 1880	Justice of the Peace (Santa Rosa Township)	Elected 2 Nov 1880	2	7-8
Laughlin, A. D.	Thompson, T. L.; Clark, J. P.; Mills, E. T.; Fulkerson, Richard	2,000	18 Oct 1879	Justice of the Peace (Santa Rosa Township)	Elected 4 Oct 1879 at a special election	1	541-542
Laughlin, A. D.	Henry, James; McReynolds, James; Gale, Otis; Burger, C. H.	5,000	26 Jul 1886	Notary Public	Appointed 23 Jul 1886 by [George Stoneman], Governor of California	2	548-549

74

Principal Name	Sureties	Amount ($)	Date	Office	Notes	Book	Page(s)
Laughlin, A. D.	Wright, Joseph; Latapie, E.	5,000	27 Jul 1878	Notary Public	Appointed & commissioned 25 Jul 1878	1	434
Laughlin, A. D.	Johnson, George A.; Mills, E. T.; Prindle, William; Roney, J. M.; Noonan, George P.	5,000	28 Jul 1882	Notary Public	Appointed 26 Jul 1882 by George C. Perkins, Governor of California	2	135-136
Laughlin, A. D.	Coulter, S. T.; Farmer, C. C.; Baker, Henry; Finlaw, W.; Shepherd, A.; Flippin, J. T.; Loucks, A. H.	5,000	4 Aug 1880	Notary Public	Appointed 26 Jul 1880 by the Governor of California	1	581-582
Laughlin, A. D.	Armstrong, J. B.; Ferguson, E. C.; Noonan, George P.; Philbee, James	2,000	4 Nov 1879	Justice of the Peace (Santa Rosa Township)	Appointed 4 Nov 1879 by the Board of Supervisors, vice C. B. Cox, resigned	1	550-551
Laughlin, A. D.*	McReynolds, James; Hoskins, T. D.; Story, S. C.; Philips, Walter; Hodge, A. L.	5,000	2 Aug 1884	Notary Public	Appointed 23 Jul 1884 by George Stoneman, Governor of California	2	326-327
Laughlin, A. D.*	McFadyen, A.; Noonan, George P.	5,000	21 Jul 1890	Notary Public	Appointed 16 Jul 1890 by the Governor of California	4	92
Laughlin, A. D.*	McFadyen, A.; Noonan, George P.	5,000	21 Jul 1890	Notary Public	Appointed 16 Jul 1890 by the Governor of California	4	170
Laughlin, A. D.*	Hodge, A. L.; Hall, L. J.; Overton, A. P.	5,000	23 Jul 1888	Notary Public	Appointed 20 Jul 1888 by R. W. Waterman, Governor of California	3	253-255
Laughlin, Alex. D.	Laughlin, James H.; Laughlin, John M.	5,000	31 Jul 1876	Notary Public	Appointed 22 Jul 1876 by the Governor of California	1	224-225
Law, J.J.	Chauvet, J.; Poppe, Charles J.	1,000	20 Feb 1888	Constable (Sonoma Township)	Appointed 6 Feb 1888 by the Board of Supervisors	3	229-230
Law, J.J.	Chauvet, Joshaua; Poppe, Charles J.	1,000	7 Dec 1888	Constable (Sonoma Township)	Elected 6 Nov 1888	4	22
Lawrence, James A.	Bingham, A. W.	200	14 Nov 1864	School Tax Collector (Stoney Point School District)	Appointed [?] Nov 1864 by the Board of Trustees of the Stoney Point School District for the purpose of liquidating the indebtedness of said District to Miss Ann Bryant for the balance of her salary due her as teacher in said District levied in accordance with section 7 of the School Law approved 22 Mar 1864 and for school year ending 31 Aug 1864	B	461
Laymance, I. C.	Green, A. M.; Miller, George	1,000	15 Sep 1863	Constable (Mendocino Township)	Elected [2 Sep 1863]	B	353
Laymance, Isaac C.	Clack, John W.; Smith, Silvester	200	2 Mar 1861	Road Overseer (portion of Mendocino Township)	Appointed 21 Feb 1861 by the Board of Supervisors	B	140
Laymance, J. C.	Clark, C.; Skaggs, A.	1,000	15 Sep 1862	Constable [Mendocino Township]	Elected [3 Sep 1862]	B	303
Leard, J. B.	Newland, Frank; Mead, James A.	1,000	1 Dec 1888	Constable (Mendocino Township)	Elected 6 Nov 1888	3	285-286
Leard, J. B.	Hassett, J. D.; Mead, J. A.	1,000	2 Dec 1886	Constable (Mendocino Township)	Elected 2 Nov 1886	3	88-89
Leard, J. B.*	Barnes, E. H.; Cummings, William	1,000	1 Dec 1890	Constable (Mendocino Township)	Elected 4 Nov 1890	4	128
Leard, J. B.*	Bond, J. W.; Barnes, E. H.	1,000	1 Dec 1892	Constable (Mendocino Township)	Elected 8 Nov 1892	4	219

Principal Name	Sureties	Amount ($)	Date	Office	Notes	Book	Page(s)
Lee, Oliver	Cavanagh; Porter, Thomas A. D.; Laughlin, M. N.; Grove, David	5,000	29 Dec 1856	Justice of the Peace (Russian River Township)	Elected 4 Nov 1856	A	184
Lee, Oliver	Bledsoe, A. C.; Cavanagh, John; Ormsby, John S.; Power, S. T.; Cockrill, L. D.; Hill, James M.; Hoen, B.	5,000	8 Oct 1857	Justice of the Peace (Russian River Township)	Elected 2 Sep 1857, accepted by W. B. Hagans, Chairman of the Board of Supervisors	A	218-221
Lee, William G.	Millar, J. M.; Hudspeth, J. M.	10,000	1 Oct 1857	Superintendent of Common Schools	Elected 2 Sep 1857, accepted by W. B. Hagans, Chairman of the Board of Supervisors	A	287-289
Lee, William G.	White, William H.; Judson, John	1,000	16 Mar 1867	Justice of the Peace (Analy Township)	Elected 16 Oct 1867 for the term of two years	B	561-562
Lee, William G.	Canfield, William D.; Speck, Jacob	5,000	25 Sep 1854	Justice of the Peace (Analy Township)	Elected 6 Sep 1854	A	21-22
Lee, William G.	Kuffel, Isaac; Stockdale, Hugh	1,000	25 Sep 1861	Justice of the Peace [Analy Township]	Elected 4 Sep 1861	B	176
Lee, William G.	Easley, Warham; Millar, J. M.	5,000	28 Sep 1855	Assessor	Elected 5 Sep 1855	A	130
Lee, William G.	White, William H.; Arthur, C. R.	2,000	30 Nov 1869	Justice of the Peace (Analy Township)	Elected 20 Oct 1869	C	16
Lee, William G.	White, William H.; Hoag, Jared C.	1,000	30 Sep 1862	Justice of the Peace (Analy Township)	Elected 3 Sep 1862	B	294
Lee, William G.	White, John; Reed, William M.	5,000	6 Mar 1856	Assessor	Elected 5 Sep 1855	A	142
Leek, William G.	Kessing, C.; Shane, Adam	5,000	5 Jan 1875	Road Overseer (Santa Rosa Township)	Appointed 5 Jan 1875 by the Board of Supervisors	1	67-68
Leek, William G.	Kessing, C.; Shane, A.	5,000	9 Jan 1874	Road Overseer (Santa Rosa Road District)	Appointed 7 Jan 1874 by the Board of Supervisors		
Legendre, Lewis	Dow, Joseph G.; Fuller, William M.	1,000	13 May 1850	Constable (Sonoma County)	Elected 9 May 1850, witness R. B. Butler	A	66
Leigh, A. G.	Remmel, Charles; Stites, A. H.	1,000	1 Dec 1884	Constable (Washington Township)	Elected 4 Nov 1884	2	395-396
Leppo, J. R.*	Carithers, D. N.; Ware, A. B.	5,000	15 May 1890	Notary Public	Appointed 8 May 1890	4	84
Lester, Eli	Rudesill, J. P.; Levy, Michel	1,000	30 Nov 1860	Justice of the Peace (Cloverdale Township)	Elected 6 Nov 1860, witnesses James P. Montray & R. F. Hafford	B	133-134
Lester, Eli	Levy, Michel; Pixley, William	1,000	7 Oct 1858	Justice of the Peace (Washington Township)	Elected 1 Sep 1858	A	345
Lester, Eli	Riley, A. P.; Levy, Michel	1,000	8 Oct 1859	Justice of the Peace (Cloverdale Township)	Elected 7 Sep 1859	B	39
Lewis, G. W.	Hill, William McPherson; Rogers, W. K.	2,000	13 Sep 1873	Constable (Sonoma Township)	Elected 3 Sep 1873	B	704-705
Lewis, George W.	Walker, John; Overton, A. P.; McReynolds, James; Taylor, John S.	20,000	16 Nov 1882	Assessor	Elected 7 Nov 1882	2	153-155
Lewis, George W.	Burris, David; Rogers, W. K.	10,000	17 Sep 1879	Assessor	Elected 3 Sep 1879	1	476-477

Principal Name	Sureties	Amount ($)	Date	Office	Notes	Book	Page(s)
Lewis, H. H.	Shipley, R. J.; Young, James	100	2 Aug 1859	Road Overseer (Road District No. 17, Analy Township)	Appointed	B	5
Lewis, John	Pauli, G. T.; Cornelius, George H. H.	1,000	22 Sep 1879	Constable (Sonoma Township)	Elected 3 Sep 1879	1	492-493
Lewis, John	Cornelius, George H. H.; Schetter, Otto	1,000	26 Aug 1878	Constable (Sonoma Township)	Appointed [7 Aug 1878 by the Board of Supervisors], vice George P. Gammon, resigned	1	438-439
Lewis, John	Pauli, G. T.; Schetter, Otto	2,000	4 Oct 1877	Constable (Sonoma Township)	Appointed 1 Oct 1877 [by the Board of Supervisors to fill a vacancy]	1	348-349
Lewis, Lewis C.	Kendall, John; Denman, Ezekiel; McCracken, J. C.; Haydon, S. C.; Mock, John L.; Walker, John K. Bowles, Joseph M.; Faught, Willis	5,000	20 Sep 1861	Coroner	Elected 4 Sep 1861	B	223-224
Lewis, Lewis C.	Faught, Wiliam; Martin, S. M.	5,000	26 Nov 1856	Justice of the Peace (Petaluma Township)	Elected 4 Nov 1856	A	161
Lewis, Lewis C.	Bryant, W. S.; McGuire, Charles; Reyburn, L. C.; Barnes, Michael, Jr.	2,000	4 Oct 1858	Justice of the Peace (Petaluma Township)	Elected 1 Sep 1858	A	335
Lewis, Lewis C.	Faught, William; Lewis, Martin	5,000	5 Jun 1855	Justice of the Peace (Petaluma Township)	Appointed [?] [?] 1855 to fill the vacancy occasioned by the resignation of Ezekiel C. Denman, includes oath of office dated 5 Jun 1855	A	100
Lewis, M. G.	Lewis, Joshua H.; Keller, George H.; Singley, James	5,000	24 Feb 1852	Justice of the Peace (Petaluma Township)	Elected, includes oath of office dated 24 Feb 1852	A	44
Lindsay, Calvin	Lindsay, J. J.; Clark, W. S.	2,000	13 Dec 1871	Justice of the Peace (Russian River Township)	Elected 18 Oct 1871	C	135-136
Lindsay, Calvin	Lindsay, Jasper J.; Gould, John	1,000	2 Oct 1869	Constable (Russian River Township)	Elected 1 Sep 1869	B	634
Linville, H. H.	Hendley, John; Pyatt, Thomas H.	200	[?] Feb 1864	Road Master (District No. 1, Santa Rosa Township)	Appointed by the Board of Supervisors, includes undated oath of office	B	444
Linville, H. H.	Cook, J. G.; Cook, J. B.	1,000	21 Oct 1865	Road Master (Santa Rosa Township)	Elected 6 Sep 1865		
Linville, H. H.	Mothersead, A. J.; Linville, Byram	1,000	3 Oct 1859	Justice of the Peace (Santa Rosa Township)	Elected 7 Sep 1859	B	36
Linville, Hiram H.	Carr, Nelson; Crane, James E.; Beaver, Henry	5,000	21 Sep 1855	Justice of the Peace (Santa Rosa Township)	Elected 5 Sep 1855	A	114
Linville, Hiram H.	Clark, J. P.; Barnes, M.	200	7 Nov 1862	Road Master (District No. 1, Santa Rosa Township)	Appointed 7 Nov 1862 by the Board of Supervisors, includes oath of office dated 7 Nov 1862	B	326
Lippett, Frank K. *	Lippett, E. S.; Poehlman, Conrad	5,000	17 Nov 1890	Notary Public	Appointed & commissioned 11 Nov 1890 by R. W. Waterman, Governor of California	4	176

Principal Name	Sureties	Amount ($)	Date	Office	Notes	Book	Page(s)
Lippitt, E. S.	Mecham, H.; Fritsch, John	5,000	10 Oct 1882	Notary Public	Appointed 9 Oct 1882 by George C. Perkins, Governor of California, includes oath of office dated 10 Oct 1882	2	137-138
Lippitt, E. S.	Fritsch, John; Whitney, A. P.	5,000	11 Oct 1880	Notary Public	Appointed & commissioned 8 Oct 1880 by George C. Perkins, Governor of California, includes oath of office dated 11 Oct 1880	1	583-584
Lippitt, E. S.	Mecham, H.; Fritsch, John	5,000	16 Oct 1878	Notary Public	Appointed 7 Oct 1878 by William Irwin, Governor of California, for the term of two years, includes oath of office dated 16 Oct 1878	1	445-446
Lippitt, E. S.	Poehlmann, Conrad; Fritsch, John	5,000	17 Nov 1886	Notary Public	Appointed 11 Nov 1886 by George Stoneman, Governor of California, includes oath of office dated 16 Nov 1886	3	13-15
Lippitt, E. S.	Mecham, H.; Fritsch, John	5,000	21 Oct 1884	Notary Public	Appointed 14 Oct 1884 by George Stoneman, Governor of California, includes oath of office dated 21 Oct 1884	2	338-339
Lippitt, E. S.	Mecham, H.; Fritsch, John	5,000	29 Sep 1874	Notary Public	Appointed 25 Sep 1874 by the Governor of California, includes oath of office dated 29 Sep 1874	1	64-66
Lippitt, E. S.	Mecham, H.; Denman, E.	5,000	3 Oct 1876	Notary Public	Appointed 25 Sep 1876 by William Irwin, Governor of California, witness Frank W. Shattuck, includes oath of office dated 3 Oct 1876	1	225-226
Lippitt, E. S.	Hill, William; Mecham, H.	5,000	9 Oct 1872	Notary Public	Appointed		
Lippitt, Frank K.*	Lippitt, E. S.; Poehlmann, C.	5,000	17 Nov 1888	Notary Public	Appointed & commissioned 15 Nov 1888 by R. W. Waterman, Governor of California, includes oath of office dated 17 Nov 1888	3	263-265
Littler, Charles W.	Doyle, M.; Bowles, J. M.; Johnson, Fred; Brown, Daniel	2,000	20 May 1861	Constable (Petaluma Township)	Elected 6 Nov 1860; Cyrus Rohrer demanded release from prior bond requiring a new bond to be given	B	154-155
Littler, Charles W.	Doyle, M.; Wood, N. B.; Rohrer, Cyrus; Peter, Jordan	2,000	26 Nov 1860	Constable (Petaluma Township)	Elected 6 Nov 1860	B	107
Livreau, Joseph	Gird, Henry S.; Pyatt, Thomas H.	1,000	1 Dec 1856	Constable (Washington Township)	Elected 4 Nov 1856	A	179
Livreau, Joseph	Heald, H. G.; Godwin, A. C.	1,000	3 Oct 1853	Constable (Washington Township)	Elected 7 Sep 1853	A	64
Logan, W. C.	Clark, J. P.; McMinn, John; Mills, A. J.; Roney, J. M.; Weatherington, H.; Foster, Joseph; Gale, O.; Jacobs, Eli	2,000	24 Sep 1877	Constable (Santa Rosa Township)	Elected 5 Sep 1877	1	331-333
Long, D. W.	Robinson, William; Needham, F.	1,000	11 Jan 1887	Road Overseer (Vallejo Road District comprising all of Vallejo Township)	Appointed 5 Jan 1887	3	164-165
Long, D. W.	Robinson, William; Farrell, W. F.	1,000	3 Dec 1888	Road Overseer (Vallejo Road District)	Elected 6 Nov 1888	3	294-295
Long, Ive. D.	Kinsmill, Thomas E.; Boggs, Leonard; Long, M. A.; Hooker, Joseph; Wright, W. S. M.; Hendley, John; Carrillo, Julio	5,000	3 Oct 1857	Justice of the Peace (Sonoma Township)	Elected 2 Sep 1857, accepted by W. B. Hagans, Chairman of the Board of Supervisors	A	263-266

78

Principal Name	Sureties	Amount ($)	Date	Office	Notes	Book	Page(s)
Long, Iverson D.	Ewing, W. P.; Ball, John W.; Moore, William H.	5,000	2 Oct 1854	Justice of the Peace (Sonoma Township)	Elected 6 Sep 1854	A	23
Long, Iverson D.	Snoddy, B. A.; Rohrer, Fred; Rupe, Samuel H.	5,000	24 Sep 1855	Justice of the Peace (Sonoma Township)	Elected 5 Sep 1855	A	152
Long, Marcus A.	Prewett, John; Griggs, Joseph H.	1,000	3 Dec 1860	Justice of the Peace (Russian River Township)	Elected 6 Nov 1860	B	129
Long, N.	Pauli, G. T.; Bates, H. F.	1,000	27 Nov 1860	Constable (Sonoma Township)	Elected 6 Nov 1860, witness William Ellis	B	115
Long, N. J. T.	Dyer, C.; Wiseman, D. J.; Akers, S.; Linihan, Jerry	2,000	14 Oct 1871	Constable (Sonoma Township)	Elected 6 Sep 1871	C	91
Long, N. J. T.	Bright, S. B.; Bates, H. F.; Akers, Stephen	1,000	24 Sep 1855	Constable (Sonoma Township)	Elected 5 Sep 1855	A	128
Long, N. J. T.	Pauli, G. T.; Leiding, Fred	1,000	24 Sep 1859	Constable (Sonoma Township)	Elected 7 Sep 1859, witness G. L. Wratten	B	22
Long, N. J. T.	Ellis, William; Lennehen, Jerry; McDonald, Angus; Oettl, Franz	2,000	25 Sep 1867	Constable (Sonoma Township)	Elected 4 Sep 1867	B	587
Long, N. J. T.	Brockman, Israel; Galusha, N. H.; Berggren, John F.	1,000	29 Nov 1856	Road Overseer (Sonoma Township)	Appointed		
Long, N. J. T.	Carriger, Nicholas; Ryan, Mortimer; Linnehan, Jerry	2,000	29 Sep 1869	Constable (Sonoma Township)	Elected 1 Sep 1869, witness William E. McConnell	B	631
Long, Nicholas	Munday, B. B.; Bates, Henry F.	1,000	24 Sep 1861	Constable (Sonoma Township)	Elected 4 Sep 1861, witness William Ellis	B	173
Long, Nicholas	Pauli, G. T.; Lenehen, Jerry	1,000	6 Mar 1866	Constable (Sonoma Township)	Appointed 16 Feb 1866 by the Board of Supervisors	B	546
Long, Nicholas J. T.	Bates, H. F.; Brockman, Israel	1,000	30 Sep 1857	Constable (Sonoma Township)	Elected 2 Sep 1857, accepted by W. B. Hagans, Chairman of the Board of Supervisors	A	283-284
Longmore, William	Hopper, Thomas; Walker, John; Watson, James, Sr.; Hitchcock, Hollis	20,000	13 Nov 1886	Assessor	Elected 2 Nov 1886, witness J. F. Mulgrew	3	10-12
Longmore, William	Watson, James, Sr.; Doran, W. M.	2,000	2 Mar 1881	Deputy Assessor	Appointed [?] 1881 by George W. Lewis, Assessor	2	93-94
Longmore, William *	Markham, Andrew; Walker, John; Hopper, Thomas; Shea, Con	20,000	28 Nov 1890	Assessor	Elected 4 Nov 1890, witness L. W. Juilliard	4	167
Loofbourrow, Elias	Fisk, John C.; Beatty, John C.	2,000	21 Aug 1877	Justice of the Peace (Salt Point Township)	Appointed 8 Aug 1877 [by the Board of Supervisors to fill a vacancy]	1	275-276
Lovell, F. A.	Lovell, H. L.; Thompson, M. S.	5,000	1 Dec 1856	Justice of the Peace (Vallejo Township)	Elected 4 Nov 1856	A	172
Lovell, Fayette A.	Thompson, M. S.; Singley, James	5,000	15 May 1857	Justice of the Peace (Vallejo Township)	Appointed [?] May 1857 by the Board of Supervisors	A & A	57 & 207
Lowry, J. J. *	Barham, H. W.; Himebauch, Henry	2,000	[?] [?] 1882	Constable (Santa Rosa Township)	Elected 7 Nov 1882	2	197-198

Principal Name	Sureties	Amount ($)	Date	Office	Notes	Book	Page(s)
Luce, Jirah	Turner, John; Rosenberg, W.; Bostwick, N. W.; Brown, H. K.	2,000	25 Oct 1877	Justice of the Peace (Mendocino Township)	Elected 17 Oct 1877	1	358-359
Luce, Jirah	Brown, H. K.; Turner, John	1,000	9 May 1876	Justice of the Peace [Mendocino Township]	Appointed 4 May 1876 by the Board of Supervisors [to fill the vacancy occasioned by the resignation of H. M. Wilson]	1	212-213
Lusk, S. B.	Lovell, H. L.; Grinter, George W.	3,000	29 May 1860	Road Overseer (Vallejo District, comprising Vallejo Township)	Appointed 11 May 1860 by the Board of Supervisors for the term of one year, witness S. Payran	B	88
Luth, Fred. H.*	Walker, John; Ullrich, George	1,000	2 Dec 1892	Justice of the Peace (Analy Township)	Elected 8 Nov 1892	4	255
Lynch, William	Huie, George W.; Sroufe, John	1,000	23 Sep 1867	Constable (Vallejo Township)	Elected 4 Sep 1867, witness S. Payran	B	574
Lynn, John J.	Short, J. R.; Thompson, M. S.	5,000	29 Sep 1855	Justice of the Peace (Vallejo Township)	Elected 5 Sep 1855	A	131
Mahan, John	Lunsford, R. B.; Helm, S. W.; Lakey, Andrew	500	23 Sep 1865	Road Master (Road District No. 4, Mendocino Township)	Elected 6 Sep 1865	B	480
Mahler, Philip	Pauli, G. T.; Glassen, Louis	1,000	19 Sep 1862	Justice of the Peace (Sonoma Township)	Elected 3 Sep 1862, includes oath of office certification dated 19 Sep 1862	B	288
Mahler, Philip	Pauli, G. T.; Glassen, Louis	2,000	31 Oct 1863	Justice of the Peace (Sonoma Township)	Elected [21 Oct 1863], witness Harold Lud. Kamp	B	385
Mallen, John E.	Hart, Blair; Mallen, Margret (Mrs.)	1,000	29 Nov 1890	Road Overseer (Lakeville Road District, Vallejo Township)	Elected 4 Nov 1890	4	126
Manning, N. E.	Yarbrough, C. D.; Guerne, George E.; Williams, R.	2,000	1 Jan 1874	Justice of the Peace (Redwood Township)	Elected 15 Oct 1873	**B**	766-767
Manning, N. E.	Coon, R. W.; Armstrong, J. B.	5,000	19 Nov 1887	Notary Public	Appointed 17 Nov 1887	3	205-207
Markle, R. B.	Brown, George W.; Carson, Robert W.; Caldwell, William	2,000	27 Nov 1863	Justice of the Peace (Cloverdale Township)	Elected [21 Oct 1863], witness J. Ramey	B	405
Marshall, Robert A.	Haupt, Charles; Montague, Hugh	1,000	12 Dec 1888	Constable (Salt Point Township)	Elected 6 Nov 1888	4	36
Marshall, Robert A.	Haupt, Charles; Montague, Hugh	1,000	13 Dec 1886	Constable (Salt Point Township)	Elected 2 Nov 1886	3	123-125
Martin, F. McG. (Mrs.)*	Hopper, Thomas; Stuart, A. McG.; Austin, James; Forsyth, Robert; Coulter, S. T.	5,000	10 Dec 1890	Superintendent of Public Schools	Elected 4 Nov 1890, witness L. W. Juilliard	4	166
Martin, Fannie McG.	Clewe, F.; Duhring, F.	5,000	19 Nov 1886	Superintendent of Public Schools	Elected 2 Nov 1886	3	15-17
Martin, Horace B.	Barnes, M.; Boyce, J. F.; Martin, R. M.; Arnold, G. W.; Shattuck, F. W.; Gallagher, Jacob M.; Ellis, John J.; Hoen, Berthold; Campbell, J. A.; Carrillo, Julio	5,000	21 Sep 1861	Surveyor	Elected 4 Sep 1861 for the term of two years from the first Monday of October 1861 [7 Oct 1861]	B	212

Principal Name	Sureties	Amount ($)	Date	Office	Notes	Book	Page(s)
Martin, James	Bryant, Daniel S.; Linnehan, Jerry	1,000	22 Sep 1862	Justice of the Peace (Sonoma Township)	Elected 3 Sep 1862, includes oath of office certification dated 22 Sep 1862	B	283
Martin, S. M.	Cavanagh, John; Overton, A. P.	2,000	10 Nov 1866	Justice of the Peace (Petaluma Township)	Appointed 6 Nov 1866 by the Board of Supervisors	B	555
Martin, S. M.	Fritsch, John; Rudesill, J. A.; Carder, D. D.; Zartman, William; McCune, James	5,000	30 Sep 1857	Justice of the Peace (Petaluma Township)	Elected 2 Sep 1857, accepted by W. B. Hagans, Chairman of the Board of Supervisors	A	222-223
Martin, Samuel	Crane, Robert; Rambo, Jacob	5,000	1 Dec 1856	Justice of the Peace (Vallejo Township)	Elected 4 Nov 1856	A	176
Martin, Samuel	Matthews, William B.; Holman, J. A.	5,000	1 Oct 1855	Justice of the Peace (Vallejo Township)	Elected 5 Sep 1855	A	126
Martin, Silas M.	Lewis, Lewis C.; Ayers, William; Purvine, Charles	5,000	5 Sep 1855	Justice of the Peace (Petaluma Township)	Elected 5 Sep 1855	A	129
Mason, Matthew	Kiernan, Michael; Stanford, Philip	1,000	21 Sep 1869	Constable (Bodega Township)	Elected [1 Sep 1869], witness W. H. Menefee, includes oath of office dated 21 Sep 1869	C	37
Mason, Matthew	Rainey, A. C.; Hudspeth, J. M.	1,000	5 Feb 1869	Constable (Bodega Township)	Appointed, includes oath of office dated 5 Feb 1869	B	624
Mass, Claus	Barnes, Jehu; Starr, Elmon G.	1,000	14 Jun 1878	Pound Master (Vallejo Pound District)	Appointed 6 May 1878 by the Board of Supervisors, witness Frank W. Shattuck	1	429-430
Mather, William	Gannon, James P.; Hayden, E. W.; Litchfield, Martin; Wightman, C.; Morris, Joseph H. P.	1,000	6 Feb 1890	Pound Master (Sebastopol Pound District)	Appointed 3 Feb 1890 by the Board of Supervisors	4	74
Matthews, George H.	Thompson, Thomas L.; Matthews, C. W.	200	3 Nov 1863	Road Master (District No. 2, Santa Rosa Township)	Elected 2 Sep 1863	B	372
Matthews, O. B.	McReynolds, John; Rudesill, John A.	6,000	10 May 1860	Road Overseer (Petaluma District)	Appointed 10 May 1860 by the Board of Supervisors for the term of one year	B	84
Matthews, O. B.	McHenry, James	500	19 Jun 1861	Road Overseer (Petaluma Road District No. 1)	Appointed, includes oath of office dated 19 Jun 1861	B	158
Maupin, R. A.	Boggs, L. W.; Vallejo, Salvador; Peabody, E. T.	1,000	23 May 1850	District Attorney (7th Judicial District)	Elected 1 Apr 1850	A	57-58
Maxey, Joseph B.	Boggs, W. M.; Boggs, J. B.; Rupe, Samuel H.; Caldwell, J. V.	1,000	29 Sep 1855	Constable (Sonoma Township)	Elected 5 Sep 1855	A	122
McClellan, M. T.	Hendley, John; Farmer, E. T.	2,000	[?] Nov 1863	Justice of the Peace (Salt Point Township)	Elected [21 Oct 1863], witness William L. Anderson		
McClish, James L.	Miller, W. P.; McClish, John	1,000	27 Jun 1885	Pound Master (Pound District No. 6)	Appointed 3 Jun 1885 [by the Board of Supervisors]	2	481-482
McClish, Thomas	Gallagher, Jacob M.; Hudson, Thomas W.	200	[?] Nov 1862	Road Master (District No. 1, Mendocino Township)	Appointed, includes oath of office dated 4 Nov 1862	B	331

Principal Name	Sureties	Amount ($)	Date	Office	Notes	Book	Page(s)
McClish, Thomas	Morgan, Charles; Wood, N. H.	200	21 Sep 1861	Road Overseer (District No. 1, Mendocino Township)	Elected 4 Sep 1861	B	235
McCluskey, William	King, John; Samuels, James	1,000	25 Nov 1884	Constable (Mendocino Township)	Elected 4 Nov 1884	2	375-376
McConnell, William E.	Burris, David; Tivnen, John; Rogers, W. K.; Snyder, J. R.; Carriger, Nicholas; Oettl, F.	10,000	13 Sep 1873	District Attorney	Elected 3 Sep 1873	B	705-707
McConnell, William E.	McConnell, G. M.; Pauli, G. T.; Linnihan, Jerry; Dillon, C. H.; Lyon, A. G.; Snoddy, B. A.; Dyer, Claybern; Bates, H. F.; Townsend, William M. A.; Goodman, Willis	5,000	15 Feb 1868	Notary Public	Commissioned 1 Feb 1868 by H. H. Haight, Governor of California	B	613
McConnell, William E.	Davis, E. L.; Noonan, George P.; Farmer. E. T.; Wright, W. S. M.	10,000	15 Sep 1877	District Attorney	Elected 5 Sep 1877	1	284-286
McConnell, William E.	Townsend, William M. A.; Dillon, C. H.; Linihan, Jerry; Wiseman, D. J.; Wegener, Edward; Lyon, A. G.	5,000	25 Jun 1870	Notary Public	Commissioned 22 Jun 1870 by H. H. Haight, Governor of California, includes oath of office dated 25 Jun 1870	C	53-54
McCorkle, M. K.	Wright, W. S. M.; Cocke, William E.	2,000	[?] Jan 1868	Justice of the Peace (Santa Rosa Township)	Elected 16 Oct 1867	B	568
McCracken, Jasper	Capell, B. B.; Baruch, Henry	1,000	17 Feb 1877	Road Overseer (Mill Creek District)	Appointed 9 Feb 1877 by the Board of Supervisors, witness W. W. Moreland	1	251-252
McCracken, William J.	Davis, B. J.; Gerkhardt, H. F.; Ontis, John; Menehan, M.; Walker, W. J.	2,000	19 Sep 1877	Constable (Cloverdale Township)	Elected 5 Sep 1877	1	327-328
McCracken, William J.	Kier, H.; Davis, B. J.; Menihan, M.; Walker, W. J.	2,000	8 Dec 1876	Constable (Cloverdale Township)	Appointed 16 Nov 1876	1	226-227
McCutchan, J. B.	Mitchell, R. T.; Prewett, James	1,000	10 Mar 1866	Justice of the Peace (Russian River Township)	Appointed 16 Feb 1866 by the Board of Supervisors	B	541
McCutchan, J. B.	Bruner, Philip; McCutchan, David; Hembree, Andrew J.; Davis, L. T.	2,000	12 Feb 1878	Justice of the Peace (Russian River Township)	Appointed 7 Feb 1878 [by the Board of Supervisors]	1	394-395
McCutchan, J. B.	Mackinder, George; Graham, J. W.; McCutchan, William C.; McCullough, Michael	1,000	24 Nov 1882	Justice of the Peace (Russian River Township)	Elected 7 Nov 1882	2	189-190
McCutchan, William C.	Hembree, Andrew T.; Throp, John	1,000	13 Mar 1866	Constable [Russian River Township]	Appointed 16 Feb 1866 by the Board of Supervisors	B	542
McCutchan, William C.	Hembree, A. T.; Mothersead, A. J.	1,000	21 Sep 1867	Constable [Russian River Township]	Elected [4 Sep 1867], witness J. B. McCutchan	B	578
McDonald, A. C.	Vallejo, M. G.; O'Farrell, Jasper	20,000	6 Jul 1850	City Treasurer (City of Sonoma)	Elected 28 May 1850	A	71
McDonald, A. C.	Fine, I. H.; Fine, A.; Cameron, John	10,000	9 Apr 1850	Treasurer	Elected 1 Apr 1850	A	55
McDonald, Alexander C.	Brockman, Israel; Ray, John G.; Cooper, James	15,000	18 Sep 1851	Treasurer	Elected 3 Sep 1851	A	53

Principal Name	Sureties	Amount ($)	Date	Office	Notes	Book	Page(s)
McDonald, Frank	Gibbons, Edward (Dr.); Safley, J. H.	2,000	29 Nov 1884	Justice of the Peace (Knight's Valley Township)	Elected 4 Nov 1884	2	390-392
McDonald, William	Fike, Nathan; Cooke, Robert	1,000	1 Oct 1862	Justice of the Peace [St. Helena Township]	Elected [3 Sep 1862], signed name as William McDonnell	B	290
McDowell, A.*	Wood, William B.; Ross, Agness	200	3 Nov 1863	Road Master (District No. 3, Analy Township)	Appointed by the Board of Supervisors, includes oath of office dated 3 Nov 1863	B	373
McElhaney, J. M.*	Bell, J. S.; Ferguson, H. O.; Daly, John; Bond, J. W.	5,000	31 Dec 1891	Notary Public	Appointed & commissioned 19 Dec 1891 by H. H. Markham, Governor of California	4	195
McFadden, George C.	Bell, Henry; Pool, Henry J.	1,000	1 Oct 1858	Justice of the Peace (Russian River Township)	Elected 1 Sep 1858	A	331
McFadden, George C.	McCollough, S. G.; Pool, Henry J.	1,000	3 Oct 1859	Justice of the Peace (Russian River Township)	Elected 7 Sep 1859	B	38
McGee, James H.	Glenn, J. H.; Sacry, D. S.; Gray, J. W.; Clark, J. P.	5,000	[?] Mar 1883	Notary Public	Appointed & commissioned 23 Mar 1883	2	288-289
McGee, James H.	Gray, James W.; Cox, C. B.; Farmer, E. T.; Roney, J. M.	5,000	26 Mar 1885	Notary Public	Appointed 21 Mar 1885 [by George Stoneman, Governor of California], witness F. G. Nagle	2	467-468
McGee, James H.	Sacry, David S.; Smith, James M.; Gray, J. W.; McCooper, William	2,000	3 Mar 1875	Justice of the Peace (Santa Rosa Township)	Appointed 2 Mar 1875 by the Board of Supervisors, [vice J. T. Cannon, resigned]	1	96-97
McGee, James H.	Gray, James W.; Roney, J. M.; Cox, C. B.; Noonan, George P.	5,000	5 Apr 1887	Notary Public	Appointed & commissioned 1 Apr 1887 [by Washington Bartlett, Governor of California], includes oath of office dated 7 Apr 1887	3	157-159
McGee, James H.	Martin, Richard M.; Sacry, D. S.; Kohle, A.; Neblett, E.	2,000	6 Nov 1871	Justice of the Peace (Santa Rosa Township)	Elected 18 Oct 1871	C	99
McGee, James H.*	Gray, James W.; Roney, J. M.; Cox, C. B.; Noonan, George P.	5,000	27 Mar 1889	Notary Public	Appointed & commissioned 25 Mar 1889	4	44
McGee, James H.*	White, John M.; Sacry, D. S.; Caldwell, F. M.; Shepherd, A.; Beam, J.; Smith, A. H.	2,000	27 Oct 1875	Justice of the Peace (Santa Rosa Township)	Elected 20 Oct 1875	1	170
McGill, P. L.	Schocken, S.; Fochetti, J.	1,000	6 Dec 1888	Road Overseer (Sonoma Road District)	Elected 6 Nov 1888	4	6
McGill, Peter L.	Hall, Robert; Litzius, Louis	1,000	17 Jan 1887	Road Overseer (Sonoma Township which constitutes Sonoma Road District)	Appointed 5 Jan 1887	3	174-175
McGimpsey, John	Johnson, Nathaniel; Jones, Clayton D. P.	1,000	20 Sep 1858	Justice of the Peace (Anderson Valley Township)	Elected 1 Sep 1858, includes oath of office dated 24 Sep 1858	A	318
McGuire, P. B.	Caldwell, William; Wassum, John H.	1,000	2 Feb 1866	Justice of the Peace (Cloverdale Township)	Elected 18 Oct 1865	B	519

83

Principal Name	Sureties	Amount ($)	Date	Office	Notes	Book	Page(s)
McGuire, P. B.	Wassum, John H.; Caldwell, William	2,000	28 Oct 1865	Justice of the Peace (Cloverdale Township)	Appointed 10 Oct 1865 by the Board of Supervisors	B	500
McGuire, William C.	Jones, Thomas B.; Ontis, John	1,000	8 Nov 1865	Constable (Cloverdale Township)	Elected 6 Sep 1865	B	490
McHenry, James	Lane, John J.; Hood, T. B.	200	22 Feb 1861	Road Overseer (Sebastopol District, Annally Township)	Appointed	B	138
McHenry, James	Ingram, Thomas W.; Isom, Hugh; Forsyth, Robert; Miller, J. M.; Barnes, Aaron	5,000	8 Mar 1862	Assessor	Elected 4 Sep 1861	B	255-256
McHenry, James*	Miller, J. M.; Lane, John J.; Barnes, Aaron; Manning, William H.	5,000	17 Sep 1861	Assessor	Elected 4 Sep 1861	B	211
McIlroy, George W.	Crane, G. L.; Greening, John	2,000	22 Jan 1867	Steward of the County Hospital	Appointed 17 Jan 1867 by the Board of Supervisors	B	557
McKinnon, Alexander C.	Bouton, A. P.; Short, P. R.; Reed, J. F.	1,000	[2 Oct 1854]	Constable (Petaluma Township)	Elected	A	20
McKinnon, Alexander C.	Ames, T. N.; Stiles, J. H.; Bouton, A. P.; Samuels, J.; Reed, James F.; Fritsch, John; Zartman, William; Bates, J. W.; Bray, Francis; Brandstetter, George J.; Remond, H.; Huff, John G.; Dean, William G.; Newman, B.; Sachs, H.; Stanley, H.; Van Houton, William; Goodspeed, F.; Bassett, H.; Judkins, L. M.; Hunt, Charles; Barnes, Thomas L.; Short, J. R.; Jacobs, J. B.	12,000	27 Sep 1855	Under Sheriff	Appointed by A. C. Bledsoe, Sheriff		
McManus, Samuel P.	Melton, William; McManus, John G.; Cook, Gordon A.; West, Robert; Hassett, J. D.	5,000	13 Apr 1874	Special Assessor (Pine Flat & Healdsburg Road District)	Elected 3 Apr 1874	1	19-20
McMeans, A. C.	Wise, Henry; Taylor, John S.; Farmer, C. C.	3,000	20 Sep 1873	Superintendent of Public Instruction	Elected 3 Sep 1873	B	718-720
McMeans, A. C.	Hood, T. B.; Taylor, John S.; Boyce, J. F.	3,000	23 Sep 1875	Superintendent of Common Schools	Elected 1 Sep 1875	1	134-135
McMeans, A. C.	Overton, A. P.; Farmer, E. T.; Wright, W. S. M.; Henley, Barclay	20,000	24 Nov 1882	Auditor	Elected 7 Nov 1882	2	187-189
McMeans, A. C.	Noonan, George P.; Brittain, R. H.; Murphy, Wyman; Taylor, John S.	10,000	27 Nov 1882	Recorder	Elected 7 Nov 1882	2	194-195
McMinn, Joseph		5,000	3 Oct 1853	Justice of the Peace (Santa Rosa Township)	Elected 7 Sep 1853	A	95
McMurray, Thomas	Purvine, Charles; McMurray, Elijah S.	1,000	2 Oct 1854	Constable (Petaluma Township)	Elected 6 Sep 1854, witness E. Denman	A	19
McNair, John E.	Cooke, Martin E.; McDonald, A. C.	10,000	10 Sep 1851	District Attorney (Sonoma County)		A	29-30
McNair, John E.	Boggs, L. W.; Cameron, John	2,000	12 Apr 1851	County Attorney		A	82

84

Principal Name	Sureties	Amount ($)	Date	Office	Notes	Book	Page(s)
McNair, John E.	Brockman, Israel; Copeland, A.; Miller, G. W.	10,000	19 Sep 1854	District Attorney (Sonoma County)	Elected to fill the unexpired term of A. Clark, Esq., deceased, late District Attorney	A	93
McQuiston, Thomas	Graham, J. W.; Forsythe, Charles	1,000	17 Feb 1880	Justice of the Peace (Russian River Township)	Appointed 4 Feb 1880 [by the Board of Supervisors]	1	569-570
McQuiston, Thomas	Graham, J. W.; Davis, L. T. (Dr.)	1,000	23 Nov 1880	Justice of the Peace (Russian River Township)	Elected 2 Nov 1880	2	27-28
McQuiston, Thomas	Clark, Charles; McCullough, Michial	1,000	24 Nov 1884	Justice of the Peace (Russian River Township)	Elected 4 Nov 1884, witness T. J. Jones	2	364-365
McQuiston, Thomas	Pool, Henry J.; Barnes, E. H.	5,000	3 Nov 1875	Justice of the Peace (Russian River Township)	Elected 20 Oct 1875	1	165-166
McQuiston, Thomas	Pool, Henry J.; Davis, L. T.	1,000	8 Aug 1879	Justice of the Peace (Russian River Township)	Appointed 5 Aug 1879 [by the Board of Supervisors, vice Thomas J. Jones, resigned]	1	464-465
McReynolds, John	Clyman, Lancaster; Matthews, O. B.	3,000	10 May 1860	Road Overseer (Annally District)	Appointed 10 May 1860 by the Board of Supervisors for the term of one year	B	83
Mead, James A.	Willson, H. M.; Hassett, J. D.; Brown, H. K.; Gum, Isaac	10,000	16 Nov 1880	Supervisor (District No. 5)	Elected 2 Nov 1880	2	5-6
Mead, James A.	Rice, John H.; Bonce, Hiram	200	28 Sep 1861	Road Overseer (District No. 2, Washington Township)	Elected 4 Sep 1861, witnesses David Odell & John Roberson	B	227
Mead, James*	Cox, N. H.; Walters, Sol; Cunningham, F. Z.; Smith, H. W.	15,000	22 Nov 1890	Supervisor (District No. 4)	Elected 4 Nov 1890	4	100
Mead, W. H.	McCoy, James; Beam, J.; Gray, J. W.; Loucks, A. H.	2,000	13 Sep 1875	Constable (Santa Rosa Township)	Elected 1 Sep 1875	1	111-112
Mead, W. H.	Mathews, John; Beam, Jeremiah; Willis, T. N.; McGeorge, Robert	2,000	8 Apr 1874	Constable (Santa Rosa Township)	Appointed 7 Apr 1874 by the Board of Supervisors [to fill the vacancy occasioned by the resignation of R. Head]	1	17-18
Mead, William	Hendley, John; Barnes, M.	1,000	14 Sep 1861	Constable (Santa Rosa Township)	Elected 4 Sep 1861	B	197
Mead, William	Taylor, John S.; Roney, J. M.; Hahman, F. G.; Wright, W. S. M.; Lane, J. J.; Boyce, J. F.; Lewis, Joshua	5,000	18 Dec 1867	Coroner	Elected 4 Sep 1867	B	570-571
Mead, William	Boyce, J. F.; Martin, R. M.	1,000	18 Sep 1862	Constable [Santa Rosa Township]	Elected 3 Sep 1862	B	301
Mead, William	Boyce, John F.; Gray, William	1,000	27 Sep 1865	Constable (Santa Rosa Township)	Elected 6 Sep 1865	B	476
Mead, Wilson H.	Morris, W. H.; Wright, Joseph; Bayler, John; Mills, E. T.; Beam, J.	2,000	6 Jun 1881	Constable (Santa Rosa Township)	Appointed 6 Jun 1881 [by the Board of Supervisors], vice D. C. Rupe, resigned	2	97-99

Principal Name	Sureties	Amount ($)	Date	Office	Notes	Book	Page(s)
Means, Thomas J.	Coulter, S. T.; Lewis, H. H.	5,000	[4 Oct 1855]	Justice of the Peace (Russian River Township)	Elected 5 Sep 1855	A	150-151
Means, Thomas J.	West, Samuel I.; Kruse, James	1,000	2 Oct 1854	Constable (Russian River Township)	Elected 6 Sep 1854	A	35
Menefee, W. H.	Joy, Benjamin; Long, Joseph J.	2,000	30 Dec 1871	Justice of the Peace (Bodega Township)	Elected 18 Oct 1871, includes oath of office dated 30 Dec 1871	C	140-141
Menefee, W. H.	Hunt, B. W.; Orender, Joel	1,000	9 Aug 1869	Justice of the Peace (Bodega Township)	Appointed, witness A. Bushnell	B	627
Menefee, William H.	Patterson, A. S.; Joy, Benjamin	2,000	[?] Dec 1869	Justice of the Peace (Bodega Township)	Elected 20 Oct 1869	C	17
Merritt, John	Roberts, Charles; Morrison, Thomas	1,000	24 Feb 1877	Road Master (Petaluma Road District No. 2)	Appointed 9 Feb 1877 [by the Board of Supervisors]	1	254-255
Metzler, Theodore C.	Boyce, John F.; Neblett, Edward	1,000	14 Jul 1871	Constable (Santa Rosa Township)	Appointed 13 Jul 1871 by the Board of Supervisors for the unexpired term of Lee Wilson made vacant by his death	C	74-75
Meyer, Claus	Ferguson, R.; Reniff, A. A.	1,000	[?] Jan 1887	Pound Master (Washington Pound District comprising all of Washington Township)	Appointed 7 Jan 1887	3	179-180
Meyer, F. A.*	Meyer, Anton; Poehlmann, Conrad	5,000	27 Apr 1889	Notary Public	Appointed & commissioned 25 Apr 1889 by R. W. Waterman, Governor of California	4	54
Meyer, Frank A.*	Meyer, Anton; Poehlmann, Conrad	5,000	21 Apr 1887	Notary Public	Appointed & commissioned 14 Apr 1887 by Washington Bartlett, Governor of California	3	188-189
Middleton, A. W.	McCullough, William; Gray, J. W.; Willis, T. N.; Roney, J. M.	5,000	12 Dec 1871	Notary Public	Appointed & commissioned 1 Dec 1871 for the term of two years, includes oath of office dated 14 Dec 1871	C	121-122
Middleton, A. W.	Farmer, E. T.; Neblett, E.	2,000	2 Jan 1874	Justice of the Peace (Santa Rosa Township)	Elected 15 Oct 1873	B	772-773
Middleton, Z.	Marks, B.; Boyce, J. F.; Clark, J. P.; Farmer, E. T.	2,000	10 Nov 1863	Justice of the Peace (Santa Rosa Township)	Elected 21 Oct 1863	B	390-391
Middleton, Z.	Williamson, W. M.; Farmer, Elijah T.	1,000	14 Sep 1861	Justice of the Peace (Santa Rosa Township)	Elected 4 Sep 1861	B	198
Middleton, Z.	Farmer, E. T.; Clark, James P.	1,000	16 Sep 1862	Justice of the Peace (Santa Rosa Township)	Elected 3 Sep 1862	B	277
Middleton, Z.	Ames, C. G.; Noonan, George P.	2,000	24 Dec 1869	Justice of the Peace (Santa Rosa Township)	Elected 20 Oct 1869, includes oath of office dated 24 Dec 1869	C	23
Middleton, Z.	Farmer, E. T.; Noonan, George P.	2,000	4 Nov 1869	Justice of the Peace [Santa Rosa Township]	Appointed 3 Nov 1869 by the Board of Supervisors, [vice M. K. McCorkle, resigned]	C	1
Middleton, Z.*	Boyce, J. F.; Gray, William; Farmer, E. T.; Noonan, George P.	2,000	8 Nov 1865	Justice of the Peace (Sonoma Township)	Elected 18 Oct 1865	B	508

Principal Name	Sureties	Amount ($)	Date	Office	Notes	Book	Page(s)
Miller, George Kay	Miller, Charles C.; Badger, Joseph J.	1,000	7 Feb 1866	Justice of the Peace (Salt Point Township)	Appointed 6 Feb 1866 by the Board of Supervisors	B	520
Miller, George W.	Leavenworth, T. M.; Brockman, Israel; Cooke, Martin E.; Brockman, Joseph E.; O'Farrell, Jasper; Cooper, James; Nevill, Joseph N.	30,000	21 Nov 1854	Public Administrator	Appointed 20 Nov 1854 by Judge of the 7th Judicial District [Hon. E. W. McKinstry]	A	94
Miller, George W.	Hendley, John; Nevill, J. N.; Maupin, R. A.; Boggs, Thomas J.; Cooke, Martin E.; Brunner, Christ; Tate, T. H.; Thornley, Henry; Vasques, P. J.; Blakney, J. C.; Boughton, Benjamin Franklin; Bennet, R. W.; Ellsworth, LeGrand	30,000	24 Oct 1854	Treasurer	Elected 6 Sep 1854	A	90
Miller, George W.	Hendley, John; Randolph, Isaac N.	6,000	7 Apr 1852	Treasurer	Appointed April term 1852 by the Court of Sessions to fill the vacancy occasioned by the resignation of Alexander C. McDonald, includes oath of office dated 7 Apr 1852	A	48-49
Miller, George W.	Joost, Jacob; Blair, John	1,000	24 Feb 1892	Pound Master (Guerneville Pound District)	Appointed 4 Feb 1892 by the Board of Supervisors	4	198
Miller, Henry*	Ingram, John; Heald, H. G.	5,000	2 Oct 1854	Justice of the Peace (Russian River Township)	Elected 6 Sep 1854	A	26
Miller, Isaac	Heald, Thomas T.; Guerne, George E.	1,000	1 Nov 1877	Justice of the Peace (Redwood Township)	Elected 17 Oct 1877	1	343-345
Miller, J. M.	Willits, W. H.; Murphy, Rufus	1,000	10 Dec 1880	Justice of the Peace (Redwood Township)	Elected 2 Nov 1880	2	44-46
Miller, J. M.	Willits, W. H.; Murphy, Rufus	1,000	13 Dec 1882	Justice of the Peace (Redwood Township)	Elected 7 Nov 1882	2	262-263
Miller, J. M.	Clyman, James; Walker, John	10,000	17 Sep 1851	Justice of the Peace (Annally Township)	Elected 3 Sep 1851	A	81
Miller, J. M.	Heald, Thomas T.; Willits, W. H.	2,000	19 Sep 1879	Justice of the Peace (Redwood Township)	Elected 3 Sep 1879	1	500-501
Miller, Jacob	Heald, Thomas T.; Guerne, George E.	2,000	21 Nov 1876	Justice of the Peace (Redwood Township)	Appointed 16 Nov 1876 [by the Board of Supervisors upon the death of Squire Clover]	1	278-279
Miller, Joel	Hoen, Berthold; Atterbury, William B.	1,000	[3 Dec 1860]	Justice of the Peace (Santa Rosa Township)	Elected 6 Nov 1860	B	122
Miller, Joel	Hood, T. B.; Heisel, Paul	1,000	13 May 1862	Justice of the Peace (Santa Rosa Township)	Appointed 10 May 1862 by the Board of Supervisors, witness William H. Crowell	B	265
Miller, Joel	Williamson, William M.; Gallagher, Jacob M.; Hudson, Martin; Mothersead, A. J.; Leary, William; Hudson, Thomas; Vaughn, Daniel; Todd, S. S.; Treadway, R. M.; Lane, John J.; Lamb, Joseph	6,000	30 Sep 1857	Recorder	Elected 2 Sep 1857, accepted by W. B. Hagans, Chairman of the Board of Supervisors	A	199-206
Miller, Joseph M.	Walker, John; Dougherty, John	1,000	3 Oct 1859	Justice of the Peace (Annally Township)	Elected 7 Sep 1859	B	43

Principal Name	Sureties	Amount ($)	Date	Office	Notes	Book	Page(s)
Miner, E. D.	Shaw, Isaac E.; Kier, Harry	1,000	23 Sep 1879	Constable (Cloverdale Township)	Elected 3 Sep 1879	1	505-506
Mock, Wesley	Thayer, D. S.; Leslie, J.	200	20 Sep 1861	Road Overseer (District No. 1, Santa Rosa Township)	Appointed 10/12 Sep 1861 by the Board of Supervisors	B	231
Mock, William	Waugh, Lorenzo; Gray, Thomas C.	5,000	2 Oct 1854	Justice of the Peace (Vallejo Township)	Elected 6 Sep 1854	A	26
Mock, William	Mock, Charles; Van Winkle, T. B.	5,000	9 Oct 1855	Surveyor	Elected for a term of two years	A	121
Moore, A. P.	Glynn, F. B.; Maddux, J. P.; Glenn, Robert; Gauldin, W. W.; Barnes, W. P.; Hopper, Thomas	10,000	13 Nov 1886	Recorder	Elected 2 Nov 1886, witness A. D. Laughlin	3	4-6
Moore, A. P.	Glynn, F. B.; Maddux, J. P.; Glenn, R.; Gauldin, W. W.; Barnes, W. P.; Hopper, Thomas; Burger, C. H.; Smith, H. W.; Overton, A. P.; Harris, Jacob; Shelton, A. C.	20,000	13 Nov 1886	Auditor	Elected 2 Nov 1886, witness A. D. Laughlin	3	7-10
Moore, A. P.	Howell, O.; Ware, A. B.; Davis, W. S.; Burris, L. W.; Dunbar, J.; Hopper, J. W.; Carithers, D. N.	10,000	20 Nov 1888	Recorder	Elected 6 Nov 1888	3	269-271
Moore, A. P.	Howell, Orrin; Harris, Jacob; McGee, J. H.; Taylor, John S.; Fulkerson, John; Near, C. D.; Shea, Con; Brittain, R. H.; Carithers, D. N.; Glynn, F. B.	20,000	20 Nov 1888	Auditor	Elected 6 Nov 1888	3	271-273
Morehous, Nathan B.	Jordan, J.; Alexander, Cyrus	1,000	24 Sep 1862	Constable (Washington Township)	Elected [3 Sep 1862]	B	295
Morehouse, C. D.	Bedwell, Franklin	200	6 Nov 1861	Road Overseer (District No. 1, Washington Township)	Appointed November Term 1861 by the Board of Supervisors, witness T. H. White, includes oath of office dated 6 Nov 1861	B	238
Morehouse, Charles D.	McPherson, Charles P.; Alexander, Cyrus	200	8 Mar 1861	Road Overseer (portion of Washington Township lying east of the Russian River)	Appointed Feb 1861 Term by the Board of Supervisors	B	149
Moreland, W. W.	Brown, H. K.; Hassett, John D.	5,000	2 Mar 1878	Notary Public	Appointed & commissioned 25 Feb 1878	1	413-415
Moreland, W. W.	Carruthers, T. C.; Hassett, John D.	5,000	4 Mar 1876	Notary Public	Appointed & commissioned 25 Feb 1876 by William Irwin, Governor of California, includes oath of office dated 4 Mar 1876	1	190-191
Moreland, W. W.*	Hotchkiss, W. J.; Barnes, E. H.	5,000	29 Sep 1891	Notary Public	Appointed 23 Sep 1891 by the Governor of California	4	191
Morgan, D. B.	Caldwell, William; Davis, G. V.	1,000	17 Nov 1880	Justice of the Peace (Cloverdale Township)	Elected 2 Nov 1880	2	8-10
Morgan, D. B.	Shaw, Isaac E.; Chalfant, John E.	5,000	19 Dec 1885	Notary Public	Appointed 14 Dec 1885 by [George Stoneman], Governor of California, witness Charles H. Cooley	2	515-518
Morgan, D. B.	Kier, Harry; Shaw, Isaac E.	5,000	22 Dec 1877	Notary Public	Appointed 18 Dec 1877 by the Governor of California	1	379-380
Morgan, D. B.	Shaw, Isaac E.; Kier, Harry	5,000	23 Dec 1879	Notary Public	Appointed & commissioned 18 Dec 1879 by the Governor [of California]	1	559-560

Principal Name	Sureties	Amount ($)	Date	Office	Notes	Book	Page(s)
Morgan, D. B.	Larison, Samuel; Davis, G. V.	1,000	23 Sep 1879	Justice of the Peace (Cloverdale Township)	Elected 3 Sep 1879	1	506-507
Morgan, D. B.	Kier, H.; Shaw, Isaac E.; Shores, Leander; Davis, G. V. B.; Dixon, John; Davis, B. J.	5,000	24 Dec 1875	Notary Public	Appointed 18 Dec 1875 by William Irwin, Governor of California	1	183
Morgan, D. B.	Shaw, Isaac E.; Chalfant, John E.	5,000	24 Dec 1883	Notary Public	Appointed 18 Dec 1883 by [George] Stoneman, Governor of California	2	312-314
Morgan, D. B.	Caldwell, William; Davis, G. V.	1,000	25 Nov 1882	Justice of the Peace (Cloverdale Township)	Elected 7 Nov 1882	2	209-210
Morgan, D. B.	Shaw, I. E.; Davis, G. V.	1,000	25 Oct 1877	Justice of the Peace (Cloverdale Township)	Elected 17 Oct 1877	1	356-358
Morgan, D. B.	Larison, Samuel; Davis, G. V.	1,000	26 Nov 1884	Justice of the Peace [Cloverdale Township]	Elected 4 Nov 1884	2	386-387
Morgan, D. B.	Truett, M. K.; Larson, S.	2,000	3 Jan 1872	Justice of the Peace (Cloverdale Township)	Appointed 2 Jan 1872, vice J. P. Morris, neglected to qualify	C	143-145
Morgan, D. B.	Larison, Sam; Shores, Leander; Dixon, John; Kier, Harry	2,000	3 Jan 1874	Justice of the Peace (Cloverdale Township)	Elected 15 Oct 1873	B	764-766
Morgan, D. B.	Davis, G. V.; Shaw, I. E.	5,000	3 Jan 1882	Notary Public	Appointed 19 Dec 1881	2	115-116
Morgan, D. B.	Shores, Leander; Kier, Harrie; Larison, Samuel; Shaw, I. E.	2,000	30 Oct 1875	Justice of the Peace (Cloverdale Township)	Elected 20 Oct 1875	1	160-161
Morgan, D. B.*	Jones, T. B.; Caldwell, William	1,000	29 Nov 1869	Justice of the Peace (Cloverdale Township)	Elected 20 Oct 1869	C	13
Morgan, Irwin R.	McGuire, Cornelius; Drennan, A. J.	100	20 Aug 1859	Road Overseer (Road District No. 9, Analy Township)	Appointed by the Board of Supervisors, includes oath of office dated 20 Aug 1859	B	7
Morris, J. C.	Purrine, A. S.; Farrell, Martin	1,000	26 Sep 1879	Constable (Bodega Township)	Elected 3 Sep 1879	1	523-524
Morris, J. R.	Ellis, John J.; Clark, James P.	1,000	3 Dec 1860	Justice of the Peace (Annally Township)	Elected 6 Nov 1860, witness James W. Shattuck	B	117
Morris, J. R.	Ross, Losson; Harris, E. D.	1,000	7 Oct 1861	Justice of the Peace (Annally Township)	Elected 4 Sep 1861	B	219-220
Morris, James B.	Cady, Martin K.; Morris, Thomas D.	1,000	10 May 1888	Pound Master (Sonoma Pound District)	Appointed 10 May 1888 by the Board of Supervisors	3	243-244
Morris, James B.	Morris, T. D.; Heggie, Norman J.	1,000	2 Dec 1890	Justice of the Peace (Sonoma Township)	Elected 4 Nov 1890	4	127
Morris, James W.	Hendley, John; Green, C. C.	1,000	[?] Sep 1859	Constable (Santa Rosa Township)	Elected 7 Sep 1859	B	45
Morris, John	Morris, James B.; Craig, O. W.	1,000	23 Mar 1878	Road Master (Sonoma [Road] District, Northern Division)	Appointed 4 Mar 1878 [by the Board of Supervisors]	1	423-424

89

Principal Name	Sureties	Amount ($)	Date	Office	Notes	Book	Page(s)
Morris, John C.	Purrine, A. S.; Farrell, Martin	2,000	21 Sep 1877	Constable (Bodega Township)	Elected 5 Sep 1877	1	330-331
Morris, Joseph H. P.	Dougherty, John; Phelps, Charles W.	1,000	19 Dec 1863	Constable (Analy Township)	Elected 2 Sep 1863	B	419
Morris, Joseph H. P.	Irwin, Newton C.; Nuckolls, Nathaniel	1,000	2 Oct 1854	Constable (Annally Township)	Elected 6 Sep 1854	A	27
Morris, Joseph H. P.	Peterson, A. J.; Boyce, John F.	1,000	20 Feb 1861	Constable (Annally Township)	Appointed 20 Feb 1861 by the Board of Supervisors	B	145
Morris, Joseph H. P.	Ross, Losson; Clark, James P.	1,000	21 Sep 1861	Constable (Annally Township)	Elected 4 Sep 1861	B	192
Morris, Joseph H. P.	Orr, John; Wilson, William H.	1,000	25 Sep 1862	Constable (Analy Township)	Elected 3 Sep 1862	B	306
Morris, Joseph H. P.	Orr, John; Crawford, Adam	1,000	30 Dec 1867	Constable (Analy Township)	Elected 4 Sep 1867	B	600
Morris, W. R.*	Farmer, E. T.; Willis, T. N.; Forsyth, Robert A.; Mitchell, R. T.	6,000	30 Dec 1871	Clerk	Elected 6 Sep 1871	**B**	552-554
Morris, William R.	Hall, L. J.; Bedwell, J. C; Miller, Thomas B.; Morris, John; Woods, G.; Parmer, C. F.	5,000	26 Dec 1863	Assessor	Elected 2 Sep 1863, witness David Odell	B	418
Morris, William R.*	Hassett, J. D.; Bloom, David; Norton, L. A.; Farmer, E. T.	6,000	5 Feb 1870	Clerk	Elected 1 Sep 1869	**B**	408-409
Morrison, Oscar	Noonan, George P.; Farmer, Elijah T.	5,000	13 Mar 1882	Notary Public	Appointed 4 Feb 1882	2	126-127
Morrison, Oscar	McFadyen, Allan; Tupper, George A.	5,000	17 Oct 1887	Notary Public	Appointed & commissioned 13 Oct 1887 by the Governor of California, witness L. W. Juilliard	3	199-200
Morrison, Oscar	Justice, A. L.; Farmer, C. C.	5,000	29 Jun 1880	Auctioneer			
Morse, E. E.	Adler, Lewis; Martin, James	1,000	15 Jan 1880	Justice of the Peace (Sonoma Township)	Appointed 5 Jan 1880 by the Board of Supervisors	1	566-567
Morse, E. E.	Hill, William McPherson; Hooper, George F.	10,000	18 Nov 1880	Supervisor (District No. 1)	Elected 2 Nov 1880	2	20-21
Morse, E. E.	Hill, William McPherson; Rogers, W. K.; Haraszthy, A. F.; Leiding, C. F.	15,000	23 Nov 1882	Supervisor (District No. 1)	Elected 7 Nov 1882	2	174-175
Morse, E. E.	Burris, David; McHarvey, Charles	2,000	24 Sep 1879	Commissioner (Pueblo of Sonoma)	Appointed 16 Sep 1879, vice John Tivnen, resigned	1	536-537
Morse, E. E.	Pauli, G. T.; Barnard, N. S.	1,000	31 Oct 1877	Justice of the Peace (Sonoma Township)	Elected 17 Oct 1877	1	333-334
Morstadt, A.	Tempel, C.; Poehlmann, Conrad	2,000	26 Nov 1890	Justice of the Peace (Petaluma Township)	Elected 4 Nov 1890	4	108
Morstadt, A.	Schmitt, George; Newburgh, Edward	2,000	4 Dec 1869	Justice of the Peace (Petaluma Township)	Elected 20 Oct 1869	C	9
Morstadt, Adolph	Schmitt, George; Gerkens, J. H. L.	2,000	21 Nov 1884	Justice of the Peace (Petaluma Township)	Elected 4 Nov 1884	2	412-413

Principal Name	Sureties	Amount ($)	Date	Office	Notes	Book	Page(s)
Moss, W. H.	Bloom, D.; Meyer, S.; Hawkins, Duff G.	2,000	10 Nov 1871	Justice of the Peace (Mendocino Township)	Elected 18 Oct 1871	C	106
Moss, William H.	Mead, James A.; Baruch, Henry; Curtiss, James H.	2,000	5 Dec 1873	Justice of the Peace (Mendocino Township)	Elected 15 Oct 1873	B	751-752
Mott, William A.	Cassidey, S.; Allen, N. L.	5,000	29 Nov 1856	Constable (Petaluma Township)	Elected 4 Nov 1856	A	177
Moyce, Swift H.	Hockin, William; McClellan, James E.	1,000	18 Oct 1884	Justice of the Peace (Salt Point Township)	Appointed 3 Sep 1884 [by the Board of Supervisors, vice David Peters, deceased]	2	422-423
Moyce, Swift H.	Hockin, William; Piver, Leroy	1,000	6 Dec 1884	Justice of the Peace (Salt Point Township)	Elected 4 Nov 1884	2	402-403
Mulgrew, Felix B.	Young, John S.; Rosenberg, W.	5,000	5 Dec 1887	Notary Public	Appointed 23 Nov 1887 by R. W. Waterman, Governor [of California], witness W. M. Moulton	3	210-211
Mulgrew, J. F.*	Powell, Ransom; Barnes, E. H.; Miller, George T.; Truitt, R. K.; Truitt, J. R.; Ragan, Joel; Tombs, W. L.; Samuels, James; Bell, G. K.; Phillips, D. D.	25,000	23 Dec 1886	Clerk	Elected 2 Nov 1886	3	126-128
Mulgrew, J. F.*	Shea, Con; Towey, Peter; Hall, L. J.; Burger, C. H.; Maddux, J. P.; Noonan, George P.; Roney, J. M.; Gauldin, W. W.; Taylor, John S.; Murphy, Rufus; Hopper, Thomas; McConnell, William E.; Noonan, P. H.; Carithers, D. N.; Guerne, George E.; Hopper, J. W.	50,000	29 Nov 1890	Tax Collector	Elected 4 Nov 1890, witness A. D. Laughlin	3	348-351
Mulgrew, J. F.*	Shea, Con; Towey, Peter; Hall, L. J.; Burger, C. H.; Maddux, J. P.; Noonan, George P.; Roney, J. M.; Gauldin, W. W.; Brittain, R. H.; Taylor, John S.; Murphy, Rufus; Hopper, Thomas; Kinslow, John F.; Noonan, P. H.; Walker, John; Carithers, D. N.; Guerne, George E.; Hopper, J. W.; McConnell, William E.	60,000	29 Nov 1890	Sheriff	Elected 4 Nov 1890, witness A. D. Laughlin	3	344-348
Mulgrew, J. F.*	Noonan, George P.; Roney, J. M.; Prindle, William; Proctor, T. A.	5,000	31 Aug 1889	Notary Public	Appointed & commissioned 29 Aug 1889 by R. W. Waterman, Governor of California	4	65
Mulgrew, John F.*	Powell, R.; Truitt, John R.; Brown, H. K.; Hassett, J. D.; Samuels, James; Allen, William T.; Nalley, A. B.; Board, William; Ragan, Joel; Cunningham, F. Z.	25,000	[?] Nov 1884	Clerk	Elected 4 Nov 1884	2	339-341 & 361-363
Munday, James	Vallejo, M. G.; Woods, J. S.; Tate, T. H.	5,000	27 Nov 1856	Justice of the Peace (Sonoma Township)	Elected 4 Nov 1856, witness Martin E. Cooke	A	180
Murdock, N. E.	Meyer, Claus; Reniff, A. A.	1,000	4 Dec 1886	Justice of the Peace (Washington Township)	Elected 2 Nov 1886	3	100-101
Murphy, B. F.	Murphy, Rufus; Byrne, M.	1,000	[?] Aug 1878	Justice of the Peace (Redwood Township)	Appointed 6 Aug 1878 [by the Board of Supervisors], vice S. N. Hudson, resigned	1	439-440
Murphy, John F.	Ormsby, J. S.; Rathbun, Erskine	1,000	14 Oct 1858	Constable (Mendocino Township)	Elected 1 Sep 1858	A	351
Murphy, Patrick	Cavanagh, John; Hynes, James	2,000	18 May 1877	Road Overseer (South Vallejo Road District)	Appointed 9 May 1877 [by the Board of Supervisors, vice P. Pharris, resigned]	1	269-270

Principal Name	Sureties	Amount ($)	Date	Office	Notes	Book	Page(s)
Murphy, Patrick	Bliss, William D.; Donnelly, John	200	7 Jan 1865	Road Master (District No. 2, Vallejo Township)	Elected [8 Nov 1864], witness I. G. Wickersham	B	466-467
Murray, Thomas	Goodman, L. S.; Farrell, Martin	1,000	14 Jul 1879	Justice of the Peace (Bodega Township)	Appointed 9 Jul 1879 [by the Board of Supervisors to fill a vacancy caused by the death of J. L. Springer]	1	459-460
Murray, Thomas	Goodman, L. S.; Farrell, Martin	1,000	24 Sep 1879	Justice of the Peace (Bodega Township)	Elected 3 Sep 1879	1	516-517
Murray, Thomas	Goodman, L. S.; McCaughey, J.	1,000	26 Nov 1880	Justice of the Peace (Bodega Township)	Elected 2 Nov 1880	2	30-31
Murray, Thomas	Long, Frederick; Stump, James	2,000	29 Dec 1869	Justice of the Peace (Bodega Township)	Elected 20 Oct 1869	C	21
Myers, D. D.	Beaver, Henry; Warner, Philemon	1,000	15 Aug 1859	Justice of the Peace (Santa Rosa Township)	Appointed [?] Aug 1859 by the Board of Supervisors	B	6
Myers, D. D.	Warner, P.; Beaver, Henry	1,000	26 Sep 1859	Justice of the Peace (Santa Rosa Township)	Elected 7 Sep 1859	B	24
Myers, D. D.	Hood, Thomas B.; Williamson, William M.	1,000	30 Nov 1860	Justice of the Peace (Santa Rosa Township)	Elected 6 Nov 1860	B	109-110
Myers, Dudley D.	Beaver, Henry; Williamson, William M.	1,000	24 Sep 1858	Constable (Santa Rosa Township)	Elected 1 Sep 1858	A	316
Myrick, D. B.	Clark, Robert; Low, William	1,000	27 Sep 1862	Constable (Washington Township)	Elected 3 Sep 1862	B	311
Nagle, F. G.	Williams, James M.; Carithers, D. N.; Cox, C. B.; Noonan, George P.	5,000	29 Jan 1886	Notary Public	Appointed 26 Jan 1886 [by George Stoneman, Governor of California], witness W. D. Reynolds, includes oath of office dated 29 Jan 1886	2	528-530
Nagle, F. G.	Williams, James M.; Farmer, Elijah T.	5,000	31 Jan 1884	Notary Public	Appointed 29 Jan 1884, witness James H. McGee	2	318-319
Nagle, F. G. *	Noonan, George P.; Cox, Charles B.	5,000	2 Feb 1888	Notary Public	Appointed 26 Jan 1888	3	216-218
Nagle, F. G. *	Noonan, George P.; Cox, C. B.	5,000	27 Jan 1890	Notary Public	Appointed [?] Jan 1890	4	72
Nagle, F. G. *	Farmer, E. T.; Pauli, G. T.; Hahman, F. G.; Boyce, J. F.; Williams, James M.	5,000	3 Dec 1875	Notary Public	Appointed 1 Dec 1875 by R. Pacheco, Governor of California	1	173
Nagle, Fred G.	Williams, James M.; Farmer, Elijah T.; Grosse, Guy E.; Hahman, F. G.	5,000	12 Jan 1882	Notary Public	Appointed 10 Jan 1882	2	117-118
Nagle, Fred G.	Williams, James M.; Farmer, Elijah T.; Smallwood, Lewis W.; Cox, Charles B.	5,000	13 Jan 1880	Notary Public	Appointed 10 Jan 1880	1	562-564
Naughton, John F.	Davis, E. W.; Lougee, F. W.; Fairbanks, H. T.; Jones, William	10,000	21 Nov 1884	Recorder	Elected 4 Nov 1884	2	409-410
Naughton, John F.	Charles, J. M.; Higgins, A.; Wickersham, I. G.; Jewell, I. R.; Stewart, David; Bliss, William D.; Van Doren, J. S.; Tempel, C.	20,000	21 Nov 1884	Auditor	Elected 4 Nov 1884	2	435-436
Neely, T. L.	Barnes, E. H.; Smith, H. W.	1,000	30 Nov 1888	Constable (Mendocino Township)	Elected 6 Nov 1888	3	282-283
Nevill, Joseph N.	Cameron, John; McDonald, A. C.	5,000	15 May 1850	Assessor	Appointed	A	84

92

Principal Name	Sureties	Amount ($)	Date	Office	Notes	Book	Page(s)
Nobles, Harmon*	Stengel, Christian; Lancaster, Charles B.	1,000	10 Dec 1892	Constable (Salt Point Township)	Elected 8 Nov 1892	4	250
Noon, James T.	Noonan, George P.; Shea, Cornelius	5,000	2 Oct 1886	Notary Public	Appointed 27 Sep 1886 by George Stoneman, Governor of California, for the term of two years	2	555-556
Noonan, George P.	Willis, T. N.; Boyce, John F.; Bond, William H.; Neblett, E.; Ledwidge, John; Taylor, John; Knox, John T.	15,000	26 Nov 1869	Public Administrator	Elected 1 Sep 1869	C	15
Norton, E. M.*	Barnes, E. H.; Warfield, R. H.	5,000	9 Jun 1890	Notary Public	Appointed 31 May 1890	4	87
Norton, L. A.	May, J. J.; Thurgood, William S.; Bloom, D.; Forrister, A. J.	5,000	1 Jul 1862	Notary Public	Commissioned 23 Jun 1862 by Leland Stanford, Governor of California	B	272
Norton, L. A.	St. Clair, F. C.; Clack, J. W.	5,000	11 Feb 1881	Notary Public	Appointed 8 Feb 1881 by George C. Perkins, Governor of California	2	83-84
Norton, L. A.	Powell, R.; Barnes, E. H.	5,000	15 Jan 1879	Notary Public	Appointed 11 Jan 1879 by the Governor of California for the term of two years	1	453-454
Norton, L. A.	Gum, Isaac; Palmer, J. S.	5,000	16 Jan 1877	Notary Public	Appointed 11 Jan 1877 for two years commencing from 11 Jan 1877, witness W. W. Moreland	1	230-231
Norton, L. A.	Brown, H. K.; Clack, John W.	5,000	9 Jan 1875	Notary Public	Appointed 7 Jan 1875	1	75-76
Norton, L. A.*	Barnes, E. H.; Powell, Ransom	5,000	27 Apr 1889	Notary Public	Appointed 25 Apr 1889 by R. W. Waterman, Governor of California	4	55
Norton, Lewis A.	Molloy, Edward B.; Bloom, David	5,000	2 Mar 1870	Notary Public	Appointed 25 Feb 1870 by H. H. Haight, Governor of California, includes certificate of oath of office dated 2 March 1870	C	44-45
Norton, Lewis Adelbert	Williams, George F.; Powell, Ransom	5,000	9 Jan 1873	Notary Public	Appointed 7 Jan 1873 by Newton Booth, Governor of California, includes oath of office dated 10 Jan 1873		
Nowlin, James T.	Nowlin, Bennet; Hooper, J. M.	1,000	6 Oct 1857	Constable (Mendocino Township)	Elected 2 Sep 1857, accepted by W. B. Hagans, Chairman of the Board of Supervisors	A	293-294
Nuckolls, N.	Rathbun, J. S.; Molleson, H. P.; Carrillo, Julio	5,000	1 Oct 1855	Justice of the Peace (Annally Township)	Elected 5 Sep 1855	A	124
Nuckolls, Nathaniel	Miller, J. M.; Dougherty, John; Morris, Joseph H. P.	1,000	24 Nov 1856	Constable (Annally Township)	Elected 4 Nov 1856	A	164
Nuckolls, Nathaniel	Moore, William H.; Hendley, John	5,000	25 Sep 1854	Justice of the Peace (Annally Township)	Elected 6 Sep 1854	A	21
Nuckolls, Nathaniel	Fine, Abraham; Manning, John; Dougherty, John; Miller, J. M.; Fine, I. H.	5,000	30 Sep 1857	Assessor	Elected 2 Sep 1857, accepted by W. B. Hagans, Chairman of the Board of Supervisors	A	285-287
O'Brien, John H.	Orr, John; McGill, William	2,000	17 Sep 1878	Constable (Ocean Township)	Appointed 9 Sep 1878 [by the Board of Supervisors]	1	444-445
O'Farrell, William	Markham, Andrew; Sheridan, James	1,000	23 Jan 1888	Road Overseer (Ocean Road District)	Appointed 14 Jan 1888 by the Board of Supervisors	3	218-219
O'Farrell, William	Crayne, Daniel; Campbell, R. B.	1,000	27 Nov 1884	Constable (Bodega Township)	Elected 4 Nov 1884	2	396-397

Principal Name	Sureties	Amount ($)	Date	Office	Notes	Book	Page(s)
O'Grady, Thomas	Farrell, Martin; Hobbs, G. W.	1,000	15 Jan 1876	Road Master (Bodega Township, District No. 2)	Appointed 8 Jan 1876 by the Board of Supervisors	1	203-204
O'Grady, Thomas	Watson, James; Farrell, Martin	1,000	19 Feb 1877	Road Master (Bodega [Road] District No. 2)	Appointed 9 Feb 1877 [by the Board of Supervisors]	1	253-254
O'Hara, B. E. *	Collins, F. M.; Putnam, T. C.	1,000	6 Dec 1892	Justice of the Peace (Vallejo Township)	Elected 8 Nov 1892	4	232
O'Hara, John	Tempel, C.; Ingram, J. H.; Sullivan, James; Counihen, John; Caltoft, John; Hoar, B. F.; Clark, A.; Collins, F. M.; Comstock, William; Sherman, Frank	15,000	10 Sep 1884	Supervisor (District No. 1)	Appointed 4 Sep 1884 [by George Stoneman, Governor of California] for the unexpired term of E. E. Morse, [deceased], witness N. W. Scudder	2	341-343
O'Hara, John	St. John, S. C.; Tempel, C.	1,000	19 Nov 1880	Justice of the Peace (Vallejo Township)	Elected 2 Nov 1880	2	18-19
O'Hara, John	Tempel, C.; St. John, S. C.	1,000	2 Dec 1882	Justice of the Peace (Vallejo Township)	Elected 7 Nov 1882	2	226-227
O'Hara, John	Cronin, Patrick; Clark, A.; Lavin, James; Palmer, James M.; Needham, F.; McLaughlin, M.	15,000	25 Nov 1884	Supervisor (District No. 1)	Elected 4 Nov 1884	2	366-367
O'Keefe, William	Matthews, O. B.	200	4 Nov 1862	Road Overseer (Road District No. 2, Petaluma Township)	Appointed	B	321
O'Leary, Edward F.	Gannon, James P.; Kelly, J. W.	1,000	11 Jan 1887	Road Overseer (Analy Road District comprising all of Analy Township)	Appointed 5 Jan 1887	3	162-163
O'Leary, Edward F.	Hammy, George; Gannon, James P.; Morris, Joseph H. P.; Walker, Edward L.	1,000	9 Nov 1889	Constable (Analy Township)	Appointed 4 Nov 1889 by the Board of Supervisors	4	67
O'Neill, Henry	Geer, Cyrus V.; Müller, Joseph	1,000	8 Feb 1888	Constable (Russian River Township)	Appointed 6 Feb 1888 by the Board of Supervisors	3	224-225
Oates, James W.	Porter, William W.; McConnell, William E.; Henley, Barclay	5,000	23 Jan 1883	Notary Public	Commissioned 16 Jan 1883 by George Stoneman, Governor of California	2	276-277
Oates, James W.	Porter, William W.; Nalley, A. B.; Hoskins, T. D.; Noonan, George P.	5,000	27 Jan 1885	Notary Public	Appointed & commissioned 20 Jan 1885 by George Stoneman, Governor of California, includes oath of office dated 28 Jan 1885	2	459-460
Oates, James W. *	Campbell, John T.; Barham, J. A.	5,000	27 Jul 1892	Notary Public	Commissioned 25 Jul 1892	3	362-363
Odell, David	Fike, Nathan; Norton, L. A.	1,000	20 Sep 1862	Justice of the Peace [Washington Township]	Elected [3 Sep 1862]	B	286
Odell, David	Kilgore, A. C.; Clark, Robert	1,000	3 Dec 1860	Justice of the Peace (Washington Township)	Elected 6 Nov 1860	B	130
Odell, David	Stone, N. P.; Clark, Robert; McPherson, C. P.	1,000	30 Sep 1861	Justice of the Peace (Washington Township)	Elected 4 Sep 1861, witnesses William Fitch & H. L. Johns	B	204
Odell, David	Gird, Henry S.; McPherson, Charles P.	1,000	4 Oct 1858	Justice of the Peace (Washington Township)	Elected 1 Sep 1858	A	326

Principal Name	Sureties	Amount ($)	Date	Office	Notes	Book	Page(s)
Odell, David	Fike, N.; Alexander, Cyrus; Laymance, J. C.; Allison, George	2,000	5 Jan 1864	Justice of the Peace (Washington Township)	Elected [21 Oct 1863]	B	415
Odell, David	Campbell, David; Gird, Henry S.	1,000	6 Oct 1859	Justice of the Peace (Washington Township)	Elected 7 Sep 1859	B	47
Ogden, Eliel	Acker, R. W.; Dutton, Warren	1,000	10 Jan 1879	Road Overseer (Salt Point Township [Road District] No. 2)	Appointed 8 Jan 1879 [by the Board of Supervisors]		
Ogden, Eliel	Rien, Samuel; Sheridan, James	1,500	29 Nov 1882	Road Overseer (Ocean Township)	Elected 7 Nov 1882	2	237-239
Ogden, Eliel	Stockhoff, John H.; Rien, Samuel	1,000	7 Feb 1878	Road Master (Salt Point Township Road District No. 3)	Appointed 7 Feb 1878 by the Board of Supervisors	1	390-391
Ogle, J. Oliver	Graham, James W.; Thompson, J. D.; Crane, G. L.; Barnes, E. H.	2,000	31 Dec 1869	Justice of the Peace (Russian River Township)	Elected 20 Oct 1869	C	25
Ogle, John Oliver	Gentry, W. O.; Graham, J. W.	1,000	8 Jan 1868	Justice of the Peace (Russian River Township)	Elected [16 Oct 1867]	B	625
Orr, Frank	Orr, John; Sheridan, James	1,000	11 Feb 1886	Road Overseer (Ocean Road District comprising all of Ocean Township)	Appointed 5 Feb 1886 [by the Board of Supervisors, vice S. D. Ingram, resigned]	2	531-532
Overton, A. P.	Doyle, M.; Ellis, John J.; Schmitt, George; Berger, M.; Hopper, Thomas; Gray, Thomas C.; Hunt, Charles; Alberding, F. H.; Tempel, C.; Jackson, Jesse	5,000	23 Sep 1867	District Attorney	Elected 4 Sep 1867 for the term of two years and until his successor is elected and qualified	B	576-577
Overton, A. P.	Arthur, Charles R.; Anderson, William L.	500	30 Jun 1857	Road Overseer (Petaluma District)	Appointed 4 May 1857 by the Board of Supervisors	A	212
Overton, A. P.	Wright, W. S. M.; Laughlin, J. H.	10,000	7 Mar 1870	District Attorney	Elected 1 Sep 1869	C	47-48
Overton, A. P.	Taylor, J. M.; Alberding, Fredric H.; Ellis, John J.; Patton, Charles	5,000	8 Nov 1861	Notary Public	Appointed, witness John T. Fortson, includes oath of office dated 8 Nov 1861	B	226
Overton, A. P.	Matthews, O. B.; Haydon, S. C.	1,000	9 Oct 1855	Constable (Petaluma Township)	Elected 5 Sep 1855, witness Samuel King	A	109
Owen, J. W.	Whitney, A. P.; Cavanagh, John; Sroufe, John; Hunt, Charles	10,000	9 May 1866	Notary Public	Commissioned 2 May 1866 by F. F. Low, Governor of California	B	549
Owens, James	Clark, James; LeBaron, Harrison Melvin	1,000	1 Dec 1890	Road Overseer (Bodega Road District)	Elected 4 Nov 1890	4	116
Packwood, A. J.	Pool, Henry J.; Miller, James R.	1,000	11 Jan 1887	Road Overseer (Russian River Road District comprising all of Russian River Township)	Appointed 5 Jan 1887	3	167-168

Principal Name	Sureties	Amount ($)	Date	Office	Notes	Book	Page(s)
Packwood, A. J.	Laughlin, Leonidas; Pool, H. J.	1,000	4 Dec 1888	Road Overseer (Russian River Road District)	Elected 6 Nov 1888	3	319-320
Page, Charles A.*	Barnett, J. D.; Noonan, George P.	5,000	14 Jun 1890	Notary Public	Appointed & commissioned 13 Jun 1890 by R. W. Waterman, Governor of California, for the term of 4 years	4	89
Page, Charles A.*	Noonan, George P.; Barnett, J. D.	5,000	26 May 1888	Notary Public	Appointed & commissioned 25 May 1888, witness L. W. Juilliard	3	245-246
Pander, Henry*	Dreyfuss, Ed; Newburgh, Ed	1,000	23 Aug 1870	Secretary of the Board of Fire Delegates of the City of Petaluma	Elected 20 Aug 1870 for the term of one year	B	427-428
Park, Collins	Hoag, Jared C.; McReynolds, Jacob, Jr.	1,000	7 Feb 1866	Road Master (Road District No. 3, Analy Township)	Elected 6 Sep 1865		
Park, John C.*	Ruoff, John; Stockhoff, J. H.	1,000	10 Dec 1892	Constable (Salt Point Township)	Elected 8 Nov 1892	4	251
Park, John*	Stockhoff, John H.; Ruoff, John	1,000	29 Nov 1890	Constable (Salt Point Township)	Elected 4 Nov 1890	4	119
Park, Theodore T.	Miller, William R.; Carsin, John; Miller, William; Piver, Leroy	2,000	16 Sep 1873	Constable (Salt Point Township)	Elected 3 Sep 1873	B	743-744
Parkerson, C. J.	Richards, W. E.; Cozzens, D.	1,000	8 Dec 1888	Road Overseer (Mendocino Road District)	Elected 6 Nov 1888	4	19
Parkerson, Carter J.	Bell, G. K.; Phillips, G. D.	1,000	13 Jan 1887	Road Overseer (Mendocino Road District comprising all of Mendocino Township)	Appointed 5 Jan 1887	3	171-172
Parks, Abraham H.	Parks, David H.; Hall, Henry	1,000	10 Dec 1884	Constable (Analy Township)	Elected 4 Nov 1884	2	444-445
Parks, H. G.	Knowles, Joseph; Hendley, John	200	[?] Feb 1861	Road Overseer (Coleman Valley District, Bodega Township)	Appointed 21 Feb 1861 by the Board of Supervisors	B	144
Parks, H. G.	Lane, J. J.; Smith, S. S.; Abelbeck, F. D.; Farmer, J. H.; Spencer, Thomas; Ames, C. G.; Clark, J. P.; Hayes, R. K.; Holman, J. H.; Farmer, C. C.	5,000	18 Aug 1870	Auctioneer	Applied for a license as an auctioneer for the town of Santa Rosa	C	55-56
Parks, H. G.	White, J. M.; Farmer, C. C.; Roney, J. M.; Hoag, O. H.; Armstrong, J. B.; Rice, J. B.; Campbell, J. T.; Loucks, A. H.	5,000	18 Aug 1881	Auctioneer		2	107-108
Parks, H. G.	Atterbury, William B.; Noonan, George P.; Kohle, August	2,000	21 Sep 1867	Constable (Santa Rosa Township)	Elected 4 Sep 1867	B	601
Parks, H. G.	Noonan, George P.; Hendley, John; Farmer, E. T.; Wright, W. S. M.	2,000	4 Nov 1869	Constable (Santa Rosa Township)	Elected 1 Sep 1869	C	2

Principal Name	Sureties	Amount ($)	Date	Office	Notes	Book	Page(s)
Parks, Hiram G.	Hendley, John; Farmer, E. T.; Roney, J. M.; Cocke, William E.	2,000	26 Dec 1871	Constable (Santa Rosa Township)	Elected 6 Sep 1871	C	136-138
Parmer, C. F.	Sweeney, G.; Ely, Elisha	2,000	27 Dec 1871	Justice of the Peace (Washington Township)	Elected 18 Oct 1871	C	132-133
Parmer, C. F.	Miller, Thomas B.; Board, William	1,000	31 Dec 1869	Justice of the Peace (Washington Township)	Elected 20 Oct 1869	C	20
Parmer, C. F.	Ellis, L. G.; Cook, G. A.; Stites, A. H.	2,000	8 Nov 1867	Justice of the Peace (Washington Township)	Elected 16 Oct 1867	B	588
Parmer, Henry	Parmer, C. F.; McDarment, Richard	1,000	2 Oct 1865	Constable (Washington Township)	Elected 6 Sep 1865	B	495
Parmeter, John	Thompson, Thomas L.; Fitzpatrick, Andrew	2,000	8 Jan 1873	Road Master (Bodega Road District)	Appointed 7 Jan 1873 by the Board of Supervisors		
Parmeter, John S.	Crayne, Daniel; Vanderlieth, John	1,000	10 Dec 1886	Constable (Bodega Township)	Elected 2 Nov 1886	3	119-121
Patrick, James	Matthews, C. W.; Warren, W. P.	1,000	17 Jan 1885	Road Overseer (Knight's Valley Road District)	Appointed 13 Jan 1885 [by the Board of Supervisors]	2	470-471
Patrick, James	St. Clair, F. C.; Warren, W. P.	1,000	23 Nov 1882	Road Overseer (Knight's Valley Township)	Elected 7 Nov 1882	2	239-240
Patrick, James	Ferguson, John N.; Warren, W. P.	1,000	28 Nov 1890	Road Overseer (Knight's Valley Road District)	Elected 4 Nov 1890	4	113
Patrick, James	Smith, H. W.; Warren, W. P.	1,000	4 Dec 1888	Road Overseer (Knight's Valley Road District)	Elected 6 Nov 1888	3	320-321
Patton, T. S.	McClellan, M. T.; Helmke, F.	1,000	22 Nov 1867	Justice of the Peace [Salt Point Township]	Elected 16 Oct 1867	B	597
Pauli, G. T.	Justi, Charles; Williams, Joseph A.; Hill, William McPherson; Linehan, Jerry; Lawlor, James; Oettl, F.; Green, William; Akers, Stephen; Goodman, Willis C.; Poppe, J. A.; Winkle, Henry; Neeb, John; Engler, Mathias; Murphy, James D.; Rogers, W. K.; Terry, Michael; Watriss, George E.; Burris, David; Edwards, A. S.; Whitman, G. W.	50,000	12 Sep 1873	Treasurer	Elected 3 Sep 1873	B	696-699
Pauli, G. T.	Adler, Lewis; Pohley, Joseph; Weyl, Henry J.; Litzius, Louis; Lawler, James; Tivnen, John; Linihan, Jerry; McDonald, Angus; Lammot, Alfred V.; Monahan, Patrick; Green, William; Akers, Stephen; Neeb, John; Townsend, William M. A.; Gundlach, Jacob; Winkle, Henry; Clark, J. E.; Whitman, G. W.; Gibson, John; Warfield, J. B.; Williams, Joseph A.; Justi, Charles; Hill, William McPherson; Seawell, Washington; Carriger, Nicholas; Engler, M.; Poulterer, Thomas J.; Davisson, D. D.	140,000	3 Oct 1871	Treasurer	Elected 6 Sep 1871, witness Willam E. McConnell	C	85-87

Principal Name	Sureties	Amount ($)	Date	Office	Notes	Book	Page(s)
Pauli, G. T.	Wohler, Herman; Hamilton, James P.; Linnehan, Jerry; Lammot, Alfred V.; Whitman, G. W.; Oettl, F.; Monahan, John; Carriger, Nicholas; Rogers, W. K.; Seawell, Washington; Poulterer, Thomas J.; Hill, William McPherson; Williams, Joseph A.; Justi, Charles; Clark, J. E.; Townsend, William M. A.; Leiding, C. F.; Warfield, J. B.; Engler, Mathias; Davisson, D. D.; Neeb, John; Akers, Stephen; Monahan, Patrick; Donahue, Michael; Green, William; McDonald, A.; Adler, Lewis; Biggins, James; Davies, T. R.; Munday, B. B.	70,000	9 Feb 1870	Treasurer	Elected 1 Sep 1869	C	34-36
Payran, Stephen	Hahman, F. G.; Bernhard, Isaac	1,000	16 Sep 1861	Justice of the Peace (Vallejo Township)	Elected 4 Sep 1861, witness L. C. Reyburn	B	201
Payran, Stephen	Gray, Thomas C.; Humphries, Charles	2,000	2 Nov 1867	Justice of the Peace (Vallejo Township)	Elected 16 Oct 1867, witness John Cavanagh	B	591
Payran, Stephen	Cavanagh, John; Thompson, M. S.	1,000	23 Nov 1860	Justice of the Peace (Vallejo Township)	Elected 6 Nov 1860	B	100
Payran, Stephen	Farley, F. H.; Haydon, S. C.; Siddons, J. H.; Newman, B. ; Bliss, W. D.; Thompson, M. S.; Singley, James; Vandernoot, J.	5,000	23 Sep 1857	Justice of the Peace (Vallejo Township)	Elected 2 Sep 1857, taking office from 1 Oct 1857 for one year, accepted by W. B. Hagans, Chairman of the Board of Supervisors	A	209
Payran, Stephen	Cavanagh, John; Henley, William	1,000	23 Sep 1859	Justice of the Peace (Vallejo Township)	Elected 7 Sep 1859, witness L. C. Reyburn	B	21
Payran, Stephen	Farley, Francis H.; Haydon, S. C.; Kinney, John; Towne, Smith D.; Shirley, J. Q.; Rohrer, John; Linus, John; Charles, J. M.	5,000	24 Sep 1859	Coroner	Elected 7 Sep 1859, witness L. C. Reyburn	B	30
Payran, Stephen	Thompson, M. S.; Newman, B.	1,000	28 Sep 1858	Justice of the Peace (Vallejo Township)	Elected 1 Sep 1858	A	337
Payran, Stephen	Thompson, M. S.	500	9 Aug 1856	Road Overseer (Vallejo Township)	Appointed by the Board of Supervisors		
Payran, Stephen*	Reyburn, L. C.; Hardin, J. A.; Huie, J. Thompson	2,000	8 Nov 1865	Justice of the Peace (Vallejo Township)	Elected 18 Oct 1865	B	504
Peabody, E. T.	Boggs, L. W.; Maupin, Richard A.	5,000	8 Sep 1851	Surveyor	Elected 3 Sep 1851	A	31
Peabody, E. T.	Boggs, L. W.; Carson, M. B.	5,000	9 Apr 1850	Surveyor	Elected 1 Apr 1850	A	58
Pearce, George	Towne, Smith D.; Robinson, John	5,000	11 Jan 1856	Notary Public	Appointed 7 Jan 1856, includes oath of office dated 11 Jan 1856	A	108
Pearce, George	Murray, Dennis; Nalley, A. B.; Bowles, J. M.; Brackett, J. S.; Cavanagh, John; Walsh, M.; McNamara, M.; Lawrence, H. E.	15,000	20 Nov 1886	District Attorney	Elected 2 Nov 1886, witness D. B. Fairbanks	3	35-37
Pearce, George	Jackson, Calvin; Anderson, William L.; Cook, Israel; Haydon, S. C.; Delahenty, John; Derby, Solon P.; Doyle, M.	5,000	22 Jul 1857	Notary Public	Appointed 25 Jun 1857, includes oath of office dated 22 Jul 1857	A	210-211

Principal Name	Sureties	Amount ($)	Date	Office	Notes	Book	Page(s)
Pearson, Richmond C.	Sroufe, John; Ayers, William	200	28 Sep 1861	Road Master (District No. 2, [Petaluma Township])	Elected 4 Sep 1861	B	242
Peavey, Jacob C.	Overton, A. P.; Ordway, William; Brown, S. C.; McCune, James N.	2,000	26 Nov 1860	Constable (Petaluma Township)	Elected 6 Nov 1860 for the term of one year	B	108-109
Peerman, M. H.*	Hopper, Thomas; Carithers, D. N.; Doggett, W. J.	2,000	1 Dec 1890	Constable (Santa Rosa Township)	Elected 4 Nov 1890, witness W. F. Wines	4	125
Peerman, Miles H.	Gray, J. W.; Gale, Otis; Roney, J. M.; Temple, R. A.; Warner, James	2,000	8 Sep 1887	Constable (Santa Rosa Township)	Appointed 6 Sep 1887 by the Board of Supervisors	3	195-197
Peerman, Miles H.*	Hopper, Thomas; Doggett, W. J.	1,000	5 Dec 1892	Constable (Santa Rosa Township)	Elected 8 Nov 1892	4	245
Perry, H. R.	Shaw, N. R.; Ward, J. T.	1,000	6 Dec 1888	Constable (Bodega Township)	Elected 6 Nov 1888	4	7
Peters, David	McMale, Richard; Ruoff, John	2,000	13 Aug 1883	Justice of the Peace (Salt Point Township)	Appointed 9 Aug 1883 [by the Board of Supervisors, vice E. Blackford, resigned]	2	297-298
Petray, G. W.	Barnes, E. H.; Calhoon, J. W.	1,000	17 May 1860	Justice of the Peace (Russian River Township)	Appointed 12 May 1860 by the Board of Supervisors	B	81-82
Petray, G. W.*	Barnes, E. H.; Graham, J. W.	1,000	13 Nov 1865	Justice of the Peace (Russian River Township)	Elected 18 Oct 1865	B	492
Petray, G. W.*	Mothersead, A. J.; Petray, R. A.	1,000	20 Nov 1865	Justice of the Peace (Russian River Township)	Appointed 17 Nov 1865 by the Board of Supervisors, includes oath of office dated 20 Nov 1865	B	512
Pettis, W. H.	Heald, G. W.; Purdy, T. V.	5,000	31 Oct 1877	Auctioneer		1	338-339
Pettit, Amos	Palmer, C. H.; Lefebvre, O. M.; Oliver, J. S.; Mooney, T.	2,000	28 Feb 1876	Constable (Analy Township)	Elected 1 Sep 1875	1	187-188
Pettit, Amos	Hoag, Jared C.; Carroll, Patrick	1,000	3 Jan [1870]	Constable (Analy Township)	Elected [1] Sep 1869	C	27
Pettit, Amos	Hoag, O. H.; Oliver, John S.; Crose, John M.; Hall, C. T.	2,000	5 Nov 1873	Constable (Analy Township)	Elected 3 Sep 1873	B	728-729
Pettus, James E.	Lewis, M. G.; Veeder, C. H.	5,000	[?] [?] 1853	Notary Public	Appointed	A	78
Pettus, James E.	Edwards, Uriah; Robberson, John S.	1,000	[?] Oct 1858	Justice of the Peace (Ukiah Township)	Elected 1 Sep 1858	A	343
Pettus, James E.	Singley, James; McClure, William A.	5,000	1 Oct 1853	Justice of the Peace (Petaluma Township)	Elected	A	79
Pettus, James E.	Bramlett, William B.; Briggs, Moses C.; Potter, William; Short, John R.	5,000	5 Apr 1858	Justice of the Peace (Ukiah Township)	Appointed November Term 1857 by the Board of Supervisors	A	303
Peugh, D. B.	Wescott, Oliver; Carr, William	1,000	5 Dec 1890	Road Overseer (Redwood Road District)	Elected 4 Nov 1890	4	155

Principal Name	Sureties	Amount ($)	Date	Office	Notes	Book	Page(s)
Pharis, P. H.	McDevit, Charles; Sparks, G. W.	1,000	22 Mar 1877	Road Master (South Vallejo Township)	Appointed 21 Mar 1877 [by the Board of Supervisors]	1	266-267
Pharis, P. H.	Peterson, A. J.; Head, Robinson; Hixson, Andrew	1,000	6 Jan 1875	Road Master (Vallejo Township)	Appointed 6 Jan 1875 by the Board of Supervisors, witness John T. Fortson	1	69-70
Phillips, D. D.	Bloom, D.; Board, William	1,000	24 Dec 1869	Constable (Mendocino Township)	Elected 1 Sep 1869	C	38
Phillips, D. D.	Vaughn, Thomas H.; Board, William	100	8 Dec 1859	Road Overseer (Road District No. 30, Mendocino Township)	Appointed 25 Nov 1859 by the Board of Supervisors	B	66
Phillips, D. D.*	Hudson, T. W.; Wilson, H. M.	1,000	14 Oct 1865	Constable ([Mendocino Township])	Elected [6 Sep 1865], witness Joseph Albertson	B	507
Philpott, J. F.	Luebberke, H.; Philpott, B. F.	1,000	5 Dec 1888	Constable (Russian River Township)	Elected 6 Nov 1888	4	2
Phinney, T. W.	Benitz, William; Helmke, F.	1,000	3 Mar 1866	Justice of the Peace (Salt Point Township)	Appointed [?] Feb 1866 by the Board of Supervisors	B	538
Phinney, T. W.	Benitz, William; Kalkmann, H. L. F.	1,000	4 Oct 1862	Justice of the Peace [Salt Point Township]	Elected 3 Sep 1862	B	296
Phinney, T. W.	Reisch, P. M.; Benitz, William	2,000	5 Nov 1863	Justice of the Peace [Salt Point Township]	Elected 21 Oct 1863	B	392
Pickett, D. L.	Easley, Warham; Boyce, J. F.	1,000	15 Nov 1855	Constable (Annally Township)	Appointed 9 Nov 1855 by the Board of Supervisors	A	117
Pickett, Henry A.	Schetter, Otto; Clark, George W.	1,000	24 Dec 1880	Justice of the Peace (Sonoma Township)	Elected 2 Nov 1880	2	49-50
Pickle, John A.	Graham, James W.; Thomas, Henry	2,000	20 Sep 1873	Constable (Russian River Township)	Elected 3 Sep 1873	1	7-8
Pickle, John A.*	Yates, J. W.; Graham, J. W.	2,000	13 Dec 1871	Constable (Russian River Township)	Elected 6 Sep 1871	C	124-126
Pierpont, Robert R.	Hopkins, Robert	5,000	10 Oct 1850	Notary Public		A	42
Piggott, A. K.	O'Farrell, John; Roche, Thomas	5,000	20 Oct 1855	Justice of the Peace (Bodega Township)	Elected	A	146
Piggott, A. K.	Carrillo, Julio; Hendley, John	1,000	24 Sep 1858	Justice of the Peace (Bodega Township)	Elected 1 Sep 1858		
Piggott, A. K.	Potter, Samuel, Jr.; Thurston, Erastus T.; Carrillo, Julio	5,000	6 Feb 1858	Justice of the Peace (Bodega Township)	Appointed February Term 1858 by the Board of Supervisors, includes oath of office dated 25 Mar 1858		
Piggott, A. K.	Watson, James; O'Farrell, John	1,000	8 Nov 1859	Justice of the Peace (Bodega Township)	Appointed 8 Nov 1859 by the Board of Supervisors	B	64
Pippin, B. G.*	Wescott, Oliver; Coon, R. W.	1,000	2 Dec 1892	Constable (Redwood Township)	Elected 8 Nov 1892	4	239
Pippin, T. C.	Bagley, John W.; Williams, Reuben; Roney, J. M.; Longley, R. G.	2,000	13 Sep 1873	Constable (Redwood Township)	Elected 3 Sep 1873	B	714-715

Principal Name	Sureties	Amount ($)	Date	Office	Notes	Book	Page(s)
Pippin, T. C.	Heald, Thomas T.; Bagley, J. W.	1,000	28 Mar 1872	Constable (Redwood Township)	Appointed 3 Jan 1872 by the Board of Supervisors [to fill the vacancy occasioned by the neglect of Reuben Williams to qualify]		
Pippin, Thomas C.	Bagley, J. W.; Willits, W. H.; Williams, Reuben; Alden, B. F.	2,000	17 Sep 1877	Constable (Redwood Township)	Elected 5 Sep 1877	1	303-304
Pippin, Thomas C.	Bagley, J. W.; Guerne, George E.	2,000	26 Sep 1875	Constable (Redwood Township)	Elected 1 Sep 1875	1	153-154
Pixley, William	Seaman, Jesse F.; Matheson, Roderick	100	15 Aug 1858	Road Overseer (Road District No. 2, Cloverdale)	Appointed	A	344
Plumly, M. W.	Henry, James; Tomasini, Julian	1,000	20 Nov 1880	Justice of the Peace (Salt Point Township)	Elected 2 Nov 1880	2	21-22
Plumly, M. W.	Liebig, Fred; Henry, James	1,000	28 Dec 1880	Justice of the Peace (Salt Point Township)	Elected 2 Nov 1880	2	54-55
Pond, C. H.*	Young, John; Prince, J. B.	5,000	12 Feb 1892	Notary Public	Appointed 10 Feb 1892 by the Governor of California	4	197
Pool, H.J.	Willis, T. N.; Laughlin, J. H.	1,000	16 Feb 1877	Road Master (Russian River Road District)	Appointed 9 Feb 1877 [by the Board of Supervisors]	1	240-242
Pool, H.J.	Lindsay, J.J.; Mitchell, R. T.	1,000	17 Jan 1880	[Road] Overseer (Russian River Road District)	Appointed 7 Jan 1880 [by the Board of Supervisors]		
Pool, H.J.	Davis, T. T.; Clark, Charles	1,000	20 Jan 1879	Road Overseer (Russian River [Road] District)	Appointed 8 Jan 1879		
Pool, H.J.	Lindsay, J.J.; Graham, J. W.; Gaines, W. C.; Clark, W. S.	2,000	23 Nov 1880	Road Overseer (Russian River Township)	Elected 2 Nov 1880	2	64-65
Pool, H.J.	Kennedy, G. H.; Maddux, L. D.	1,500	25 Jan 1873	Road Master (Russian River Road District)	Appointed 7 Jan 1873 by the Board of Supervisors		
Pool, H.J.	Bedwell, Franklin; Wilson, M. A.; Grove, W. H.; Graham, James W.; Mitchell, R. T.; Barnes, Thomas J.	15,000	25 Nov 1882	Supervisor (District No. 5)	Elected 7 Nov 1882	2	205-207
Pool, H.J.	Hopkins, Thomas J.; Graham, James W.	1,000	9 Jan 1875	Road Overseer (Russian River Township)	Appointed 5 Jan 1875 by the Board of Supervisors	1	76-78
Pool, Henry J.	Mitchell, R. T.; Davis, L. T.	1,000	16 Feb 1878	Road Overseer (Russian River Road District)	Appointed 7 Feb 1878 [by the Board of Supervisors]	1	400-401
Pool, Henry J.	Maddux, J. Parker; Mitchell, R. T.	1,000	3 Feb 1874	Road Overseer (Russian River [Road] District)	Appointed 6 Jan 1874 by the Board of Supervisors		
Pool, John	Clar, Laurence F.; Murphy, Rufus	1,000	28 Nov 1888	Constable (Redwood Township)	Elected 6 Nov 1888	4	18
Pool, John*	Wescott, Oliver; Joost, Jacob	1,000	5 Dec 1890	Constable (Redwood Township)	Elected 4 Nov 1890	4	153
Pool, W. H.	Luebberke, H.; Bell, H.	1,000	18 Jul 1889	Constable (Russian River Township)	Appointed 5 Jul 1889 by the Board of Supervisors, vice J. F. Philpott, resigned	4	62

Principal Name	Sureties	Amount ($)	Date	Office	Notes	Book	Page(s)
Pope, C. A.	McCollough, S. G.; Pool, Henry J.	1,000	1 Oct 1858	Constable (Russian River Township)	Elected 1 Sep 1858 for the term of one year	A	321
Poppe, Robert A.	Leiding, C. F.; McHarvey, Charles	5,000	21 Nov 1882	Notary Public	Appointed & commissioned 17 Nov 1882 by George C. Perkins, Governor of California	2	152-153
Poppe, Robert A.	Leiding, C. F.; Poppe, Catherine	5,000	6 Apr 1887	Notary Public	Appointed & commissioned 1 Apr 1887 by Washington Bartlett, Governor of California	3	148-150
Poppe, Robert A.*	Leiding, C. F.; McHarvey, C.	5,000	29 Mar 1889	Notary Public	Appointed 25 Mar 1889 by the Governor of California	4	48
Poppe, Robert Albion	Leiding, C. F.; McHarvey, Charles; Cornelius, George H. H.	5,000	19 Nov 1880	Notary Public	Commissioned 15 Nov 1880 by George C. Perkins, Governor of California	2	13-15
Potter, Samuel	Watson, James; Smith, John K.; Marks, Berry; Dougherty, John; Willis, T. N.; Boyce, J. F.; Bliss, William D.; Wise, Henry; McReynolds, James; Martin, R. M.; Hoen, B.; Hahman, F. G.; Jones, F. S.; Sears, F.; Roney, J. M.; Forsyth, Robert; Holman, John H.; Lane, J. J.; Ware, George W.; Lawton, John W.; Taylor, John S.; Pauli, G. T.	25,000	[17 Feb 1868]	Sheriff	Elected 4 Sep 1867, witness Thomas H. Pyatt	B	608-609
Potter, Samuel	Watson, James; Smith, John K.; Marks, Berry; Dougherty, John; Willis, T. N.; Boyce, J. F.; Bliss, William D.; Wise, Henry; McReynolds, James; Martin, R. M.; Hoen, B.; Hahman, F. G.; Jones, F. S.; Sears, F.; Roney, J. M.; Forsyth, Robert; Holman, John H.; Lane, J. J.; Ware, George W.; Lawton, John W.; Taylor, John S.; Pauli, G. T.	25,000	[17 Feb 1868]	Sheriff & ex officio Tax Collector	Elected 4 Sep 1867, witness Thomas H. Pyatt	B	606-607
Potter, Samuel	Hahman, F. G.; McReynolds, James; McReynolds, Jacob, Jr.; Farmer, E. T.; Wise, Henry; Bostwick, N. W.; Martin, R. M.; Roney, J. M.; Willis, T. N.; Lawton, John W.; Watson, James; Dougherty, John; Forsyth, Robert; Taylor, John S.; Hewitt, H. T.; Neblett, E.; Sedgley, Jotham; Hopper, Thomas; Beacom, Thomas; Rien, Samuel	25,000	[3 Mar 1870]	Sheriff	Elected 1 Sep 1869	C	42-43
Potter, Samuel	Hahman, F. G.; McReynolds, James; McReynolds, Jacob, Jr.; Farmer, E. T.; Wise, Henry; Bostwick, N. W.; Martin, R. M.; Roney, J. M.; Willis, T. N.; Lawton, John W.; Watson, James; Dougherty, John; Forsyth, Robert; Taylor, John S.; Hewitt, H. T.; Neblett, E.; Sedgley, Jotham; Hopper, Thomas; Beacom, Thomas; Rien, Samuel	25,000	[3 Mar 1870]	Sheriff & ex officio Tax Collector	Elected 1 Sep 1869	C	40-41
Potter, Samuel, Jr.	Pyatt, Thomas H.	500	16 Nov 1855	Road Overseer (Bodega District No. 4)	Appointed by the Board of Supervisors		
Potter, William	Swift, E.; Carder, D. D.	100	19 Mar 1859	Road Overseer (Road District No. 13)	Appointed 12 Mar 1859 by the Board of Supervisors to serve for one year from that date	A	371

Principal Name	Sureties	Amount ($)	Date	Office	Notes	Book	Page(s)
Potter, William	Ayers, Robert; Mayfield, A. J.	200	19 Sep 1863	Road Overseer (District No. 1, Anally Township)	Elected 2 Sep 1863	B	359
Powell, Joab	Peters, A. N.; Gray, Thomas	2,000	9 Oct 1871	Constable (Vallejo Township)	Elected 6 Sep 1871	C	89
Powell, John	Bowles, J. M.; Fairbanks, H. T.	2,000	11 Nov 1871	Justice of the Peace (Vallejo Township)	Elected 18 Oct 1871		
Powell, John	Bowles, J. M.; Bransford, Z. W.; Powell, Moses	2,000	4 Dec 1869	Justice of the Peace (Vallejo Township)	Elected 20 Oct 1869, witness F. W. Shattuck	C	10
Pressley, John G.	Smith, R. Press; White, J. M.; Caldwell, F. M.; Farmer, E. T.; Simms, J. R.	5,000	30 Apr 1875	Notary Public	Appointed & commissioned 26 Apr 1875	1	104-105
Preston, Robert J.	Baur, John; Pearce, George	5,000	9 May 1876	Auctioneer			
Prewett, James	Cockrill, L. D.; Smith, A. H.	5,000	1 Oct 1855	Justice of the Peace (Russian River Township)	Elected 5 Sep 1855	A	125
Prewett, James	Richardson, Achilles; Hoen, Berthold	5,000	2 Oct 1854	Justice of the Peace (Russian River Township)	Elected 6 Sep 1854	A	32
Prewett, James	Ross, William; Manion, William	1,000	23 Jun 1862	Justice of the Peace (Russian River Township)	Appointed 23 Jun 1862 by the Board of Supervisors	B	297
Prewett, James	Carson, Lindsey; Dow, J. G.	5,000	27 Nov 1852	Justice of the Peace (Russian River Township)	Elected 2 Nov 1852	A	74
Prewett, James		5,000	3 Oct 1853	Justice of the Peace (Russian River Township)	Elected 7 Sep 1853	A	95
Price, Andrew	Weaver, C. W.; Hall, S. J.	1,000	9 Feb 1891	Justice of the Peace (Mendocino Township)	Elected 31 Jan 1891	4	183
Price, Andrew*	Weaver, C. W.; Jacobs, G. H.	5,000	8 Feb 1890	Notary Public	Appointed 7 Feb 1890 by the Governor of California	4	75
Price, E. W.	Hembree, A. J.; Bell, Henry	1,000	27 Jul 1889	Pound Master (Russian River Pound District)	Appointed 25 Jul 1889 by the Board of Supervisors, vice J. C. Shane, resigned	4	63
Price, J. K.	Powers, D.P.; Stump, Daniel A.; Allen, O. S.; Himebauch, Joseph	2,000	[31 Dec 1875]	Constable (Salt Point Township)	Elected 1 Sep 1875	1	184
Price, J. K.	Powers, D. P.; Stump, Daniel A.	1,000	5 Jan 1876	Constable (Salt Point Township)	Appointed 4 Jan 1876 [by the Board of Supervisors] to serve until the first Monday of March 1876	1	185
Price, James A.	Miller, G. W.; Vasquez, P. J.	5,000	12 May 1855	Constable (Sonoma Township)	Appointed 1 May 1855 by the Board of Supervisors to hold office until the next regular election, includes oath of office dated 12 May 1855	A	99
Price, John	Bishop, T. C.; Samuels, James	1,000	1 Oct 1879	Justice of the Peace (Mendocino Township)	Elected 3 Sep 1879	1	538-539

Principal Name	Sureties	Amount ($)	Date	Office	Notes	Book	Page(s)
Price, John	Hudson, Thomas W.; Bloom, Jonas	2,000	28 Dec 1869	Justice of the Peace (Mendocino Township)	Elected 20 Oct 1869	C	28
Price, John	Barker, John; Jacobs, G. H.	1,000	28 Nov 1882	Justice of the Peace (Mendocino Township)	Elected 7 Nov 1882	2	218-220
Price, John	Hall, L. J.; McPherson, L.	1,000	4 Dec 1880	Justice of the Peace (Mendocino Township)	Elected 2 Nov 1880	2	41-43
Price, John	Powell, R.; Bailhache, John N.	2,000	6 Nov 1877	Justice of the Peace (Mendocino Township)	Elected 17 Oct 1877	1	346-347
Price, John	Truitt, R. K.; Bell, A. K.	1,000	8 Dec 1888	Justice of the Peace (Mendocino Township)	Elected 6 Nov 1888	4	15
Price, John*	Powell, Ransom; McManus, John G.	2,000	[8 Nov 1865]	Justice of the Peace (Mendocino Township)	Elected 18 Oct 1865	B	484
Price, John*	May, J. J.; McManus, J. G.	2,000	28 Oct 1863	Justice of the Peace (Mendocino Township)	Elected 21 Oct 1863	B	394
Price, Joseph K.	Charles, George A.; Muller, William	2,000	13 Dec 1871	Constable (Timber Cove Precinct)	Elected 6 Sep 1871	C	142-143
Price, Joseph K.	McCune, Samuel; Piver, Leroy	2,000	17 Jun 1876	Constable (Salt Point Township)	Appointed [4] May 1876 by the Board of Supervisors [to fill a vacancy]	1	220-221
Price, Joseph K.	Marshall, Hugh; Kenny, Patrick	2,000	19 Nov 1877	Constable (Salt Point Township)	Elected 5 Sep 1877	1	378-379
Price, Joseph K.	Hargrave, Scipio; McClellan, M. T.	1,000	2 Oct 1869	Constable (Salt Point Township)	Elected 1 Sep 1869	B	635
Price, Joseph K.	Stockhoff, John H.; Charles, G. A.	1,000	28 Nov 1879	Constable (Salt Point Township)	Elected 3 Sep 1879	1	558-559
Prince, Morrice	Lodge, J. D.	5,000	[?] Nov 1882	Auctioneer		2	141-142
Prince, Thomas R.	Walters, William; Hatfield, John	200	[?] Nov 1862	Road Master (District No. 2, Mendocino Township)	Appointed, witness Thomas Spencer, includes oath of office dated 5 Nov 1862	B	328
Proctor, D. D.	Cox, C. B.; Proctor, T. J.	5,000	19 Jun 1886	Notary Public	Appointed & commissioned 7 Jun 1886 [by George Stoneman, Governor of California]	2	542-543
Proctor, D. D.	Craig, D. N.; Pare, L.	1,000	28 Nov 1890	Justice of the Peace (Bodega Township)	Elected 4 Nov 1890	4	120
Proctor, Ira	Brown, H. K.; Wright, A.	1,000	[13 Nov 1885]	Pound Master (Manzanita Pound District in Mendocino Township)	Appointed 3 Nov 1885 by the Board of Supervisors	2	506-507
Proctor, Ira	Ferguson, H. O.; Barnes, E. H.	1,000	28 Nov 1890	Road Overseer (Mendocino Road District)	Elected 4 Nov 1890	4	112

Principal Name	Sureties	Amount ($)	Date	Office	Notes	Book	Page(s)
Proctor, T. W.	Canan, W. S.; Brown, H. K.; West, Robert; Turner, John; Miller, George; Grater, John F.	2,000	12 Sep 1873	Constable (Mendocino Township)	Elected 3 Sep 1873	B	715-717
Proctor, Thomas J.	McReynolds, James; Gray, James W.; Farmer, E. T.; Carithers, D. N.; Clark, D.	15,000	27 Nov 1882	Supervisor (District No. 3)	Elected 7 Nov 1882	2	195-197
Purcell, George E.*	Norton, William H.; Fletcher, Duncan	1,000	9 Dec 1882	Constable (Salt Point Township)	Elected 7 Nov 1882	2	273-274
Purrine, A. S.	Shaw, Nelson R.; Cerini, John	1,000	22 Jan 1879	Road Overseer (Bodega [Road] District No. 2)	Appointed 8 Jan 1879 [by the Board of Supervisors]		
Purrine, A. S.	Shaw, N. R.; Cerini, John	2,000	9 Feb 1878	Road Master (Bodega Township, District No. 2)	Appointed 8 Feb 1878 [by the Board of Supervisors]	1	399-400
Purrine, Andrew S.	Blume, F. G.; Hegeler, H.	100	12 May 1859	Road Overseer (Road District No. 28, Bodega Township)	Appointed	A	376
Purrine, Andrew S.	Green, C. C.; Zilhart, William H.	100	9 Apr 1860	Road Overseer (Road District No. 28, Bodega Township)	Appointed [?] Feb 1860 by the Board of Supervisors	B	75
Pyatt, Thomas H.	Williamson, William M.; West, Samuel; Hoen, Berthold; Green, C. C.; Cameron, Daniel E.; Ellis, James M.; Morris, Joseph H. P.; Martin, H. B.; Beaver, Henry; Warner, P.	5,000	[?] [?] 1859	Recorder	Elected 7 Sep 1859	B	25-27
Pyatt, Thomas H.	Wise, Henry; Holman, John H.; Powell, R.; Thompson, Thomas L.; Farmer, E. T.; Bernhard, Samuel; Hendley, John; Alberding, Fredric H.; Atterbury, William B.; Ellis, James M.	5,000	[?] [?] 1863	Auditor	Elected 2 Sep 1863	B	433-434
Pyatt, Thomas H.	Bledsoe, A. C.; Browne, Daniel; Hendley, John; Boyce, J. F.; Farmer, E. T.; Barnes, M.; Henderson, J. W.; Ross, William; Thompson, Thomas L.; Williamson, James R.	5,000	13 Sep 1861	Recorder	Elected 4 Sep 1861 for the term of two years and five months from the first Monday in October 1861 [7 Oct 1861], ending on the first Monday in March 1864 [7 Mar 1864]	B	182-183
Pyatt, Thomas H.	Hendley, John; Boyce, J. F.; Framer, E. T.; Barnes, M.; Sansom, E.	2,500	14 Sep 1861	Auditor	Elected 4 Sep 1861 as Recorder and ex officio Auditor	B	184
Pyatt, Thomas H.	Potter, Samuel, Jr.	500	16 Nov 1855	Road Overseer (Santa Rosa District No. 6)	Appointed by the Board of Supervisors		
Pyatt, Thomas H.	May, J. J.; Grant, John D.; Hahman, F. G.; Bowles, J. M.; Hill, William McPherson; Boyce, J. F.; Norton, L. A.; Marks, B.; Thompson, A. W.; Caldwell, William	5,000	20 Oct 1863	Recorder	Elected 2 Sep 1863	B	435-436
Pyatt, Thomas H.	Hendley, John; Hoen, Berthold	1,000	24 Sep 1858	Justice of the Peace (Santa Rosa Township)	Elected 1 Sep 1858	A	314
Pyatt, Thomas H.	Carrillo, Julio; Hahman, F. G.; Boyce, J. F.; Fulkerson, Richard; Hoen, Berthold; Williamson, William M.; Mize, Merrill; Patten, Thomas B.; Ellis, James M.	5,000	3 Oct 1857	Justice of the Peace (Santa Rosa Township)	Elected 2 Sep 1857, accepted by W. B. Hagans, Chairman of the Board of Supervisors	A	270-274
Quigley, B. H.	Young, James; Seawell, William H.	200	24 [Nov] 1860	Road Overseer (Anally District)	Appointed 22 Nov 1860 by the Board of Supervisors for the term of one year	B	139

Principal Name	Sureties	Amount ($)	Date	Office	Notes	Book	Page(s)
Quinlan, Martin*	Quinlan, P. D.; Doran, William M.	2,000	1 Apr 1878	Deputy Assessor (Bodega, Ocean, & Salt Point Townships & part of Analy Township)	Appointed 5 Mar 1878, bound unto George W. Sparks, Assessor	1	425-426
Ragsdale, J. W.*	Lemmon, Allen B.; Barnett, J. D.; Burris, L. W.; Brown, Harry C.	5,000	29 Mar 1889	Notary Public	Appointed 28 Mar 1889	4	46
Ragsdale, James W.	Shaw, Isaac E.; Cooley, Charles H.; Brush, W. T.; Dixon, John	5,000	29 Jan 1881	Notary Public	Commissioned 24 Jan 1881 by George C. Perkins, Governor of California	2	57-58
Ragsdale, James Wilson	Byington, H. W.; Tupper, G. A.; Glenn, J. H.; Fowler, John H.; Barnett, J. D.	5,000	19 Mar 1887	Notary Public	Appointed & commissioned 17 Mar 1887 by Washington Bartlett, Governor of California	3	137-139
Railsback, Caleb	Mecham, H.; Denman, E.	5,000	10 Jan 1874	Road Master (Petaluma Township)	Appointed, includes oath of office dated 10 Jan 1874		
Rain, William G.	Nevill, J. N.; Miller, G. W.	1,000	30 Sep 1854	Constable (Sonoma Township)	Elected 6 Sep 1854	A	87
Rainey, R. S.	Townsend, William M. A.; Tivnen, John	1,000	30 Sep 1865	Constable (Sonoma Township)	Elected [6 Sep 1865], witness Philip Mahler	B	496
Rains, Gallant	Merritt, John; Gale, Otis	1,000	13 Jan 1885	Road Overseer (Petaluma Road District)	Appointed 13 Jan 1885 [by the Board of Supervisors]	2	447-448
Rains, Gallant	Winters, L.; Spotswood, A.	1,000	2 Jun 1888	Pound Master (Petaluma Pound District)	Appointed 10 May 1888 by the Board of Supervisors	3	248-250
Rains, Gallant	Morsehead, Phillip; Bishop, T. C.	1,000	5 Jan 1887	Road Overseer (Petaluma Township)	Appointed 5 Jan 1887	3	160-161
Rains, Gallant	Spotswood, Andrew; Cooper, Campbelle	1,000	8 Dec 1888	Road Overseer (Petaluma Road District)	Elected 6 Nov 1888	4	20
Rains, James K. P.	Davis, G. V.; Caldwell, William	1,000	18 Nov 1880	Road Overseer (Cloverdale Township)	Elected 2 Nov 1880	2	75-76
Ramey, James	Gould, T. J.; Levy, Michel	1,000	18 Sep 1861	Justice of the Peace (Cloverdale Township)	Elected [4 Sep 1861], witness Eli Lester	B	200
Ramey, James	Markle, R. B.; Smith, S. H.	1,000	19 Sep 1862	Justice of the Peace (Cloverdale Township)	Elected [3 Sep 1862], witness J. J. Johnson	B	285
Ramey, James	Thompson, J. A. C.; Caldwell, William; Wormer, M.	2,000	4 Jan 1864	Justice of the Peace (Cloverdale Township)	Elected [21 Oct 1863]	B	410
Ramsey, William	Thompson, J. D.; McManus, John G.	1,000	25 Sep 1861	Constable (Russian River Township)	Elected 4 Sep 1861	B	174
Randolph, Isaac N.	Hiland, O. A.; Long, J. D.; Boughton, B. F.; Boggs, J. B.	5,000	24 Nov 1852	Justice of the Peace (Sonoma Township)	Elected 2 Nov 1852, includes oath of office dated 24 Nov 1852	A	52
Ray, E.	Hall, D. W.; Shelford, John	2,000	30 Sep 1871	Constable (Cloverdale Township)	Elected 6 Sep 1871	C	147-148
Ray, Elijah	Dodge, W. R.; McClintick, S.	1,000	17 Sep 1862	Constable (Cloverdale Township)	Elected [3 Sep 1862], witness J. Ramey	B	302

Principal Name	Sureties	Amount ($)	Date	Office	Notes	Book	Page(s)
Ray, Elijah	Levy, Michel; Hammond, William R.	1,000	18 Sep 1861	Constable (Cloverdale Township)	Elected [4 Sep 1861], witness Eli Lester	B	195
Ray, Elijah	Cooper, John; Shores, Leander	1,000	22 Sep 1869	Constable (Cloverdale Township)	Elected 1 Sep 1869	B	632
Ray, Elijah	Levy, Michel; Taylor, Alexander	1,000	24 Nov 1860	Constable (Cloverdale Township)	Elected 6 Nov 1860	B	104-105
Redmond, Patrick	Hewitt, H. T.; Morrow, James; Noonan, George P.	5,000	26 Aug 1870	Auctioneer	Applied for a license as an auctioneer for the town of Santa Rosa	C	57-58
Reed, G. W.	Weston, H. L.; Lightner, J. M.; Bliss, William D.; Codding, G. R.	2,000	4 Jan 1864	Justice of the Peace (Petaluma Township)	Elected [21 Oct 1863]	B	413-414
Reiners, C. A.	Thayer, John; Truitt, R. K.	1,000	16 Jun 1886	Pound Master (Dry Creek Pound District in Mendocino Township)	Appointed 7 Jun 1886 [by the Board of Supervisors]	2	540-541
Remmel, Charles	Stites, A. H.; Hamilton, Emmor	1,000	14 Mar 1877	Constable (Washington Township)	Appointed 8 Feb 1877 [by the Board of Supervisors, vice J. C. Ensign, resigned]	1	265-266
Remmel, Charles	Murrell, John L.; Parker, J. L.; Ellis, L. G.; Wood, J. J.	2,000	20 Sep 1877	Constable (Washington Township)	Elected 5 Sep 1877	1	291-292
Remmel, Charles	Stites, A. H.; Ellis, L. G.	1,000	26 Sep 1879	Constable (Washington Township)	Elected 3 Sep 1879	1	524-526
Reniff, A. A.	Brown, H. K.; Fried, Henry	1,000	1 Nov 1877	Justice of the Peace (Washington Township)	Elected 17 Oct 1877	1	342-343
Reyburn, L. C.	Cavanagh, John; Hunt, Charles; Edwards, Uriah; Bradley, G. L.; Tustin, Samuel	2,000	22 Nov 1860	Justice of the Peace (Petaluma Township)	Elected 6 Nov 1860	B	136-137
Reyburn, L. C.	Cavanagh, John; Henley, William	2,000	23 [Sep] 1859	Justice of the Peace (Petaluma Township)	Elected 7 Sep 1859, witness S. Payran	B	32
Reyburn, L. C.	Cavanagh, John; Hunt, Charles	2,000	23 Sep 1861	Justice of the Peace (Petaluma Township)	Elected 4 Sep 1861, witness J. Chandler	B	208
Reyburn, L. C.	Ellis, J. J.; Anderson, W. L.	2,000	4 Oct 1858	Justice of the Peace (Petaluma Township)	Elected 1 Sep 1858	A	336
Reyburn, L. C.*	Towne, Smith D.; Singley, James; Commins, Edward; Huie, J. Thompson; Edwards, Thomas; Ellis, John J.; Clark, Almer; Sroufe, John; Flanery, William E.; Gill, George; Evans, M. R.; Tempel, C.; Poehlmann, Martin; Cavanagh, John; Bond, J. S.; Morrison, Thomas; Trinque, W. D.; Burnett, William; Alberding, Fredric H.; Conrad, Simon; Newman, B.; Cowen, Philip; Sroufe, D. W.; Payran, S.; Huie, George W.; Atterbury, William B.; Hunt, Charles; Carrillo, Julio	15,000	3 Mar 1864	Public Administrator	Elected 2 Sep 1863	B	445-448
Reynolds, James A.	Grant, John D.; Sondheimer, Emanuel; Engel, H. S.; Hooper, V. C. W.; Thurgood, William S.; Bagley, John W.; Heald, Thomas T.	5,000	11 Feb 1858	Notary Public	Appointed 2 Feb 1858 by the Governor of California, includes oath of office dated 12 Feb 1858	A	300

Principal Name	Sureties	Amount ($)	Date	Office	Notes	Book	Page(s)
Reynolds, James A.	Ray, John G.; Hendley, John; Mckamy, James W.; Brewster, J. A.	5,000	2 Dec 1852	Assessor	Elected	A	64
Reynolds, James A.	Chambers, Thomas K.; Singley, James	5,000	21 Sep 1854	Justice of the Peace (Sonoma Township)	Elected 6 Sep 1854	A	22
Reynolds, James A.	Rupe, Samuel H.; Boggs, W. M.; McKamey, J. W.; Menefee, N. McC.	5,000	29 Dec 1855	Deputy Sheriff	Appointed by A. C. Bledsoe, Sheriff		
Reynolds, James A.	Cecil, John F.; Beck, Robert; Long, Ive. D.	5,000	29 Sep 1855	Justice of the Peace (Sonoma Township)	Elected 5 Sep 1855	A	135
Reynolds, W. B.	Truitt, R. K.; Ragsdale, J. W.	5,000	15 Dec 1883	Notary Public	Appointed 13 Dec 1883 by the Governor of California	2	304-305
Reynolds, W. B.	Brown, H. K.; Newland, F.	5,000	15 Dec 1887	Notary Public	Appointed 14 Dec 1887 by the Governor of California, witness J. W. Rose	3	212-213
Reynolds, W. B.	Truitt, Roland K.; Brown, H. K.	5,000	17 Dec 1885	Notary Public	Appointed 14 Dec 1885 by George Stoneman, Governor of California, witness A. E. Cochran	2	513-515
Reynolds, W. D.	Carithers, D. N.; Proctor, T. J.; McConnell, William E.; Wilson, W. Y.; Bishop, T. C.	5,000	29 Jul 1884	Notary Public	Appointed 24 Jun 1884	2	329-330
Reynolds, W. D.	Proctor, T. J.; Cooper, S. R.	5,000	3 Jul 1886	Notary Public	Appointed 25 Jun 1886 [by George Stoneman, Governor of California]	2	546-547
Reynolds, W. D.*	Mailer, J. C.; Brooke, T. J.	5,000	3 Jul 1890	Notary Public	Appointed 30 Jun 1890 for the term of 4 years	4	91
Reynolds, W. D.*	Gardner, D. P.; McDonald, M. L.; Harris, Jacob	5,000	9 Jul 1888	Notary Public	Appointed 2 Jul 1888 by the Governor of California, witness A. D. Laughlin	3	250-252
Reynolds, William B.	Brown, H. K.; Truitt, Roland K.	5,000	16 Dec 1881	Notary Public	Appointed 13 Dec 1881 by the Governor of California	2	114-115
Reynolds, William B.	Bailhache, John N.; Samuels, James	5,000	18 Dec 1879	Notary Public	Appointed 13 Dec 1879	1	556-557
Richardson, A. J.	Muther, Frank; Dolan, Peter	2,000	20 Nov 1884	Constable (Santa Rosa Township)	Elected 4 Nov 1884	2	368-369
Richardson, A. J.	Noonan, P. H.; Allen, S. I.; Warner, James; Hoag, O. H.	2,000	30 Sep 1885	Constable (Santa Rosa Township)	Elected 4 Nov 1884, a new bond was filed because the sureties on his original bond dated 20 Nov 1884 withdrew (Frank Muther) and became insolvent (Peter Dolan)	2	491-492
Richardson, Joseph H.	McMinn, John; Gray, James W.; Kohle, A.; Smith, R. Press, Jr.	2,000	18 Sep 1873	Constable (Santa Rosa Township)	Elected 3 Sep 1873	B	709-711
Richardson, Joseph H.	Farmer, C. C.; Gray, J. W.	2,000	30 Sep 1871	Constable (Santa Rosa Township)	Elected 6 Sep 1871	C	80
Richardson, W. M.*	Boyd, W. H.; Haupt, Charles; Smith, J. P.	5,000	15 Apr 1890	Notary Public	Commissioned 5 Apr 1890 by R. W. Waterman, [Governor of California]	4	81
Ricksecker, L. E.*	Walker, John; Burnett, E.; Fowler, John H.	10,000	11 Dec 1890	Surveyor	Elected 4 Nov 1890	4	178
Ridenhour, L. W.	McPeak, Anthony; Ridenhour, William R.	1,000	13 Apr 1885	Pound Master (Redwood Pound District)	Appointed 7 Apr 1885 [by the Board of Supervisors]		

Principal Name	Sureties	Amount ($)	Date	Office	Notes	Book	Page(s)
Rien, Samuel	Goodman, L. S.; Hoag, O. H.	1,000	2 Mar 1877	Road Master (Ocean Township)	Appointed 9 Feb 1877 [by the Board of Supervisors]	1	259-260
Rien, Samuel	Acker, R. W.; Hoag, O. H.	1,000	4 Jan 1876	Road Master (Ocean Township)	Appointed 4 Jan 1876 by the Board of Supervisors	1	200-201
Rien, Samuel	Parmeter, John; Miller, L. W.	1,000	6 Jan 1874	Road Overseer (Ocean Road District)	Appointed 6 Jan 1874 by the Board of Supervisors		
Rien, Samuel	Phelps, A.; Estes, H.	1,000	7 Feb 1878	Road Master (Ocean Township)	Appointed 7 Feb 1878 [by the Board of Supervisors]	1	384-385
Rien, Samuel*	Ingram, S. D.; McKenzie, John	1,000	6 Jan 1875	Road Overseer (Ocean Township)	Appointed 5 Jan 1875 by the Board of Supervisors	1	71-72
Riese, Frederick	Derby, A. B.; Spotswood, Robert	5,000	25 Oct 1877	Auctioneer	Witness Frank W. Shattuck	1	350-352
Roberson, John	McDarment, Richard; Morris, William R.; Kilgore, William M.	1,000	17 Sep 1861	Constable [Washington Township]	Elected [4 Sep 1861], witness David Odell	B	191
Roberts, Charles	Tempel, C.; Martin, John	1,000	24 Feb 1877	Road Master (Petaluma Road District No. 3)	Appointed 9 Feb 1877 [by the Board of Supervisors]	1	256-257
Robertson, James O.	Akers, Stephen; Goodman, Willis	1,000	20 Sep 1862	Constable (Sonoma Township)	Elected 3 Sep 1862, includes oath of office certification dated 20 Sep 1862	B	307
Robertson, John	Schloss, S.; Brians, William	1,000	18 Sep 1879	Constable (Redwood Township)	Elected 3 Sep 1879	1	483-484
Robinson, George	Watson, James; Potter, Samuel, Jr.	5,000	1 Oct 1855	Justice of the Peace (Bodega Township)	Elected 5 Sep 1855	A	127
Rochford, Thomas	Browne, Daniel	500	7 May 1862	Road Overseer (Petaluma District No. 1, Petaluma Township)	Appointed	B	267
Rodgers, J. P.	Doyle, M.; Bowles, J. M.	5,000	11 Jul 1878	Notary Public	Appointed 8 Jul 1878 by the Governor of California for the term of two years, includes oath of office dated 13 Jul 1878	1	431-432
Rodgers, J. P.	Bowles, J. M.; Doyle, M.	5,000	24 Jul 1876	Notary Public	Appointed	1	223
Rodgers, J. P. *	Bowles, J. M.; McNamara, M.	5,000	1 Jun 1888	Notary Public	Appointed & commissioned 19 May 1888 by R. W. Waterman, Governor of California	3	246-248
Rodgers, J. P. *	Bowles, J. M.; McNamara, M.	[?]	1 Jun 1892	Notary Public	Appointed & commissioned 25 May 1892	4	201
Rodgers, John P.	Doyle, M.; Bowles, J. M.	5,000	11 Jun 1884	Notary Public	Appointed & commissioned 23 May 1884 by George Stoneman, Governor of California	2	325-326
Rodgers, John P.	Bowles, J. M.; Steitz, Henry	5,000	24 May 1882	Notary Public	Appointed & commissioned 20 May 1882 by George C. Perkins, Governor of California, includes oath of office dated [?] May 1882	2	133-135
Rodgers, John P.	Bowles, J. M.; Fairbanks, H. T.	5,000	5 Jun 1886	Notary Public	Appointed & commissioned 22 May 1886 by George Stoneman, Governor of California, includes oath of office dated 5 Jun 1886	2	538-539

Principal Name	Sureties	Amount ($)	Date	Office	Notes	Book	Page(s)
Roe, William*	Goodman, L. S.; Smith, George W.	1,000	3 Dec 1892	Constable (Bodega Township)	Elected 8 Nov 1892	4	235
Rogers, J. P.	Berger, M.; Crane, J. H.	500	20 Jul 1875	Deputy District Attorney	Appointed 17 Jul 1875, witness E. L. Lippitt	1	108-109
Rogers, John P.	Watson, James, Sr.; Cunninghame, William J.	1,000	10 Oct 1867	Constable (Bodega Township)	Elected 4 Sep 1867	B	583
Rogers, John P.	Smith, William; Cockrill, L. D.	1,000	3 Oct 1859	Constable (Annally Township)	Elected 7 Sep 1859 for the term of one year	B	50
Rogers, W. K.	Winkle, Henry; Pauli, G. T.; Phariss, P. H.; Goss, Leonard	10,000	13 Sep 1873	Supervisor (District No. 1)	Elected 3 Sep 1873	B	699-701
Rogers, W. K.	Phariss, P. H.; Pauli, G. T.; Lynch, C.; Lynch, J.	10,000	22 Nov 1876	Supervisor (District No. 1)	Elected 7 Nov 1876	1	280-282
Rohrer, Calvin	Cornwell, C.; Merritt, Charles	1,000	14 Feb 1863	Constable (Vallejo Township)	Appointed 6 Feb 1863 by the Board of Supervisors to serve until his successor shall be duly elected and qualified, includes oath of office dated 14 Feb 1863	B	333
Rohrer, Calvin	Rohrer, Frederick; Rohrer, Cyrus	1,000	17 Sep 1861	Constable (Vallejo Township)	Elected 4 Sep 1861, witness S. Payran	B	194
Rohrer, Calvin	Rohrer, Cyrus; Hardin, J. A.	1,000	23 Nov 1860	Constable (Vallejo Township)	Elected 6 Nov 1860	B	99
Rohrer, Calvin	Merritt, Charles; Alberding, Fredric H.	1,000	23 Sep 1863	Constable (Vallejo Township)	Elected 2 Sep 1863	B	361
Rose, J. W.	Hassett, J. D.; Rosenberg, W.	5,000	15 Jan 1886	Notary Public	Appointed 12 Jan 1886 [by George Stoneman, Governor of California], witness W. B. Reynolds	2	521-523
Rose, J. W.	Ruffner, William; Curtiss, J. H.	5,000	16 Jan 1884	Notary Public	Appointed 15 Jan 1884 by the Governor of California	2	311-312
Rose, J. W.	Willson, H. M.; Ruffner, William	5,000	19 Jan 1882	Notary Public	Appointed 16 Jan 1882 by the Governor of California for the term of two years, vice himself, term expired	2	120-121
Rose, J. W.	Bailhache, John N.; Clack, John W.	5,000	24 Jan 1880	Notary Public	Appointed 15 Jan 1880 by the Governor of California	1	564-565
Rose, J. W.*	Mead, James A.; Raabe, M.	5,000	12 Jan 1888	Notary Public	Appointed 11 Jan 1888 by [R. W. Waterman], Governor of California	3	213-214
Rose, J. W.*	Mead, James A.; Delano, I. A.	5,000	13 Jan 1890	Notary Public	Appointed 11 Jan 1890 by the Governor of California	4	71
Rosebrough, C. E.	Crigler, William E.; Brush, William T.	1,000	[?] Jan 1887	Road Overseer (Cloverdale Road District comprising all of Cloverdale Township)	Appointed 5 Jan 1887	3	168-169
Rosebrough, C. E.	Yordi, Fred; Field, John	1,000	4 Dec 1888	Road Overseer (Cloverdale Road District)	Elected 6 Nov 1888	3	323-324
Roseburg, A.	Taft, H. C.; Wiswell, J. A.	5,000	28 Dec 1870	Auctioneer	Doing business along with D. W. Sroufe as auctioneers in Petaluma under the name and firm of Roseburg & Sroufe; See 1870 D. W. Sroufe file	C	66

Principal Name	Sureties	Amount ($)	Date	Office	Notes	Book	Page(s)
Roseburgh, Allen	Gaston, Hugh; Dalton, William H.	1,000	14 Feb 1878	Road Master (Petaluma Township, Road District No. 3)	Appointed 7 Feb 1878 by the Board of Supervisors, witness Frank W. Shattuck, includes oath of office dated 14 Feb 1878	1	397-399
Roseburgh, Allen	Gaston, Hugh; Dalton, William H.	1,000	14 Jan 1879	Road Master (Petaluma Road District No. 3)	Appointed 8 Jan 1879 [by the Board of Supervisors]		
Ross, William	Brockman, Israel; McNair, John E.	5,000	12 Mar 1853	Notary Public	Appointed and commissioned by John Bigler, Governor of California, includes certification of oath of office dated 12 Mar 1853	A	80-81
Ross, William	Hendley, John; Tupper, G. A.; Goldfish, B.; Hewett, H. T.; Boyce, J. F.; Taylor, John S.	5,000	15 Feb 1866	District Attorney	Elected 6 Sep 1865	B	521
Ross, William	Cooke, Martin E.; Shattuck, Frank W.	5,000	25 Jun 1853	Notary Public	Appointed and commissioned by the Governor of California, includes certification of oath of office dated 25 Jun 1853		
Ross, William	Hoen, Berthold; Maupin, R. A.	5,000	26 Nov 1855	Notary Public	Appointed and commissioned 6 Nov 1855 by the Governor of California, includes oath of office dated 27 Nov 1855	A	141-142
Ross, William	Harrison, R.; Bliss, William D.; Wright, W. S. M.; Green, C. C.; Warner, Philemon; Barry, John; Carder, D. D.; Edwards, Uriah; Barnes, Thomas L.; Ellis, John J.	10,000	29 Nov 1858	District Attorney	Appointed 23 Nov 1858 by the Board of Supervisors to fill the vacancy occasioned by the decease of William G. Gordon	A	358
Ross, William	Brockman, Israel; Hartman, J. William; Case, J. M.; Hendley, John	10,000	5 Feb 1855	District Attorney (Sonoma County)	Appointed 5 Feb 1855	A	43-44
Ross, William	Hendley, John; Lane, John J.; Warner, Philemon; Hoag, J. C.; Emerson, Henry; Phillips, D. D.; Parks, William T.	5,000	5 Feb 1864	District Attorney	Elected 2 Sep 1863	B	438-439
Rupe, D. C.	Holmes, Henderson P.; Griggs, Joseph H.; Smith, John K.; Clark, D.; Smallwood, L. W.; Latapie, E.	2,000	22 Sep 1877	Constable (Santa Rosa Township)	Elected 5 Sep 1877	1	323-325
Rupe, David C.	Munday, B. B.; Hay, A. M.	200	[?] Sep 1863	Road Master (Sonoma Township)	Elected 2 Sep 1863	B	382
Rupe, David C.	Hardin, James A.; Hopper, Thomas; Hall, L. B.; Griggs, J. H.	2,000	[?] Sep 1879	Constable (Santa Rosa Township)	Elected 3 Sep 1879	1	475-476
Rupe, David C.	Griggs, J. H.; Thompson, Thomas L.; White, J. M.; Foster, Joseph	2,000	22 Sep 1875	Constable (Santa Rosa Township)	Elected 1 Sep 1875	1	144-146
Russell, H. A.	Hall, J. W.; Carithers, D. N.	1,000	1 Dec 1888	Road Overseer (Fulton Road District)	Elected 6 Nov 1888	3	280-281
Russell, H. A.	Forsyth, Robert; Harris, Jacob	1,000	13 Feb 1888	Road Overseer (Fulton Road District)	Appointed 9 Feb 1888 by the Board of Supervisors	3	226-227
Russell, H. A.	Carithers, D. N.; Hall, J. W.	1,000	17 Jan 1885	Road Overseer (Santa Rosa Road District)	Appointed 13 Jan 1885 [by the Board of Supervisors]	2	453-454
Russell, H. A.	Griggs, J. H.; Carithers, D. N.	1,000	8 Jan 1880	Road Overseer (Santa Rosa Road District No. 1)	Appointed 7 Jan 1880 [by the Board of Supervisors]		
Russell, Hugh A.	Hall, J. W.; Carithers, D. N.	1,000	25 Nov 1890	Road Overseer (Fulton Road District)	Elected 4 Nov 1890	4	99

Principal Name	Sureties	Amount ($)	Date	Office	Notes	Book	Page(s)
Russell, W. F.	Forsyth, B.; Brooke, T. J.; Cooper, S. R.; Davis, George W.	5,000	6 Apr 1887	Notary Public	Appointed & commissioned 2 Apr 1887 by Washington Bartlett, Governor of California	3	150-152
Rust, Horace	Rambo, Jacob; Bushnell, Amasa	200	1 Jun 1864	Road Master (District No. 2, Analy Township)	Appointed, includes oath of office dated 1 Aug 1864		
Rutherford, A. G.	Thurston, John M.; Carrillo, Julio	1,000	18 Oct 1859	Constable (Bodega Township)	Elected 7 Sep 1859 for the term of one year	B	63
Rutherford, George	Potter, Samuel, Jr.; Coulter, J. P.	2,000	[?] Jun 1860	Road Overseer (Bodega District)	Appointed 18 Jun 1860 by the Board of Supervisors for the term of one year		
Ryan, John	Carrillo, Julio; McGuire, Cornelius	1,000	4 Oct 1858	Constable (Anally Township)	Elected 1 Sep 1858	A	327
Sabine, R. H.	King, William; Brown, Richard	1,000	29 Nov 1890	Justice of the Peace (Ocean Township)	Elected 4 Nov 1890	4	124
Sackett, D. A.	Oman, George W.; Charles, J. M.	100	24 Feb 1860	Road Overseer (Road District No. 26)	Appointed 24 Feb 1860 by the Board of Supervisors	B	71
Sackett, D. A.	Bowles, J. M.	500	9 Apr 1862	Road Overseer (Vallejo Road District, Vallejo Township)	Appointed, includes oath of office dated 9 Apr 1862	B	267
Sacry, E. C.	Sweeney, G.; Critchfield, G. W.	2,000	16 Mar 1872	Justice of the Peace (Washington Township)	Appointed [6 Feb 1872 by the Board of Supervisors]	C	161-163
Sacry, G. M.*	Powell, Ransom; McManus, John G.	2,000	8 Nov 1865	Justice of the Peace (Mendocino Township)	Elected 18 Oct 1865	B	506
Sacry, George M.	Marks, B.; Carter, L.	2,000	30 Nov 1863	Justice of the Peace (Russian River Township)	Elected 21 Oct 1863	B	397
Sales, John*	Zimmerman, George; Shelton, Abraham Cooper; Ayers, William; Scott, J. C.; Martin, A. P.; Goatley, A.	15,000	29 Nov 1890	Supervisor (District No. 2)	Elected 4 Nov 1890	4	123
Samuels, James	Bloom, D.; Martin, J. M.	200	26 Apr 1861	Road Overseer (Russian River Township included in Sotoyome School District)	Appointed, includes oath of office dated 26 Apr 1861	B	152
Samuels, James	Sondheimer, E.; Binns, J. D.	100	7 Mar 1860	Road Overseer (Road District No. [?], Russian River Township)	Appointed	B	72
Sargent, Henry	Tucker, B. Frank; Norton, L. A.	1,000	24 Sep 1861	Constable [Mendocino Township]	Elected 4 Sep 1861	B	217
Sargent, J. C.	Shea, Cornelius; Roney, J. M.	2,000	28 Nov 1884	Justice of the Peace (Santa Rosa Township)	Elected 4 Nov 1884	2	388-389
Savage, George N.	Hewitt, H. T.; Young, James B.	5,000	19 Mar 1875	Auctioneer	Proposed to become an auctioneer 19 Mar 1875	1	98-99
Scales, A. W.	McReynolds, James; Dougherty, B. G.; Wilson, W. H.; Allen, B. B.	1,000	12 Feb 1870	Constable (Analy Township)	Appointed 9 Feb 1870 by the Board of Supervisors, [vice William Monroe, refused to qualify]	C	30

Principal Name	Sureties	Amount ($)	Date	Office	Notes	Book	Page(s)
Schroyer, Aaron	Mayer, August; Call, G. W.	1,000	22 Oct 1879	Road Overseer (Fort Ross Road District)	Appointed 6 Oct 1879 by the Board of Supervisors	1	552-553
Schweitzer, A. R.	Luttringer, Joseph; Durand, Victor	1,000	29 Jul 1885	Justice of the Peace (Salt Point Township)	Appointed 9 Jul 1885 by the Board of Supervisors, [vice S. H. Moyce, resigned]	2	507-508
Scott, David B.	Duncan, Alexander; Orr, John	5,000	18 Sep 1873	Surveyor	Elected 3 Sep 1873	B	720-721
Scudder, N. W.	Wilsey, Henry; Van Doren, J. S.	5,000	1 Feb 1882	Notary Public	Appointed & commissioned 30 Jan 1882 by George C. Perkins, Governor of California	2	122-123
Scudder, N. W.	Poehlmann, Conrad; Steitz, Henry	5,000	2 Feb 1884	Notary Public	Appointed 29 Jan 1884 by George Stoneman, Governor of California, witness J. P. Rodgers	2	319-320
Scudder, N. W.	Van Doren, J. S.; Hildburgh, L.	5,000	6 Feb 1880	Notary Public	Appointed & commissioned 29 Jan 1880 by George C. Perkins, Governor of California, includes oath of office dated 6 Feb 1880	1	567-569
Scudder, N. W.*	O'Hara, John; Wickersham, Fred. A.; Bowles, J. M.; Denman, E.	2,000	30 Nov 1892	Justice of the Peace (Petaluma Township)	Commissioned 25 Jul 1892	4	215
Seaton, D. M.	Fairbanks, H. T.; Towne, S. D.	5,000	17 Oct 1879	Notary Public	Commissioned 13 Oct 1879 by William Irwin, Governor of California, includes oath of office dated 17 Oct 1879	1	543-544
Seaton, D. M. W.	Fairbanks, H. T.; Miner, W. E.	5,000	20 Sep 1873	Notary Public	Commissioned 17 Sep 1873 by Newton Booth, Governor of California	B	724-725
Seaton, D. M. W.	Pearce, George; Fairbanks, H. T.	1,000	22 Mar 1874	Deputy District Attorney	Appointed 2 Mar 1874 by W. E. McConnell, District Attorney, witness Frank W. Shattuck	1	13-14
Seaton, D. M. W.	Whitney, A.P.; Bowles, J. M.	5,000	9 Nov 1870	Notary Public	Commissioned 1 Nov 1870 by H. H. Haight, Governor of California, includes certificate of oath of office dated 9 Nov 1870	C	61-62
Seaton, Daniel M. W.	Towne, Smith D.; Tuttle, B. F.; Ellis, John J.; Doyle, M.	5,000	30 Oct 1868	Notary Public	Appointed 27 Oct 1868 by H. H. Haight, Governor of California, includes oath of office dated 30 Oct 1868	B	620
Seawell, Emmet*	Brooke, T. J.; McConnell, William E.	5,000	24 Oct 1890	Notary Public	Appointed 21 Oct 1890 for the term of 4 years, witness J. R. Leppo	4	174
Seawell, Emmet*	Taylor, John S.; Maddux, J. P.; Gauldin, W. W.; Near, C. D.; Carithers, D. N.	15,000	26 Nov 1892	District Attorney	Elected 8 Nov 1892	4	210
Seawell, Emmett*	Brooke, T. J.; Hardin, James A.	5,000	10 Oct 1888	Notary Public	Appointed & commissioned 4 Oct 1888 by R. W. Waterman, Governor of California	3	257-258
Seawell, W. N.	Harris, Jacob; Reed, J. H.	2,000	12 Dec 1885	Justice of the Peace (Santa Rosa Township)	Appointed 10 Dec 1885 by the Board of Supervisors, [vice J. C. Sargent, deceased]	2	510-512
Seawell, W. N.	Proctor, T. J.; Forsyth, Robert; Gale, Otis; Reed, W. C.; Young, B. S.; Mock, Wesley	2,000	16 Nov 1886	Justice of the Peace (Santa Rosa Township)	Elected 2 Nov 1886	3	1-3
Seawell, W. N.	Hopper, Thomas; Brooke, T. J.	2,000	28 Nov 1890	Justice of the Peace (Santa Rosa Township)	Elected 4 Nov 1890, witness Ben. S. Wood	4	118
Seawell, W. N.	Forsyth, R.; Taylor, John S.; Harris, Jacob	2,000	3 Dec 1888	Justice of the Peace (Santa Rosa Township)	Elected 6 Nov 1888	3	311-312

Principal Name	Sureties	Amount ($)	Date	Office	Notes	Book	Page(s)
Seawell, William N.*	Smith, R. Press; Dunbar, John; Wilson. E. A.; Lee, W. H.	2,000	1 Dec 1892	Justice of the Peace (Santa Rosa Township)	Elected 8 Nov 1892	4	217
Sedgley, Jotham	Hoag, Jared C.; Wilson, William H.	200	22 Nov 1864	Road Master (District No. 1, Analy Township)	Appointed 22 Nov 1864 by the Board of Supervisors, includes oath of office dated 22 Nov 1864		
See, William	Farmer, Elijah T.; Wise, Henry	2,000	20 May 1867	Steward of the County Hospital	Appointed [?] May 1867 by the Board of Supervisors [to fill the vacancy occasioned by the removal of G. W. McIlroy]	B	586
Sellards, C. V.	Stillwell, V.; McReynolds, J.	1,000	1 Dec 1888	Constable (Analy Township)	Elected 6 Nov 1888	4	16
Seymour, L. B.	Orr, John; Rien, Samuel	1,000	1 Feb 1879	Road Overseer (Ocean Township)	Appointed 8 Jan 1879 [by the Board of Supervisors]		
Seymour, L. B.	Hammy, George; Dayton, John J.; Duncan, A.; Rien, Samuel; Orr, John	1,500	25 Nov 1880	Road Overseer (Ocean Township)	Elected 2 Nov 1880	2	80-81
Seymour, Levi Burton	Orr, John; Duncan, Samuel M., Jr.	1,000	17 Jan 1880	Road Overseer (Ocean Township)	Appointed 8 Jan 1880 [by the Board of Supervisors]		
Shane, Adam	Lindsay, J. J.; Grove, W. H.	1,000	1 Dec 1886	Justice of the Peace (Russian River Township)	Elected 2 Nov 1886	3	86-87
Shane, Adam	Bruner, Phillip; Lindsay, J. J.	1,000	14 Dec 1888	Justice of the Peace (Russian River Township)	Elected 6 Nov 1888	4	25
Shane, Adam	Bell, Henry; Lindsay, J. J.	1,000	4 Dec 1890	Justice of the Peace (Russian River Township)	Elected 4 Nov 1890	4	154
Shane, Adam*	Bell, Henry; Jacobsen, J. H.	1,000	5 Dec 1892	Justice of the Peace (Russian River Township)	Elected 8 Nov 1892	4	224
Shane, James C.	Hembree, A. J.; Bell, Henry	1,000	27 Mar 1889	Pound Master (Russian River Pound District)	Appointed 12 Mar 1889 by the Board of Supervisors	4	47
Shane, James C.*	Philpott, B. F.; Bell, Henry	1,000	24 Feb 1891	Constable (Russian River Township)	Appointed 9 Feb 1891 by the Board of Supervisors	4	186
Shane, James C.*	Philpott, B. F.; McClelland, J. H.	1,000	24 Feb 1891	Pound Master (Russian River Pound District)	[Appointed] 9 Feb 1891 by the Board of Supervisors, [vice E. W. Price, removed from the county]	4	185
Sharkey, John	Vasques, P. J.; Brackett, J. S.	1,000	30 Sep 1853	Constable (Sonoma Township)	Received certificate of election dated 20 Sep 1853	A	30
Shattuck, D. O.*	Pauli, G. T.; Leiding, C. F.	3,000	1 Jul 1863	Trustee (Town of Sonoma)	Elected 18 May 1863	B	51
Shattuck, David O.*	Leiding, C. F.; Pauli, G. T.	3,000	31 May 1862	Trustee (City of Sonoma)	Elected 19 May 1862	B	14
Shattuck, Dickson P.	Kavanaugh, N.; Thornley, Henry	1,000	27 Nov 1860	Constable (Sonoma Township)	Elected 6 Nov 1860, witness William Ellis	B	125-126

114

Principal Name	Sureties	Amount ($)	Date	Office	Notes	Book	Page(s)
Shattuck, F. W.	Poehlmann, Conrad; Cowen, Philip; Benson, J. H.; Bowles, J. M.; Merritt, John	5,000	23 Oct 1887	Notary Public	Appointed & commissioned 13 Oct 1887 by R. W. Waterman, Governor of California, for the term of two years, witness J. P. Rodgers, includes oath of office dated 23 Oct 1887	3	204-205
Shattuck, Francis W.	Robinson, C. J.; Jackson, Calvin; Hartman, J. W.; Schmitt, G.; Towne, Smith D.; Siddons, J. H.; Hunt, Charles; Edwards, Thomas; Rexford, E. A.; Cooper, B. F.	5,000	26 May 1859	Notary Public	Appointed 12 May 1859 by the Governor of California for the term of two years	A	382
Shattuck, Frank W.	Bowles, J. M.; Doyle, M.	5,000	1 Aug 1876	Notary Public	Appointed 22 Jul 1876 by the Governor of California for the term of two years		
Shattuck, Frank W.	Berger, M.; Tempel, C.	2,000	11 Nov 1871	Justice of the Peace (Petaluma Township)	Elected 18 Oct 1871	C	107-108
Shattuck, Frank W.	Tuttle, B. F.; Daly, James	2,000	12 May 1866	Justice of the Peace (Petaluma Township)	Appointed 11 May 1866 by the Board of Supervisors to fill the vacancy occasioned by the resignation of W. Henry Jones for the remainder of said Jones' term	B	548
Shattuck, Frank W.	Zimmerman, George; Bowles, J. M.; Shelton, A. C.; Maynard, F. T.; Meyerholtz, H.	5,000	14 Aug 1880	Notary Public	Appointed 9 Aug 1880 by George C. Perkins, Governor of California	1	582-583
Shattuck, Frank W.	Tempel, C.; Naughton, Hubert	2,000	17 Dec 1873	Justice of the Peace (Petaluma Township)	Elected 15 Oct 1873, witness John Cavanagh	B	756-757
Shattuck, Frank W.	Hill, William; McGuire, A.; Tempel, C.; Hopper, Tom	5,000	17 Sep 1870	Notary Public	Appointed 8 Sep 1870 by H. H. Haight, Governor of California, for the term of two years from the date of appointment, witness Arthur Shattuck, includes oath of office dated 17 Sep 1870	C	59-60
Shattuck, Frank W.	Maynard, F. T.; Palmer, J. M.; Carpenter, L. F.; Soldate, J. A.; Haskins, T. J.	5,000	18 Oct 1883	Notary Public	Appointed & commissioned 15 Oct 1883 by George Stoneman, Governor of California, for the term of two years	2	314-316
Shattuck, Frank W.	Hardin, James A.; Jackson, Jesse; Cahen, A. S.; Davis, Levi; Bond, J. L.; Hunt, Charles; Berger, M.; Duerson, J. H.; Mannheim, H.; Tempel, C.	5,000	25 Aug 1868	Notary Public	Appointed & commissioned 21 Aug 1868 for the term of two years, includes oath of office dated 25 Aug 1868		
Shattuck, Frank W.	Evans, M. R.; Delahenty, John; Fritsch, John; Stafford, N. O.; Brown, S. C.; McVicar, C. M. C.; Wickersham, I. G.; Rudesill, J. A.; Carder, D. D.; Anderson, William L.	5,000	25 Sep 1857	Justice of the Peace (Petaluma Township)	Elected 2 Sep 1857, taking office from 1 Oct 1857 for one year, accepted by W. B. Hagans, Chairman of the Board of Supervisors	A	213-214
Shattuck, Frank W.	Shattuck, David O.; Griffith, James A.	5,000	26 Nov 1852	Justice of the Peace (Sonoma Township)	Elected 2 Nov 1852, includes oath of office dated 26 Nov 1852	A	68-69
Shattuck, Frank W.	Bowles, J. M.; Tempel, C.; Merritt, John; Bernhard, Isaac	5,000	27 Jul 1878	Notary Public	Appointed 25 Jul 1878 by William Irwin, Governor of California, for the term of two years, witness J. P. Rodgers, includes oath of office dated 27 Jul 1878	1	435-436
Shattuck, Frank W.	Singley, James; Haydon, S. C.; Thompson, M. S.; Anderson & Robberson	5,000	28 Nov 1856	Justice of the Peace (Petaluma Township)	Elected 4 Nov 1856	A	172
Shattuck, Frank W.	Shattuck, David O., Sr.; Brewster, John A.	5,000	3 May 1853	Notary Public	Appointed and commissioned 5 Apr 1853 by the Governor of California, includes certification of oath of office dated 3 May 1853		

Principal Name	Sureties	Amount ($)	Date	Office	Notes	Book	Page(s)
Shattuck, Frank W.	Bowles, J. M.; Poehlmann, C.; Haskins, T. J.; Tempel, C.; Merritt, John	5,000	30 Oct 1885	Notary Public	Appointed & commissioned 28 Oct 1885 by George Stoneman, Governor of California, includes oath of office dated 30 Oct 1885	2	501-503
Shattuck, Frank W.	Tighe, Kelly; Carpenter, L. F.; Bernhard, Isaac; Newburgh, E.	2,000	8 Nov 1878	Justice of the Peace (Petaluma Township)	Appointed 7 Nov 1878 by the Board of Supervisors to fill the unexpired term made vacant by the removal of O. T. Baldwin	1	446-447
Shattuck, Frank W.	Huie, George W.; Sroufe, John	2,000	9 Apr 1868	Justice of the Peace (Petaluma Township)	Appointed 7 Apr 1868 by the Board of Supervisors, vice B. F. Tuttle, Esqr., resigned, to hold office during the unexpired term of said B. F. Tuttle and until his successor is elected and qualified, includes oath of office dated 9 Apr 1868	B	617
Shaw, John R.	Archambeau, Peter T.; Livreau, Joseph; Singley, R. R.; Cozzens, D.; Hooper, J. M.; Harrison, R.; Myers, S.	5,000	1 Dec 1856	Justice of the Peace (Washington Township)	Elected 4 Nov 1856	A	182
Shaw, N. R.	Brumfield, George P.; McCollough, S. G.	1,000	[4 Oct] 1858	Justice of the Peace (Russian River Township)	Elected 1 Sep 1858	A	332
Shaw, Nelson R.	Campbell, R. B.; Purrine, A. S.	1,000	19 Jan 1883	Constable (Bodega Township)	Appointed 10 Jan 1883 by the Board of Supervisors, [vice Julius Steele, failed to qualify]	2	281-282
Shearer, Henry		5,000	11 Mar 1854	Justice of the Peace (Vallejo Township)	Elected 15 Mar 1854	A	35
Shearer, John	Veale, W. R.; Wharff, D.	4,000	23 Nov 1882	Road Overseer (Vallejo Township)	Elected 7 Nov 1882	2	232-234
Shelford, Peter L.	Heald, Jacob G.; Sissengood, John	1,000	16 Feb 1878	Road Overseer (Cloverdale Road District)	Appointed 7 Feb 1878 [by the Board of Supervisors]	1	404-405
Shelford, Peter L.	Crigler, W. E.; Davis, B. J.	1,000	17 Feb 1877	Road Overseer (Cloverdale Road District)	[Appointed] 9 Feb 1877 by the Board of Supervisors	1	247-248
Sherman, Caleb	Patterson, A. S.; Kuffle, Isaac	1,000	27 Nov 1860	Constable (Analy Township)	Elected 6 Nov 1860, witnesses L. C. Reyburn & E. Latapie	B	135
Sherman, Caleb	Finley, S. J.; Arnold, G. W.	1,000	6 Feb 1862	Justice of the Peace (Bodega Township)	Appointed	B	253
Sherman, Caleb	Henckell, George; McHenry, James	1,000	6 Oct 1862	Justice of the Peace (Bodega Township)	Elected 3 Sep 1862, witness William L. Anderson, includes oath of office dated 6 Oct 1862	B	293
Shiell, Frank R.	Parks, D. H.; Stanley, J. P.	1,000	[?] Jul 1886	Justice of the Peace (Analy Township)	Appointed 8 Jul 1886 by the Board of Supervisors, [vice L. D. Cockrill, deceased]	2	550-551
Shinn, S. M.	Mothersead, A. J.; Cavanaugh, John	1,000	3 Oct 1859	Justice of the Peace (Russian River Township)	Elected 7 Sep 1859 for the term of one year	B	49

Principal Name	Sureties	Amount ($)	Date	Office	Notes	Book	Page(s)
Shinn, S. M.	Rosenberg, M. J.; Calhoon, John W.	1,000	5 Oct 1861	Justice of the Peace (Russian River Township)	Elected [4 Sep 1861]	B	218-219
Shipley, R. J.	Warner, Philemon; Carter, Landon	100	3 Aug 1859	Road Overseer (Road District No. 20, Russian River Township)	Appointed	B	5
Shirley, John Q.	Kalkmann, Philipp	100	[4 Jun 1858]	Road Overseer (Southern District of Vallejo Township)	Appointed by the Board of Supervisors, witness S. Payran	A	310
Shores, James M.	Davis, Gary V.; Shaw, Isaac E.; Mitchell, Charles E.; Byron, Peter	2,000	17 Sep 1875	Constable [Cloverdale Township]	Elected 1 Sep 1875	1	123-125
Shores, James M.	Davis, G. V.; Worth, Claiborn; Davis, B. J.; Cooper, John	2,000	20 Sep 1877	Constable (Cloverdale Township)	Elected 5 Sep 1877	1	328-330
Simmons, J. R.	Brown, A.; Shoemake, Omer	1,000	14 [Jan 1886]	Road Overseer (Redwood [Road] District)	Appointed 12 Jan 1886 [by the Board of Supervisors, vice J. W. Bagley, resigned]	2	523-525
Sims, J. C.*	McGee, James H.; Taylor, John S.; Ware, A. B.; Hopper, Thomas	5,000	[?] Nov 1888	Notary Public	Commissioned 15 Nov 1888 by R. W. Waterman, Governor of California, witness Charles E. Runyon	3	265-267
Sims, J. C.*	Roney, J. M.; Noonan, George P.; Smith, R. Press; Davis, G. V.	5,000	18 Nov 1890	Notary Public	Appointed & commissioned 17 Nov 1890	4	97
Singley, R. R.	McPherson, William B.; Ormsby, J. S.; Levalley, D. T.	1,000	1 Dec 1856	Constable (Washington Township)	Elected 4 Nov 1856	A	181
Singley, Rhees R.	Ray, John G.; Heald, H. G.	1,000	2 Oct 1854	Constable (Washington Township)	Elected 6 Sep 1854	A	33
Sink, W. D.	Sink, D.; Gould, T. J.	1,000	3 Oct 1865	Road Master (Cloverdale Township)	Elected 6 Sep 1865	B	371
Sink, William H.	Sink, Daniel; Sink, William D.	1,000	5 Oct 1863	Constable (Cloverdale Township)	Elected [2 Sep 1863], witness J. Ramey	A	334
Sitton, Thomas H.	Sackett, David A.; Bryant, W. S.	1,000	4 Oct 1858	Constable (Vallejo Township)	Elected 1 Sep 1858	4	60
Skaggs, George*	Roney, J. M.; Mulgrew, J. F.; Davis, W. S.; Striening, M. J.; Burris, L. W.	5,000	7 Jun 1889	Notary Public	Appointed & commissioned 3 Jun 1889 by R. W. Waterman, Governor of California	1	208-209
Skillman, Theodore	Merritt, John; Hill, William	2,000	15 Jan 1876	Road Master (Petaluma Road District)	Appointed 8 Jan 1876 by the Board of Supervisors	2	379-380
Small, J. B.	Muldry, Martin; Agnew, S. J.	1,000	25 Nov 1884	Justice of the Peace (Sonoma Township)	Elected 4 Nov 1884	3	129-131
Small, Joe B.*	Winkle, Henry; Muldry, Martin	1,000	27 Dec 1886	Justice of the Peace (Sonoma Township)	Elected 2 Nov 1886	2	175-177
Smith, A. B.*	Cox, C. B.; Prindle, William; Loucks, A. H.; Reed, J. H.	2,000	25 Nov 1882	Constable (Santa Rosa Township)	Elected 7 Nov 1882		

Principal Name	Sureties	Amount ($)	Date	Office	Notes	Book	Page(s)
Smith, Alexander H.	Smith, Isaac P.; Slusser, Levi S. B.	2,000	29 Sep 1853	Constable (Russian River Township)	Elected 7 Sep 1853		
Smith, F. A.	Overton, A. P.; Walker, John; Carithers, D. N.	15,000	23 Nov 1888	Supervisor (District No. 5)	Elected 6 Nov 1888	3	273-275
Smith, G. Canning	Godwin, A. C.; Singley, R. R.	5,000	1 Oct 1855	Justice of the Peace (Big River Township Mendocino County)	Elected 5 Sep 1855	A	120
Smith, George N.*	Codding, George C.; Hopkins, S. J.; Bryant, C. G.; Ivancovich, George	5,000	6 Oct 1892	Notary Public	Appointed & commissioned 30 Sep 1892	4	206
Smith, John K.	Smith, Robert E.; Henderson, Mathew	100	15 May 1858	Road Overseer (Road District No. 21, Bodega)	Appointed	A	309
Smith, John K.	Smith, Jacob; Hood, Thomas B.	1,000	19 Nov 1860	Justice of the Peace (Bodega Township)	Elected 6 Nov 1860	B	92
Smith, Nathan	Hammond, Wiliam R.; Hafford, R. F.	200	5 Dec 1860	Road Overseer (Road District No. [?], Cloverdale Township)	Appointed	B	141
Smith, S. H.	Gould, T. J.; Whitman, J. H.	200	26 Nov 1862	Road Master (District No. [?], [?] Township)	Appointed	B	336
Smith, Soloman H.	Whitman, J. H.; Ramey, J.	200	[15 Nov 1861]	Road Overseer (Cloverdale Township)	Elected [4 Sep 1861], witness Eli Lester	B	230
Smith, Solomon	Gould, T. J.; Ray, E.	250	[20 Jun 1861]	Road Master (Cloverdale Township)	Appointed by the Board of Supervisors from 17 Jun 1861, includes oath of office dated 20 Jun 1861	B	228
Smith, Stephen, 2nd	Campbell, Peter; Hendley, John	5,000	6 Oct 1851	Justice of the Peace (Bodega Township)	Elected 3 Sep 1851	A	67-68
Smith, William F.	Hendley, John; Ellis, John J.; Barnes, Michael; Potter, Samuel; Pyatt, Thomas H.; Shattuck, Frank W.; Cocke, William E.	10,000	5 Aug 1861	District Attorney	Appointed 5 Aug 1861 by the Board of Supervisors to fill the vacancy occasioned by the resignation of R. C. Flournoy, includes undated oath of office	B	166-167
Smyth, C. S.	Doyle, M.; Taylor, John S.; Roney, J. M.; Henley, Barclay	5,000	20 Nov 1882	Superintendent of Schools	Elected 7 Nov 1882	2	149-150
Smyth, C. S.	Bell, J. S.; Burris, D.	3,000	6 Jan 1880	Superintendent of Schools	Appointed 5 Jan 1880 [by the Board of Supervisors], vice E. W. Davis, resigned	1	560-561
Smyth, Charles S.	Underhill, John G.; Fulkerson, Richard; McReynolds, James	3,000	23 Sep 1879	Superintendent of Schools	Elected 3 Sep 1879, witness A. D. Laughlin	1	497-498
Snell, J. G.	Short, John R.; Smith, John P.	1,000	4 Oct 1858	Justice of the Peace (Ukiah Township)	Elected 1 Sep 1858		
Snider, Charles C.	Hooper, V. C. W.; Sondheimer, E.; Engel, H. S.; Hudson, Thomas W.	5,000	28 Sep 1859	Assessor	Elected 7 Sep 1859	B	48
Snook, W. P.	Miller, George; Sargent, Henry; Brown, H. K.; Clack, John W.; Hooten, Martin V.	5,000	15 Jun 1876	Auctioneer		1	219-220
Snook, W. P.	Brown, H. K.; Zane, A. J.	1,500	15 May 1875	Constable (Mendocino Township)	Appointed 7 May 1875 by the Board of Supervisors, [vice J. W. Bell, resigned]	1	107-108

Principal Name	Sureties	Amount ($)	Date	Office	Notes	Book	Page(s)
Snook, W. P.	Hassett, J. D.; Powell, R.; Bell, J. S.; Hudson, T. W.	2,000	21 Sep 1877	Constable (Mendocino Township)	Elected 5 Sep 1877	1	322-323
Snook, W. P.	Gladden, W. N.; Cook, G. A.; Zane, A. J.; Mead, James A.	1,000	25 Sep 1879	Constable (Mendocino Township)	Elected 3 Sep 1879	1	517-518
Snook, William P.	Meyer, Samuel; McManus, John G.	1,000	26 Nov 1869	Constable (Mendocino Township)	Elected 1 Sep 1869	C	5
Snow, J.	Fritsch, John; Keating, Michael M.; Poehlmann, Conrad; Fairbanks, H. T.	2,000	19 Nov 1880	Justice of the Peace (Petaluma Township)	Elected 2 Nov 1880	2	23-24
Snow, J.	Maynard, F. T.; Wickersham, I. G.	5,000	21 Oct 1881	Notary Public	Appointed & commissioned 13 Oct 1881 by George C. Perkins, Governor of California	2	104-105
Snow, J.	Fritsch, John; Poehlmann, Conrad	2,000	23 Nov 1882	Justice of the Peace (Petaluma Township)	Elected 7 Nov 1882	2	165-166
Snow, Joshua	Wiswell, Nelson; Kelty, George	1,000	13 Sep 1862	Justice of the Peace (Vallejo Township)	Elected 3 Sep 1862, witness J. Chandler	B	280
Snow, Joshua	Maynard, Frank T.; Leavy, Robert; Davis, W. K.	2,000	2 Dec 1869	Justice of the Peace (Petaluma Township)	Elected 20 Oct 1869	C	14
Snow, Joshua	Charles, J. M.; Cowen, Philip; Hartman, J. W.; Bliss, William D.	2,000	9 Nov 1863	Justice of the Peace (Vallejo Township)	Elected 21 Oct 1863 for the term of two years from 1 Jan 1864	B	393
Solomon, Charles	Walker, John; Morris, Joseph H. P.	1,000	13 Jan 1892	Justice of the Peace (Analy Township)	Appointed 12 Jan 1892 [by the Board of Supervisors to fill the vacancy that had existed for some time caused by the death of Justice Berry]	4	194
Sparks, G. W.	Hill, William McPherson; Rogers, W. K.	2,000	13 Sep 1873	Constable (Sonoma Township)	Elected 3 Sep 1873	B	703-704
Sparks, G. W.	Schocken, S.; Haraszthy, A. F.	1,000	24 Nov 1884	Constable (Sonoma Township)	Elected 4 Nov 1884	2	372-373
Sparks, G. W.	Schocken, S; McMackin, James	1,000	5 Dec 1888	Constable (Sonoma Township)	Elected 6 Nov 1888	3	316-317
Sparks, G. W.*	Schocken, S.; McMackin, James	1,000	1 Dec 1890	Constable (Sonoma Township)	Elected 4 Nov 1890	4	117
Sparks, George W.	Rogers, W. K.; Lennox, James W.; Hill, William McPherson; Craig, O. W.; Edwards, A. S.	10,000	[?] Sep 1875	Assessor	Elected 1 Sep 1875	1	132-134
Sparks, George W.	McMackin, James; Schocken, Solomon	1,000	1 Dec 1886	Constable (Sonoma Township)	Elected 2 Nov 1886	3	84-85
Sparks, George W.	Weyl, Henry; Haraszthy, A. F.	1,000	18 Jul 1883	Pound Master (Sonoma Township)	Appointed 7 Jun 1883 [by the Board of Supervisors]		
Sparks, George W.	Rogers, W. K.; Phariss, P. H.; Craig, O. W.; Pauli, G. T.	10,000	18 Sep 1877	Assessor	Elected 5 Sep 1877	1	325-326
Sparks, George W.	Oettl, F.; McDonell, Angus	2,000	6 Nov 1871	Constable (Sonoma Township)	Elected 6 Sep 1871	C	101
Sparks, George W.*	McGill, P. L.; Schocken, S.	1,000	29 Nov 1882	Constable (Sonoma Township)	Elected 7 Nov 1882	2	212-213

119

Principal Name	Sureties	Amount ($)	Date	Office	Notes	Book	Page(s)
Sparks, George W.*	Schocken, S.; McMackin, James	1,000	5 Dec 1892	Constable (Sonoma Township)	Elected 8 Nov 1892	4	229
Sparrow, Edward D.	Chalfant, John E.; Kier, Henry	5,000	25 Oct 1882	Notary Public	Appointed & commissioned 15 Sep 1882	2	138-139
Spelling, Carl*	Tupper, G. A.; Lewis, George W.	5,000	11 Apr 1887	Notary Public	Appointed & commissioned 1 Apr 1887 by Washington Bartlett, Governor of California	3	185-186
Spelling, Carl*	Bishop, T. C.; Lewis, George W.	5,000	12 Feb 1887	Notary Public	Appointed & commissioned 3 Feb 1887 by Washington Bartlett, Governor of California	3	133-135
Spelling, Carl*	Byington, H. W.; Tuttle, G. C.; Coughran, W.; Allen, S. I.; Lewis, G. W.; Mulgrew, J. F.; Gray, J. W.	5,000	8 May 1889	Notary Public	Appointed 25 Apr 1889 by the Governor of California	4	57
Spencer, Gustavus*	Wiswell, J. A.; Ellis, J. J.	1,000	22 Aug 1868	Secretary of the Board of Fire Delegates of the City of Petaluma	Elected 20 Aug 1868	B	469-470
Spencer, Thomas	Thurgood, William S.; Forrister, A.J.	1,000	15 Sep 1862	Justice of the Peace [Mendocino Township]	Elected [3 Sep 1862]	B	279
Spencer, Thomas	McCoy, John; Tucker, B. Frank	1,000	17 Sep 1861	Justice of the Peace [Mendocino Township]	Elected 4 Sep 1861	B	199
Springer, James L.	Caseres, Cyrus; Goodman, L. S.	2,000	15 Nov 1873	Justice of the Peace (Bodega Township)	Elected 15 Oct 1873	B	758-760
Springer, James L.	Cheney, E. H.; Stump, James	1,000	25 Oct 1877	Justice of the Peace (Bodega Township)	Elected 17 Oct 1877	1	340-342
Springer, James L.	Cheney, E. H.; Stump, James	2,000	3 Nov 1875	Justice of the Peace (Bodega Township)	Elected 20 Oct 1875	1	162-163
Springer, James L.	Potter, Samuel, Jr.; Ingraham, Samuel W.	1,000	3 Oct 1859	Justice of the Peace (Bodega Township)	Elected 7 Sep 1859	B	37
Springer, James L.	Joy, Benjamin; Taylor, Despard	2,000	30 Nov 1871	Justice of the Peace (Bodega Township)	Elected 18 Oct 1871	C	116-117
Spurr, D. F.	Caldwell, William; Larison, Samuel	1,000	30 Nov 1886	Justice of the Peace (Cloverdale Township)	Elected 2 Nov 1886	3	72-73
Spurr, D. F.	Larison, S.; Caldwell, William	1,000	8 May 1886	Justice of the Peace (Cloverdale Township)	Appointed 5 May 1886 [by the Board of Supervisors, vice D. B. Morgan, deceased]	2	536-537
Sroufe, D. W.	Taft, H. C.; Wiswell, J. A.	5,000	28 Dec 1870	Auctioneer	Doing business along with A. Roseburg as auctioneers in Petaluma under the name and firm of Roseburg & Sroufe	C	66
Sroufe, David W.	Ellis, John J.; Sroufe, John; Edwards, Thomas	5,000	26 Jan 1864	Auctioneer	Applied for a license	B	443
Stanley, Harrison	Lusk, Salmon B.; Jackson, Calvin	500	21 Dec 1855	Overseer of Roads and Highways	Appointed by the Board of Supervisors (Donald McDonald, Stephen Acres, and William Allen) to serve a term of one year from 8 Nov 1855 and until a successor is appointed or chosen, witness James B. Southard		
Steadman, Amos	Rosenberg, M. J.; Buckland, Marvin	1,000	22 Nov 1860	Constable (Russian River Township)	Elected 6 Nov 1860, witness G. W. Petray	B	97

Principal Name	Sureties	Amount ($)	Date	Office	Notes	Book	Page(s)
Stengel, Christion	Seawell, James B.; Seawell, David Henry	1,000	3 Feb 1873	Road Master (Salt Point Road District)	Appointed 7 Jan 1873 by the Board of Supervisors		
Stephens, Daniel B.	Laughlin, M. N.; Storey, George	500	18 Oct 1865	Road Master (Road District No. 1, Mendocino Township)	Elected	B	485
Stevens, Ward S.	Beaver, Henry; Hixon, Andrew	2,000	9 Dec 1871	Constable (Redwood Township)	Appointed 10 Nov 1871 by the Board of Supervisors	C	111-112
Steward, James S.		5,000	6 Oct 1853	Justice of the Peace (Bodega Township)	Elected 7 Sep 1853	A	46
Stewart, Charles	Hoag, S. Cushing; Wood, William B.	200	14 Dec 1861	Road Overseer (District No. 3, Annally Township)	Appointed	B	252
Stewart, David	Poehlmann, C.; Bowles, J. M.; Lynch, H. A.; Whitney, A. P.; Dalton, W. H.; Lougee, F. W.	15,000	25 Jun 1880	Supervisor (District No. 1)	Appointed & commissioned 23 Jun 1880 by George C. Perkins, Governor of California	1	578-579
Stites, A. H.	Morris, W. R.; McDarment, R.	300	29 Sep 1862	Road Master (Road District No. 2, Washington Township)	Elected [3 Sep 1862]	B	335
Stites, Alexander Hill	Remmel, Charles; Ellis, Leander G.	4,000	5 Mar 1881	Deputy Assessor	Appointed [?] [?] 1881 by George W. Lewis, Assessor	2	90-91
Stockhoff, J. H.	Miller, W. R.; Dibble, William	1,000	5 Jan 1876	Road Overseer (Salt Point Township, [District No. 1])	Appointed [7 Jan 1876] by the Board of Supervisors	1	202-203
Stockhoff, John H.	Schroyer, Aaron; Call, George W.	1,000	26 Feb 1877	Road Overseer (Salt Point Road District No. 1)	Appointed 9 Feb 1877 [by the Board of Supervisors]	1	261-262
Stockhoff, John H.	Ogden, Eliel; Rien, Samuel	1,000	7 Feb 1878	Road Master (Salt Point Township Road District No. 1)	Appointed 7 Feb 1878 by the Board of Supervisors	1	386-387
Stockoff, John H.	Call, G. W.; Schroyer, Aaron	1,000	18 Jan 1879	Road Overseer (Salt Point Road District No. 2)	Appointed 8 Jan 1879 [by the Board of Supervisors]		
Stockoff, John H.	Call, G. W.; Schroyer, Aaron	1,000	24 Jan 1880	Road Overseer (Salt Point Road District No. 1)	Appointed 7 Jan 1880 [by the Board of Supervisors]		
Stockwell, Eben S.	Bonnell, B. F.; Clark, Cardwell	1,000	15 Sep 1862	Constable [Mendocino Township]	Elected [3 Sep 1862]	B	299
Stofen, P. N.	Noonan, George P.; Gauldin, W.W.; Walker, John; Seegelken, E. A.; Ort, Julius; Overton, A. P.; Roney, J. M.; Brown, Daniel; Doyle, M.; Laughlin, J. M.	100,000	30 Nov 1888	Treasurer	Elected 6 Nov 1888	3	303-306
Stofen, Peter N.*	Doyle, M.; Overton, A. P.; Shea, Con.; Brush, J. H.; Hitchcock, Hollis	100,000	5 Dec 1892	Treasurer	Elected 8 Nov 1892	4	234

Principal Name	Sureties	Amount ($)	Date	Office	Notes	Book	Page(s)
Stoffen, P. H.*	Doyle, M.; Hopper, Thomas; Laughlin, James H.; Taylor, John S.; Maddux, J. P.; McConnell, William E.; Curtis, Allen A.; Shelton, A. C.; Barnes, John; Overton, A. P.	100,000	5 Dec 1890	Treasurer	Elected 4 Nov 1890, witness A. D. Laughlin	4	169
Stone, W. P.*	Lancel, Anselme; Kloppenburg, C. William	1,000	10 Dec 1890	Constable (Bodega Township)	Elected 4 Nov 1890	4	160
Straney, Frank M.	Hardin, James A.; Allen, Samuel I.	1,000	5 Mar 1880	Road Overseer (Santa Rosa Road District No. 3)	Appointed 4 Mar 1880 [by the Board of Supervisors], vice John Hughes, removed [from office because of incompetence]		
Stump, James	Potter, Samuel, Jr.; Carrillo, Julio	1,000	23 Jan 1857	Constable (Bodega Township)	Elected 4 Nov 1856	A	184-185
Stump, Samuel W.	McCaughey, James; McCrea, John	2,000	20 Dec 1871	Constable (Bodega Township)	Elected 6 Sep 1871	C	126-127
Stump, Samuel W.	Joy, Benjamin; Fitzpatrick, Andrew	2,000	6 Oct 1873	Constable (Bodega Township)	Elected 3 Sep 1873	**B**	742-743
Stump, Samuel W.*	Samsel, Hiram; McCaughey, James	1,000	13 Dec 1869	Constable (Bodega Township)	Elected 1 Sep 1869	C	19
Stumpf, J. C.	Potter, Samuel; Rien, Samuel	200	7 Oct 1862	Road Master (District No. 1, Bodega Township)	Elected 3 Sep 1862, includes oath of office dated 7 Oct 1862	B	324
Stumpf, Johann C.	Ross, William; Brown, John	200	27 Sep 1861	Road Master (District No. 1, Bodega Township)	Elected 4 Sep 1861	B	232
Sumner, J. R.	Whitney, A. P.	5,000	30 Oct 1871	Auctioneer		C	97
Susenbeth, J. C.	Poehlmann, Conrad; Hildburgh, L.	2,000	2 Nov 1875	Justice of the Peace (Vallejo Township)	Elected 20 Oct 1875	1	156-157
Swain, R. M.*	Doyle, M.; Allen, S. I.	5,000	18 Apr 1889	Notary Public	Appointed & commissioned 2 Apr 1889 by R. W. Waterman, Governor of California	4	51
Swain, Robert	Cohn, I. H.; Sutton, H. D.	1,500	28 Sep 1865	Road Master (District No. 1, Petaluma Township)	Elected 6 Sep 1865	B	477
Swan, George O.	Carroll, Patrick; Oliver, J. S.; Mooney, Thomas	1,000	30 Dec 1880	Constable (Analy Township)	Elected 2 Nov 1880	2	60-61
Swett, Frank H.	Allen, S. I.; Finlaw, W.; Taylor, John S.; Savage, C. W.	5,000	7 Oct 1884	Notary Public	Appointed 26 Sep 1884, witness O. H. Hoag	2	334-335
Taggart, John, Jr.	Murphy, Rufus; Hoag, O. H.	2,000	17 Sep 1877	Constable (Redwood Township)	Elected 5 Sep 1877	1	283-284
Tarbett, F. B.	Clark, W. S.; Davis, L. T. (Dr.)	1,000	23 Nov 1880	Justice of the Peace (Russian River Township)	Elected 2 Nov 1880	2	47-49

Principal Name	Sureties	Amount ($)	Date	Office	Notes	Book	Page(s)
Tarbett, Foster B.	Davis, L. T.; Campbell, J. H.	1,000	22 Sep 1879	Justice of the Peace (Russian River Township)	Elected 3 Sep 1879	1	507-508
Tarwater, M. W.	Harris, Jacob; McCann, John	1,000	[20 Sep 1879]	Constable (Knight's Valley Township)	Elected 3 Sep 1879	1	472-473
Taylor, F. E.	Wilsey, Henry; Fernald, Johnson	5,000	17 Feb 1872	Auctioneer		C	155-156
Taylor, Simon	Sawyer, Israel; Burton, John	5,000	30 Dec 1856	Justice of the Peace (Ukiah Township)	Elected 4 Nov 1856	A	183
Taylor, William	Wilkinson, J.; Taylor, Despard	200	21 Dec 1863	Road Master (District No. 1, Bodega Township)	Elected 2 Sep 1863, witness G. Henckell, includes oath of office dated 21 Dec 1863	B	412-413
Taylor, William E.	Cooper, James; Butler, R. B.	2,000	10 May 1850	Constable (Sonoma District)	Elected 9 May 1850	A	54
Taylor, William E.	Boggs, William M.; Spriggs, Thomas	2,000	18 May 1850	Deputy Assessor	Appointed 18 May 1850, bound to Joseph N. Neville, Assessor, witness R. B. Butler		
Temple, Rufus A.	Farmer, E. T.; Juilliard, C. F.	5,000	24 Nov 1874	Notary Public	Appointed 19 Nov 1874	1	66-67
Temple, Rufus A.	Farmer, E. T.; Chamberlain, David	5,000	27 Nov 1872	Notary Public	Appointed [?] Nov 1872 by Newton Booth, Governor of California, for the term of two years		
Terrill, Samuel N.	Leffingwell, William; Freeman, John M.	5,000	26 Jun 1853	Notary Public		A	47
Terrill, Samuel N.	Lewis, M. Greene; Kent, Walter D.	5,000	4 Nov 1852	Justice of the Peace (Petaluma Township)		A	36
Thomas, Isaac R.	Ross, Losson; Thomas, Isaiah	1,000	3 Jun 1890	Pound Master (Forestville Pound District)	Appointed 3 Jun 1890 by the Board of Supervisors	4	86
Thomas, Isaiah	Carlton, Austin; Churchman, George	5,000	28 Dec 1871	Auctioneer		C	129-130
Thompson, A. W.	Hill, William; Mecham, H.	5,000	23 Oct 1866	Notary Public	Commissioned 12 Oct 1866 by Fred. F. Low, Governor of California, witness William L. Anderson, includes oath of office dated 23 Oct 1866	B	552
Thompson, Charles H.	Duncan, Samuel M.; Rien, Samuel	1,000	19 Sep 1879	Constable (Ocean Township)	Elected 3 Sep 1879	1	531-532
Thompson, J. G.	Thompson, F. P.; Underhill, John G.	1,000	11 Apr 1874	Road Overseer (Pine Flat [Road] District)	Appointed 11 Apr 1874 by the Board of Supervisors		
Thompson, J. G.	Chapman, I. N.; Grater, John F.; Hudson, T. W.; Brown, H. K.; Reynolds, William B.	5,000	18 Feb 1874	Notary Public	Appointed & commissioned 27 Jan 1874 by Newton Booth, Governor of California	1	11-13
Thompson, M. S.	Payran, Stephen; Singley, James	500	13 Apr 1857	Road Overseer (Vallejo Township)	Appointed by the Board of Supervisors		
Thompson, P. H.*	Howe, Robert; Johannsen, L. M.	15,000	3 Dec 1892	Supervisor (District No. 1)	Elected 8 Nov 1892	4	222
Thompson, Phillip R.	Godwin, A. C.; Gray, Thomas C.	5,000	2 Oct 1854	Justice of the Peace (Vallejo Township)	Elected 6 Sep 1854	A	17

123

Principal Name	Sureties	Amount ($)	Date	Office	Notes	Book	Page(s)
Thompson, Phillip R.	Latapie, E.; Thompson, T. L.; Clark, J. P.; Wise, Henry; Adams, James; McReynolds, James; Hoag, O. H.; Murphy, Rufus; Holmes, H. P.; Fulton, James; Smith, R. Press, Jr.; Phelps, A.	5,000	3 Oct 1853	Justice of the Peace (Vallejo Township)	Elected 7 Sep 1853	A	61
Thompson, R. A.		15,000	23 Sep 1879	Clerk	Elected 3 Sep 1879	1	494-496
Thompson, Ransom	Caldwell, William; Heald, J. G.	1,000	26 Nov 1890	Justice of the Peace (Cloverdale Township)	Elected 4 Nov 1890	4	109
Thompson, Ransom*	Chalfant, John E.; Ink, W. P.; Ethridge, D.; Bentley, A.; Semenza, John	5,000	16 Jun 1892	Notary Public	Appointed 7 Jun 1892, witnesses G. B. Baer & R. E. Baer	3	359-362
Thompson, Ransom*	Gerkhardt, H. F.; Yordi, Fred.	1,000	3 Dec 1892	Justice of the Peace (Cloverdale Township)	Elected 8 Nov 1892	4	238
Thompson, Reg. H.	Towne, Smith D.; Huie, J. Thompson; Doyle, M.; Kelly, George; Rexford, E. A.; Barnes, Thomas L.; Evans, M. R.	5,000	10 Jan 1860	Notary Public	Appointed & commissioned 6 Jan 1860 by John B. Weller, Governor of California, for the term of two years	B	67
Thompson, Robert A.	Harris, Jacob; Noonan, George P.; Overton, A. P.; Kelly, James W.; Laughlin, John M.; Merritt, John; Murphy, Rufus; Roney, J. M.; Goodman, L. S.; Doyle, M.	25,000	[?] Nov 1882	Clerk	Elected 7 Nov 1882	2	146-148
Thompson, Robert A.	Heisel, Paul; Harris, Jacob; Weatherington, Henry	5,000	11 Jun 1881	Clerk	Elected 3 Sep 1879, a supplemental bond substituting Paul Heisel, Jacob Harris, and Henry Weatherington for E. Latapie (died), Alma Phelps (removed from California), and Thomas L. Thompson (petitioned to be released from R. A. Thompson's original bond) as sureties on Robert A. Thompson's original bond dated 23 Sep 1879, includes Thomas L. Thompson's petition to be released from Robert A. Thompson's original bond dated 7 Jun 1881 and several Superior Court documents relating to this matter	1	594-596
Thompson, Robert A.	Holmes, H. P.; Boyce, J. F.; Davisson, D. D.; Thompson, Thomas L.; Hoag, O. H.	15,000	19 Sep 1877	Clerk	Elected 5 Sep 1877	1	290-291
Thompson, Tipton	Yates, J. W.; Espey, John, Sr.	1,000	25 Sep 1861	Justice of the Peace (Russian River Township)	Elected 4 Sep 1861	B	177
Thompson, W. P.	Henry, James; Burger, C. H.; Harris, Jacob; Bishop, T. C.	5,000	14 Feb 1887	Notary Public	Appointed & commissioned 7 Feb 1887 by Washington Bartlett, Governor of California	3	135-137
Thompson, William R. T.	Thompson, Ph. R.; Lovell, F. A	1,000	1 Dec 1856	Constable (Vallejo Township)	Elected 4 Nov 1856	A	173
Throop, Charles W.	Fairbank, James K.; Cole, J. H.	1,000	25 Jul 1884	Constable (Salt Point Township)	Appointed [5 May 1884 by the Board of Supervisors, vice George E. Purcell, resigned]	2	328-329
Throop, Charles W.	Hickman, John E.; Richardson, H. A.	1,000	6 Dec 1884	Constable (Salt Point Township)	Elected 4 Nov 1884	2	397-399

Principal Name	Sureties	Amount ($)	Date	Office	Notes	Book	Page(s)
Throop, James H.	Richardson, H. A.; Clark, John; Hickman, John E.; Haupt, Charles	5,000	10 May 1887	Notary Public	Appointed & commissioned 2 May 1887 by Washington Bartlett, Governor of California	3	189-190
Throop, James H.	Richardson, H. A.; Hickman, John E.	1,000	14 Dec 1886	Justice of the Peace (Salt Point Township)	Elected 2 Nov 1886	3	121-123
Throop, James H.	Hickman, John E.; Richardson, H. A.	1,000	6 Dec 1884	Justice of the Peace (Salt Point Township)	Elected 4 Nov 1884	2	418-420
Throop, James H.	Haupt, Charles; O'Neal, David	1,000	6 Dec 1888	Justice of the Peace (Salt Point Township)	Elected 6 Nov 1888	4	27
Throop, James H.	Parks, D. H.; Knapp, A. H.	1,000	9 Dec 1882	Justice of the Peace (Salt Point Township)	Elected 7 Nov 1882	2	257-259
Throop, James H.*	Richardson, H. A.; Rutledge, Thomas; Mulgrew, J. F.; McClellan, J. E.	5,000	21 Sep 1889	Notary Public	Appointed & commissioned 14 Sep 1889 for the term of 4 years	4	66
Throop, James H.*	Richardson, H. A.; McClellan, J. E.; Miller, Elias; O'Neal, David	5,000	25 Jul 1889	Notary Public	Appointed 11 May 1889, witness John S. Brooks	4	64
Tibbits, R. H.	Pensam, J. J.; Dopkins, Samuel	5,000	13 Apr 1857	Auctioneer		A	206
Tibbits, R. H.	Pensam, J. J.; Fritsch, John; Matthews, C. B.; Bradley, G. L.	5,000	20 May 1859	Auctioneer	Witness James Forte	B	1
Tighe, Kelly	Leddy, Patrick	20,000	12 May 1881	Public Administrator	Elected 3 Sep 1879, a supplemental bond substituting Patrick Leddy for P. Lawler as a surety on Kelly Tighe's original bond dated 17 Sep 1879, includes P. Lawler's petition to be released from Kelly Tighe's original bond dated 12 Apr 1881	2	95-97
Tighe, Kelly	Latapie, E.	1,000	16 Feb 1877	Coroner	Elected 1 Sep 1875; William B. Speers, one of the surities on Tighe's original bond approved 23 Sep 1875, died; John G. Pressley, County Judge, ordered Tighe to give an additional $1,000 bond on 16 Feb 1877, includes County Court orders & citations	1	242-243
Tighe, Kelly	Overton, A. P.; Leddy, Patrick	5,000	16 Feb 1877	Public Administrator	Elected 1 Sep 1875; William B. Speers, one of the surities on Tighe's original bond approved 23 Sep 1875, died; John G. Pressley, County Judge, ordered Tighe to give an additional $5,000 bond on 16 Feb 1877, includes County Court orders & citations	1	243-244
Tighe, Kelly	Pearce, George; Lynch, John	2,000	17 Sep 1879	Coroner	Elected 3 Sep 1879	1	471-472
Tighe, Kelly	Lynch, Charles; Erwin, N.; Maynard, F. T.; Doyle, M.; Sullivan, James; Carpenter, L. F.; Hill, William; Lawler, P.	20,000	17 Sep 1879	Public Administrator	Elected 3 Sep 1879, witness Frank W. Shattuck	1	469-471
Tighe, Kelly	Speers, William B.; Bowles, J. M.; Dalton, William H.; Matzenbach, W. B.	2,000	18 Sep 1875	Coroner	Elected 1 Sep 1875, witness Frank W. Shattuck	1	135-137

Principal Name	Sureties	Amount ($)	Date	Office	Notes	Book	Page(s)
Tighe, Kelly	Lavin, James; Connolly, M. W.; Murry, Dennis; Sullivan, James; Carroll, Patrick; Mecham, H.; Brown, Daniel; Knowles, James H.; Roberts, Charles; Derby, A. B.; Hynes, James; Lawler, Patrick; Speers, William B.; Maynard, F. T.	20,000	18 Sep 1875	Public Administrator	Elected 1 Sep 1875, witness Frank W. Shattuck	1	137-139
Tighe, Kelly	Mahony, Patrick; Morrow, David	5,000	20 Nov 1882	Coroner	Elected 7 Nov 1882	2	179-181
Tighe, Kelly	Fairbanks, H. T.; Maynard, F. T.; Hill, William; Lougee, F. W.; Smith, John B.; Whitney, A. P.; Carpenter, L. F.; Kerns, James; Ayers, William; Matzenbach, William B.; Charles, J. M.; Lynch, Charles	30,000	21 Nov 1882	Public Administrator	Elected 7 Nov 1882	2	177-179
Tighe, Kelly	Murray, Dennis; Lavin, James	2,000	26 Sep 1877	Coroner	Elected 5 Sep 1877, witness Frank W. Shattuck	1	294-295
Tighe, Kelly	Murray, Dennis; Lavin, James; Needham, Festus; Maynard, F. T.; Van der Noot, J.; Hildburgh, L.; Doyle, M.; Carroll, Patrick; Erwin, N.	20,000	26 Sep 1877	Public Administrator	Elected 5 Sep 1877, witness Frank W. Shattuck	1	293-294
Tighe, Thomas W.	Warner, James J.; Shea, Cornelius	2,000	30 Nov 1886	Constable (Santa Rosa Township)	Elected 2 Nov 1886	3	62-63
Tittemore, Charles S.	Hoag, Jared C.; Arthur, C. R.	2,000	29 Dec 1871	Constable (Analy Township)	Elected 6 Sep 1871	C	133-135
Tivnen, John	Rogers, W. K.; Duhring, F.; Weyl, H.	5,000	1 Dec 1888	Coroner	Elected 6 Nov 1888	4	4
Tivnen, John	Rogers, W. K.; Howe, Robert; Glaister, T. S.; Hall, Robert; Biggins, James	30,000	1 Dec 1888	Public Administrator	Elected 6 Nov 1888	4	5
Tivnen, John	Hooper, George F.; Hill, William McPherson	5,000	20 Nov 1884	Notary Public	Appointed 17 Nov 1884	2	411-412
Tivnen, John	Glaister, Thomas S.; Litzius, Louis; Duhring, F.	5,000	20 Nov 1886	Coroner	Elected 2 Nov 1886	3	27-28
Tivnen, John	Glaister, Thomas S.; Cornelius, George H. H.	5,000	20 Nov 1886	Notary Public	Appointed 17 Nov 1886 [by George Stoneman, Governor of California]	3	29-30
Tivnen, John	Howe, Robert; Leiding, C. F.; Weyl, H.; Rogers, W. K.; Hall, Robert; Schocken, S.	30,000	20 Nov 1886	Public Administrator	Elected 2 Nov 1886	3	24-26
Tivnen, John	Burris, David; Monahan, P.; Pauli, G. T.	5,000	23 Nov 1878	Notary Public	Commissioned 13 Nov 1878 by the Governor of California	1	448-449
Tivnen, John	Hill, William McPherson; Sears, G. C. P.; Merritt, John	10,000	24 Sep 1879	Supervisor (District No. 1)	Elected 3 Sep 1879	1	512-513
Tivnen, John	Burris, David; Rogers, W. K.	10,000	31 Jul 1879	Supervisor (District No. 1)	Appointed 24 Jul 1879 [by the Hon. John G. Pressley, County Judge, vice, W. K. Rogers, resigned]	1	462-463
Tivnen, John	Burris, David; Wegner, Edward	2,000	8 Mar 1880	Commissioner (Pueblo of Sonoma)	Appointed 6 Mar 1880 to fill the vacancy occasioned by the death of G. T. Pauli	1	570-571
Tivnen, John*	Schocken, Solomon; Weyl, Henry	5,000	23 Nov 1888	Notary Public	Appointed & commissioned 15 Nov 1888	3	275-276
Todd, Andrew Y.	Davis, Ira; Duerson, John H.	2,000	10 Feb 1874	Constable (Vallejo Township)	Appointed 2 Feb 1874 by the Board of Supervisors	1	16-17
Todd, James S.	Duerson, John H.; Davis, Ira	2,000	27 Dec 1873	Justice of the Peace (Vallejo Township)	Elected 15 Oct 1873	B	769-770

Principal Name	Sureties	Amount ($)	Date	Office	Notes	Book	Page(s)
Tombs, William H.	Carson, Lindsey; Ormsby, J. S.	1,000	1 Dec 1860	Justice of the Peace (Mendocino Township)	Elected 6 Nov 1860, witness Johnston Ireland	B	119-120
Tombs, William H.	Willson, H. M.; Powell, R.	1,000	1 Oct 1859	Justice of the Peace (Mendocino Township)	Elected 7 Sep 1859	B	40
Tombs, William H.	Mulligan, John; Rupe, Samuel H.; Wright, B. C.; Meyer, Samuel	2,000	24 Nov 1871	Justice of the Peace (Mendocino Township)	Elected 18 Oct 1871	C	105
Tombs, William H.	Bloom, D.; Smith, W. H.	2,000	7 Mar 1871	Justice of the Peace (Mendocino Township)	Appointed 6 Mar 1871 by the Board of Supervisors for the unexpired term of S. M. Hays, resigned	C	69
Tombs, William H.	Bloom, David; Clack, J. W.; Powell, Ransom	5,000	8 Dec 1871	Notary Public	Commissioned 1 Dec 1871	C	113-114
Towne, Smith D.	Siddons, James H.; Haydon, Stephen C.	5,000	1 Dec 1856	Assessor	Elected 4 Nov 1856	A	157
Towne, Smith D.	Baylis, Thomas F.; Godwin, A. C.; Newbill, P. H.	5,000	2 Oct 1854	Assessor	Elected 6 Sep 1854	A	91
Towne, Smith D.	Haydon, S. C.; Tayloe, J. Rhodes	5,000	2 Oct 1854	Assessor	Elected 6 Sep 1854	A	91
Townsend, William M. A.	Pauli, G. T.; McHarvey, Charles	2,000	17 Nov 1865	Justice of the Peace (Sonoma Township)	Elected 18 Oct 1865	B	489
Townsend, William M. A.	Pauli, G. T.; Green, William	2,000	23 Nov 1867	Justice of the Peace (Sonoma Township)	Elected [16 Oct 1867], witness William Ellis	B	567
Trosper, Arthur*	Otis, Hamilton; Trosper, F. D.	1,000	12 Dec 1892	Constable (Ocean Township)	Elected 8 Nov 1892	4	257
Trosper, F. D.*	King, William; Otis, Hamilton	1,000	8 Dec 1892	Justice of the Peace (Ocean Township)	Elected 8 Nov 1892	4	254
Troy, Daniel	Ross, Losson; Cockrill, T. G.	100	3 Apr 1858	Road Overseer (Road District No. 17 in Annally Township)	Appointed February Term 1858 by the Board of Supervisors		
Truitt, J. H.	Poor, F. G.; Stanley, S.	200	12 Sep 1863	Road Master (District No. 2, Mendocino Township)	Elected [2 Sep 1863], witness Thomas Spencer	B	374
Truitt, J. H.	Ormsby, J. S.; McManus, J. G.	100	17 Nov 1859	Road Overseer (Road District No. 4, Mendocino Township)	Appointed 9 Nov 1859	B	62
Truitt, J. H.	McManus, John G.; Clack, John W.	200	20 May 1861	Road Overseer (Healdsburg Road District)	Appointed, includes oath of office dated 20 May 1861	B	159
Truitt, James H.*	Hassett, James D.; Powell, Ransom	1,000	26 Sep 1865	Road Master (District No. 2, Mendocino Township)	Elected [6 Sep 1865], witness A. L. Boggs	B	473
Truitt, R. K.	Seawell, J. W.; Bell, A. K.	1,000	27 Nov 1886	Constable (Mendocino Township)	Elected 2 Nov 1886	3	56-57
Truitt, R. K.	Truitt, John R.; Powell, R.	4,000	4 Dec 1883	Constable [Mendocino Township]	Elected 7 Nov 1882		

Principal Name	Sureties	Amount ($)	Date	Office	Notes	Book	Page(s)
Truitt, R. K.*	Kennedy, G. H.; Ferguson, Henry O.	1,000	25 Nov 1882	Constable (Mendocino Township)	Elected 7 Nov 1882	2	192-193
Truitt, R. K.*	Truitt, John R.; Cox, N. H.	1,000	28 Feb 1885	Deputy Constable (Mendocino Township)	Bound unto J. S. Bell (Constable)	2	465
Tupper, George A.	Seegelken, E. A.; Glenn, J. H.; McFadyen, A.; DeTurk, I.; Roney, J. M.; Keser, L., Jr.; Laughlin, J. H.; Howell, Orrin; Murdock, L. A.; Fulkerson, John; Austin, James; Guerne, George E.; Hopper, Thomas; Taylor, John S.; Hitchcock, Hollis; Davis, E. W.; Carithers, D. N.; Brush, J. H.; Story, S. C.; Henry, James; Overton, A. P.; McConnell, William E.; Philips, Walter; Norton, L. A.; Taylor, O. A.; Hopper, J. W.	100,000	15 Nov 1886	Treasurer	Elected 2 Nov 1886, witness A. D. Laughlin	3	17-24
Tupper, George A.	DeTurk, I.; Byington, H. W.; Glenn, J. H.; Roney, J. M.; Seegelken, E. A.; Kinslow, John F.; Overton, A. P.; Noonan, George P.; Norton, L. A.; Story, S. C.; Beam, J.; Fisher, A. L.; McFadyen, A.; Guerne, George E.; Murdock, L. A.; Hitchcock, Hollis; Parks, D. H.; Keser, L., Jr.; Jones, William; Brown, Daniel; Walker, John; Laughlin, J. M.	100,000	17 Nov 1884	Treasurer	Elected 4 Nov 1884, witness A. D. Laughlin	2	343-347 & 347-351
Turman, Benjamin C.	Davis, Levi; Henley, William	100	21 Oct 1859	Road Overseer (Road District No. 12 in Petaluma Township)	Appointed 2 Aug 1859 by the Board of Supervisors	B	59
Tuttle, B. F.	Berger, Moses; Tempel, C.	2,000	2 Nov 1867	Justice of the Peace (Petaluma Township)	Elected 16 Oct 1867 for the term of two years from 1 Jan 1868	B	565
Ungewitter, Henry W.*	Lewis, George W.; Doyle, Frank P.	5,000	3 Dec 1892	Coroner	Elected 8 Nov 1892	4	228
Ungewitter, Henry W.*	Murphy, Rufus; Shea, Con.; McMinn, Joseph A.; Brooke, T. J.; Doran, W. M.; Hitchcock, Hollis; Walker, John	30,000	3 Dec 1892	Public Administrator	Elected 8 Nov 1892	4	230
Vallejo, U. P.	Weyl, Henry; Haraszthy, A. F.	1,000	22 Nov 1886	Constable (Sonoma Township)	Elected 2 Nov 1886	3	33-34
Van Alen, Egbert	Baker, James C.	200	4 Feb 1863	Road Overseer (District No. 2, Petaluma Township)	Appointed		
Van Doren, J. S.	Hill, William; Denman, E.	5,000	15 Oct 1881	Notary Public	Appointed & commissioned 13 Oct 1881 by George C. Perkins, Governor of California, includes oath of office dated 15 Oct 1881	2	101-102
Van Doren, John S.	Hill, William; Tempel, C.	5,000	19 Oct 1883	Notary Public	Appointed 15 Oct 1883 by George Stoneman, Governor of California, includes oath of office dated 19 Oct 1883	2	301-303
Vanderlieth, John	Pearson, William B.; Caseres, Francisco	1,000	28 Dec 1865	Constable (Bodega Township)	Elected 6 Sep 1865	B	514
Vanderlieth, John	Caseres, Francisco; Howe, E. A.	1,000	28 Sep 1863	Constable (Bodega Township)	Elected 2 Sep 1863, includes oath of office dated 28 Sep 1863	B	364-365

128

Principal Name	Sureties	Amount ($)	Date	Office	Notes	Book	Page(s)
Vanderlieth, John	Parmeter, John; Blume, F. G.	1,000	31 Jan 1868	Constable (Bodega Township)	Elected 4 Sep 1867	B	569
Varner, Samuel	Keaton, John J.; Harms, Henry	1,000	7 Dec 1888	Road Overseer (Redwood Road District)	Elected 6 Nov 1888	4	9
Varner, Samuel	Harms, Henry; Keaton, John J.	1,000	9 Oct 1888	Road Overseer (Redwood Road District)	Appointed 5 Oct 1888 by the Board of Supervisors		
Vaughan, Thomas H.	McManus, J. G.; Hassett, John D.	200	18 Sep 1861	Road Overseer (District No. 3, Mendocino Township)	Elected 4 Sep 1861	B	234
Vaughn, Wesley	Barnes, Edwin H.; Carson, Lindsey	5,000	29 Nov 1856	Justice of the Peace (Russian River Township)	Elected 4 Nov 1856	A	174
Veal, R. R.	Lavin, Timothy; Crane, R. H.	1,000	11 Nov 1865	Justice of the Peace (Vallejo Township)	Elected 18 Oct 1865	B	486
Veal, R. R. *	Clark, Almer; Veal, William	6,000	13 Dec 1865	School Tax Collector (Copeland School District No. 3, Vallejo Township)	Elected 23 Sep 1865	B	482
Veal, Richard R.	Humphries, Charles; Payran, Stephen	2,000	2 Nov 1867	Justice of the Peace (Vallejo Township)	Elected 16 Oct 1867, witness John Cavanagh	B	595
Veal, Richard R.	Clark, Almer	200	23 Nov 1864	Road Master (District No. 2, Vallejo Township)	Elected 8 Nov 1864, includes oath of office dated 23 Nov 1864	B	462
Virgin, E. F.	Austin, Amos; Berger, M.	5,000	10 Jan 1870	Auctioneer	Did business along with C. G. Bryant as auctioneers in the City of Petaluma under the name of Bryant & Virgin; See 1870 C. G. Bryant file	C	32
Walker, Alonzo	Wood, William B.; Knapp, A. H.	200	10 Feb 1865	Road Master (District No. 3, Analy Township)	Appointed 10 Feb 1865 by the Board of Supervisors	B	468
Walker, Alonzo	Hall, Henry; Tyler, Presley	5,000	10 May 1862	Assessor	Elected 4 Sep 1861	B	264
Walker, Ed. L.*	Morris, Joseph H. P.; Gannon, J. P.	1,000	5 Dec 1892	Constable (Analy Township)	Elected 8 Nov 1892	4	241
Walker, Edward L.*	Walker, John L.; Huntley, G. W.	1,000	3 Dec 1890	Constable (Analy Township)	Elected 4 Nov 1890	4	121
Walker, John	Morin, Josiah; Miller, C. S.	500	19 Nov 1855	Road Overseer	Appointed by the Board of Supervisors		
Walsworth, H. T.	Willson, H. M.; Dow, William B.	1,000	[2 Dec 1856]	Constable (Mendocino Township)	Elected 4 Nov 1856	A	159
Walsworth, Henry T.	Heald, J. G.; Hassett, J. D.	1,000	1 Oct 1855	Constable (Mendocino Township)	Elected	A	149
Walton, John*	Maxwell, J. M.; Glassen, Louis	3,000	30 Jun 1863	Trustee (Town of Sonoma)	Elected 18 May 1863	B	52
Walton, John*	Maxwell, J. M.; Glassen, Louis	3,000	31 May 1862	Trustee (City of Sonoma)	Elected 19 May 1862	B	16

Principal Name	Sureties	Amount ($)	Date	Office	Notes	Book	Page(s)
Ware, A. B.	Noonan, George P.; Farmer, E. T.; McReynolds, James; Farrell, Martin	10,000	16 Sep 1879	District Attorney	Elected 3 Sep 1879	1	467-468
Ware, George W.	Caldwell, William; Brush, William T.	200	3 Jan 1865	Road Master (Cloverdale Road District, Cloverdale Township)	Elected [8 Nov 1864], includes oath of office dated 3 Jan 1865	B	466
Warfield, George H.*	Barnes, E. H.; Powell, R.	5,000	15 Aug 1890	Notary Public	Appointed 11 Aug 1890	4	94
Warfield, R. H.	Barnes, Edwin Harrison; Norton, Lewis Adelbert	5,000	4 Apr 1887	Notary Public	Appointed & commissioned 1 Apr 1887 by Washington Bartlett, Governor of California, for the term of two years, witness A. E. Cochran	3	153-154
Warfield, R. H.*	Powell, Ransom; Barnes, E. H.	5,000	27 Mar 1889	Notary Public	Appointed 25 Mar 1889 for the term of 4 years	4	45
Warner, G.	Cassidy, J. W.; Holmes, A.; Merker, John; Cavanagh, John; Schierhold, H.; Tighe, Kelly; Kron, John; Schmitt, George; Walls, David; Davis, William; Haubrich, Leonard; Westover, O. F.; Bowles, J. M.; Hynes, James; Maynard, F. T.; Poehlmann, C.	10,000	11 Sep 1874	Supervisor [District No. 2]	Elected 2 Sep 1874 at a special election held in and for the Petaluma Township	1	60-62
Warner, James	Harris, Jacob; Austin, James	1,000	26 Dec 1883	Pound Master ([Santa Rosa Township], Pound District No. [4])	Appointed [6] [Dec] 1883 [by the Board of Supervisors]		
Warner, Philemon	Smith, William R.; Boyce, J. F.	100	29 Nov 1858	Road Overseer (Road District No. 7, northeast portion of Santa Rosa Township)			
Warren, W. P.	Ferguson, John N.; Ferguson, Henry O.	1,000	16 Mar 1888	Pound Master (Knight's Valley Pound District)	Appointed by the Board of Supervisors	A	353
					Appointed 10 Mar 1888 by the Board of Supervisors	3	236-237
Waters, James U.	Pauli, F. Albert; Burris, David	2,000	4 Dec 1871	Justice of the Peace (Sonoma Township)	Elected 18 Oct 1871	C	119-120
Watson, John, Jr.	Watson, James; Blinn, Mortimer	2,000	1 Nov 1871	Constable (Bodega Township)	Elected 6 Sep 1871	C	145-147
Watson, Milton	Knowles, D. C.; Shaw, George P.	1,000	4 Dec 1888	Road Overseer (Ocean Road District)	Elected 6 Nov 1888	4	8
Weatherington, Henry	Wilkinson, R.; Harris, Jacob; Brittain, R. H.; McMinn, John; Drennan, T. J.; Goldfish, B.; Badger, Joseph J.	10,000	18 Sep 1875	Supervisor (District No. 3)	Elected 1 Sep 1875	1	127-129
Weatherington, Richard M.	Weatherington, H.; Harris, Jacob	1,000	8 Jan 1880	Road Overseer (Santa Rosa Road District No. 2)	Appointed 7 Jan 1880 [by the Board of Supervisors]		
Weaver, Miles H.*	Lewis, I. S.; Brush, William T.	1,000	25 Nov 1890	Constable (Cloverdale Township)	Elected 4 Nov 1890	4	110
Weise, Charles C.*	Weise, Christian; Beatty, Geroge W.	1,000	2 Dec 1890	Constable (Sonoma Township)	Elected 4 Nov 1890	4	122

Principal Name	Sureties	Amount ($)	Date	Office	Notes	Book	Page(s)
Welch, Charles P.	Hopper, Wesley; McDonald, Frank	1,000	12 Dec 1882	Justice of the Peace (Knight's Valley Township)	Elected 7 Nov 1882	2	267-268
Welch, Charles P.	McDonald, Frank; Holmes, C. H.	1,000	4 Dec 1880	Justice of the Peace (Knight's Valley Township)	Elected 2 Nov 1880	2	46-47
Welch, Jackson	Walk, A. J.; Shone, Robert	1,000	20 Nov 1880	Constable (Salt Point Township)	Elected 2 Nov 1880	2	29-30
Welch, Jackson*	Walk, A. J.; Coburn, Joseph; Henry, James	1,000	29 Nov 1882	Constable ([Salt Point Township])	Elected 7 Nov 1882	2	250-252
Wescott, Oliver	Schloss, Siegmund; Sinclair, G. W.	1,000	12 Mar 1883	Constable (Redwood Township)	Appointed 7 Feb 1883 [by the Board of Supervisors], vice Roscoe McKenney, died	2	286-287
West, Samuel	Ormsby, J. S.; Chapman, H. P.	1,000	13 Nov 1856	Road Overseer (Russian River Township)	Appointed 8 Nov 1856		
Whaley, John	Bradshaw, J. A.; Cummons, M. B.	100	11 May 1859	Road Overseer (Road District No. 8, Santa Rosa Township)	Appointed	A	375
Whallen, Murray	Pearce, George; Bowles, J. M.	2,000	29 Nov 1886	Justice of the Peace (Petaluma Township)	Elected 2 Nov 1886	3	58-59
Whallon, Murray	Lougee, F. W.; Denman, E.; Brainerd, H. P.; Dinwiddie, J. L.	2,000	12 Dec 1888	Justice of the Peace (Petaluma Township)	Elected 6 Nov 1888	4	28
Whallon, Murray	Hendley, John; Boyce, John F.	2,500	26 Jan 1866	Recorder & ex officio Auditor	Elected 6 Sep 1865	B	531
Whallon, Murray	Hendley, John; Hahman, F. G.; Hewett, H. T.; Boyce, John F.	5,000	26 Jan 1866	Recorder	Elected 6 Sep 1865	B	530
Whallon, Murray	Dinwiddie, J. L.; Lawrence, H. E.; Denman, E.	2,000	26 Nov 1890	Justice of the Peace (Petaluma Township)	Elected 4 Nov 1890	4	111
Whallon, Murray	Pearce, George; Palmer, J. M.; Hardin, W. J.	2,000	9 Apr 1884	Justice of the Peace (Petaluma Township)	Appointed 8 Apr 1884 by the Board of Supervisors, [vice Joshua Snow, deceased]	2	321-322
Wheelock, C. R.	Drago, Nelson; Bones, J. F.; Beedle, L.; Kloppenburg, William; McCaughey, J.	5,000	18 May 1883	Notary Public	Appointed & commissioned 9 May 1883 by George Stoneman, Governor of California, witness Andrew J. Blaney	2	293-295
Wheelock, Charles R.	Kloppenburg, W.; Smith, George W.; Taylor, Godfrey C.; Drago, N.; McCaughey, J.	5,000	20 Jun 1881	Notary Public	Commissioned 5 May 1881 [by the Governor of California]	2	99-101
Whipple, E. L.	Clack, John W.; Phillips, D. D.	1,000	28 Apr 1874	Deputy District Attorney	Appointed 28 Apr 1874	1	22-23
White, James A.	Cheney, E. H.; Goodman, L. S.	1,000	16 Oct 1885	Constable (Bodega Township)	Appointed 5 Oct 1885 by the Board of Supervisors, vice Samuel Boyd, resigned	2	495-496
White, James F. S.	Henderson, Nath.; Case, J. M.	1,000	25 Sep 1855	Constable (Annally Township)	Elected 5 Sep 1855	A	132

Principal Name	Sureties	Amount ($)	Date	Office	Notes	Book	Page(s)
White, Thomas H.	Walker, Silas; Windsor, Jackson	1,000	14 Oct 1861	Justice of the Peace (Washington Township)	Elected 4 Sep 1861, witness J. B. Beeson	B	225
White, Thomas H.	Fike, Nathan; Alexander, Cyrus	1,000	20 Sep 1862	Justice of the Peace [Washington Township]	Elected [3 Sep 1862]	B	281
White, William H.	Vaughn, Wesley; Yates, J. W.	1,000	4 Oct 1858	Constable (Russian River Township)	Elected 1 Sep 1858	A	333
Whitehead, W. H.	Goodrich, C. B.; Leigh, A. G.	1,000	1 Dec 1884	Justice of the Peace (Washington Township)	Elected 4 Nov 1884	2	393-394
Wickersham, I. G.	Moffet, E. R.; Bassett, H.; Purvine, Charles	10,000	[?] Sep 1855	District Attorney (Sonoma County)	Elected 5 Sep 1855	A	143
Wickersham, I. G.	Doyle, M.; Merritt, C.; Hopper, Thomas	5,000	14 Jul 1859	Notary Public	Appointed by the Governor of California for the term of two years from 11 Jul 1859, includes certification of the oath of office dated 14 Jul 1859	B	4
Wickersham, I. G.	Speer, William B.; Lodge, J. D.	2,000	16 Sep 1862	Justice of the Peace (Petaluma Township)	Elected [3 Sep 1862], includes oath of office dated 18 Sep 1862	B	282
Wickersham, I. G.	Lodge, J. D.; Mechum, H.	2,000	24 Nov 1863	Justice of the Peace (Petaluma Township)	Elected 21 Oct 1863, includes oath of office dated 17 Nov 1863	B	404
Wickersham, I. G.	Lodge, J. D.; Speers, William B.	5,000	25 Jul 1861	Notary Public	Commissioned 23 Jul 1861 by John G. Downey, Governor of California, includes oath of office dated 25 Jul 1861	B	162-163
Wickersham, I. G.	Galland, J.; Lovett, O. H.; Hunt, Charles; Warner, G.	5,000	29 Jan 1856	Notary Public	Appointed and commissioned by the Governor of California, includes oath of office dated 31 Jan 1856	A	140
Wickersham, I. G.	Brown, Daniel; Doyle, M.	5,000	3 Nov 1862	Notary Public	Appointed by the Governor of California, includes oath of office dated 3 Nov 1862	B	314
Wickersham, I. G.	Bowles, J. M.; Overton, A. P.	5,000	3 Nov 1866	Notary Public	Commissioned 27 Oct 1866 by F. F. Low, Governor of California, includes oath of office dated 3 Nov 1866	B	553
Wickersham, I. G.	Pickett, J. L.; Bassett, H.; Hewlett, P. B.; Martin, S. M.; McCollough, S. G.	5,000	30 Jun 1857	Notary Public	Appointed 8 Jun 1857 by the Governor [of California] for the term of 2 years, includes oath of office dated 30 Jun 1857	A	189-190
Wickersham, I. G.	Thompson, A. W.; Speers, William B.	5,000	31 Oct 1864	Notary Public	Appointed & commissioned 27 Oct 1864 by the Governor of Califonia for the term of two years, includes oath of office dated 2 Nov 1864	B	460
Wickersham, Jesse C.	Wickersham, I. G.; Atwater, H. H.	5,000	13 Jul 1880	Notary Public	Appointed & commissioned 10 Jul 1880 by George C. Perkins, Governor of California	1	580
Wickersham, Jesse C.	Wickersham, I. G.; Atwater, H. H.	5,000	7 Sep 1875	Notary Public	Appointed 6 Sep 1875 by R. Pacheco, Governor of California, for the term of two years, includes oath of office dated 7 Sep 1875	1	112-113
Wiley, J. W.	Davis, C. P.; Ross, Losson	1,000	17 Jan 1880	Road Overseer (Analy Road District No. 2)	Appointed 8 Jan 1880 by the Board of Supervisors		
Wiley, John W.	Ross, Losson; Crawford, A.	2,000	[25 Nov 1882]	Road Overseer (Analy Township)	Elected 7 Nov 1882	2	242-243

Principal Name	Sureties	Amount ($)	Date	Office	Notes	Book	Page(s)
Wiley, John W.	Eckert, Peter; Ross, Losson	1,000	13 Jan 1885	Road Overseer (Analy Road District)	Appointed 13 Jan 1885 [by the Board of Supervisors]	2	450-451
Wiley, John W.	Gilliam, Mitchel; Ross, Losson	1,000	15 Jan 1876	Road Master (Analy Township, [District No. 2])	Appointed 8 Jan 1876 by the Board of Supervisors	1	201-202
Wiley, John W.	Ross, Losson; Davis, C. P.	3,500	15 Jan 1881	Road Overseer (Analy Township)	Appointed 6 Jan 1881	2	81-82
Wiley, John W.	Ross, Losson; Davis, C. P.	1,000	20 Jan 1879	Road Overseer (Annaly Township [Road] District No. 2)	Appointed 8 Jan 1879 [by the Board of Supervisors]		
Wiley, John W.	Davis, C. P.; Ross, Losson	1,000	21 Sep 1878	Road Overseer (Analy [Road] District No. 2)	[Appointed] 7 Feb 1878 [by the Board of Supervisors]	1	401-403
Wiley, John W.	Ross, Losson; Davis, Calvin P.	1,000	27 Feb 1877	Road Overseer (Analy [Road] District No. 2)	Appointed 9 [Feb] 1877 [by the Board of Supervisors]	1	255-256
Wiley, John W. *	Gilliam, M.; Ross, Lossen	1,000	20 Jan 1875	Road Master (Analy Township, District No. 2)	Appointed 6 Jan 1875 by the Board of Supervisors	1	87-88
Wilkins, Charles P.	Cooper, James; Brockman, Israel	1,000	6 Jun 1850	City Attorney (City of Sonoma)	Elected 9 May 1850, witnesses William M. Boggs and R. B. Butler	A	59-60
Wilks, William	Norton, L. A.; Peck, John R.; Lovejoy, Edwin L.; Thurgood, William S.; Crawford, John; May, J. J.; Fike, Nathan; Nalley, Alexander B.; Gault, Thomas L.; Linville, Byram; Carder, D. D.	10,000	[?] Jun 1862	District Attorney	Elected 4 Sep 1861	B	270-271
Wilks, William	Kessing, John F.; Maxwell, J. G.; Heisel, Paul; Hood, Thomas B.; Bostwick, N. W.; Boyce, John F.; Sigrist, Charles N.; Langdon, C. W.; Hoen, Berthold; Carrillo, Julio; Pyatt, Thomas H.; West, Samuel; Arnold, G. W.; Hendley, John	10,000	21 Dec 1861	District Attorney	Elected 4 Sep 1861	B	247-248
Williams, Harrison J.	Mathews, George; Hopper, William	300	22 Nov 1858	Road Overseer (Road District No. 20, Mendocino County)	Appointed by the Board of Supervisors	A	365
Williams, J. S.	Bowles, J. M.; Pyatt, Thomas H.	900	10 Feb 1864	Physician and Surgeon in the Hospital of Sonoma County at Santa Rosa	Awarded a contract by the Board of Supervisors to attend to the indigent sick for the sum of $450 for the term of one year from 6 Feb 1864	B	442
Williams, J. S. *	Carrillo, Julio; Bowles, J. M.	1,000	12 Dec 1862	County Hospital Physician & Surgeon	Awarded a contract by the Board of Supervisors for attending to the indigent sick as Physician & Surgeon in the County Hospital for the term of one year	B	337
Williams, James B.	Stockhoff, John H.; Liebig, Frederic	1,000	3 Dec 1886	Constable (Salt Point Township)	Elected 2 Nov 1886	3	106-107
Williams, John Q.	Jackson, Lorenzo; Waugh, Lorenzo	500	7 Oct 1865	Road Master (Road District No. 1, Vallejo Township)	Elected [6 Sep 1865]		

Principal Name	Sureties	Amount ($)	Date	Office	Notes	Book	Page(s)
Williams, John S.	Brockman, Israel; Fisher, Ed.; Richardson, A.	5,000	11 Aug 1855	Coroner	Appointed 11 Aug 1855, includes oath of office dated 11 Aug 1855	A	106
Williams, John S.	Myers, D. D.; Cattron, William C.; Lamb, Joshua E.	5,000	2 Oct 1855	Coroner	Elected 5 Sep 1855	A	137
Williams, William R.	Howe, Anthony; Thompson, S. G.	2,000	26 Sep 1874	Justice of the Peace (Mendocino Township)	Appointed [? Sep 1874]	1	65-66
Willis, Thomas N.	Farmer, E. T.; Roney, J. M.; Fulkerson, Richard; Taylor, J. S.; Fine, A.; Weller, S.; Badger, J. J.; Kohle, A.; McMinn, John; Weatherington, Henry; McCoy, James; Clark, D.; Boyce, J. F.; Nowlin, S. S.; Peterson, A. J.; Peterson, A.; Gentry, W. O.; Maddux, J. P.; Petit, A. P.; McReynolds, James; Nicoll, D. C.; Hughes, H. M.; Sullivan, M.; Smith, R. Press; Smith, John K.; Wilkinson, Reason; Fulkerson, T. S.; McReynolds, William; Maddux, L. D.; Bumpus, C. H.; Murphy, J. D.; Murphy. R.; Murphy, W.; Griggs, J. H.; Lyttaker, R. G.; Forsyth, William H.; Foster, Joseph; Story, S. C.; Hughes, John; Walker, John; Tupper, G. A.; Burris, David; Leavenworth, T. M.	80,000	15 Sep 1875	Treasurer	Elected 1 Sep 1875	1	139-144
Willson, H. M.	Hendley, John; Farmer, E. T.	5,000	11 Apr 1874	Road Overseer (Healdsburg and Pine Flat Road District)	Appointed 11 Apr 1874 by the Board of Supervisors		
Willson, H. M.	Brown, Hank K.; Clack, John W.	2,000	18 Nov 1873	Justice of the Peace (Mendocino Township)	Elected 15 Oct 1873	B	745-746
Willson, H. M.	Bloom, David; Brown, H. K.	2,000	9 Jan 1873	Justice of the Peace [Mendocino Township]	Appointed 9 Jan 1873		
Willson, H. M. *	Clack, J. W.; Mead, James A.; Brown, H. K.; McManus, J. G.	2,000	28 Oct 1875	Justice of the Peace (Mendocino Township)	Elected 20 Oct 1875	1	171
Willson, H. S.	Gregg, Isaac; Harris, Jacob; Forsythe, Charles; Armstrong, J. B.; Eveleth, J. A.; Williams, J. M.	5,000	1 Apr 1880	Notary Public	Appointed 19 Mar 1880 by the Governor of California	1	572-574
Willson, H. S.	Armstrong, J. B.; Byington, H. W.	5,000	5 Apr 1882	Notary Public	Appointed 25 Mar 1882	2	127-128
Willson, Henry M.	Hudson, Thomas W.; Heald, J. G.	5,000	[3 Dec 1856]	Justice of the Peace (Mendocino Township)	Elected	A	160
Willson, Henry M.	Aull, A. B.; Hudson, T. W.	5,000	[4 Oct 1855]	Justice of the Peace (Mendocino Township)	Elected	A	148
Willson, Henry M.	Hudson, Thomas W.; Allen, William T.	5,000	2 Oct 1854	Justice of the Peace (Mendocino Township)	Elected 6 Sep 1854	A	34
Willson, Henry M.	Molleson, Henry P.; Aull, A. B.; Espey, George T.; Heald, J. G.; Heald, Thomas T.; Walsworth, H. T.; Sondheimer, E.; Grant, John D.	5,000	21 Sep 1857	Justice of the Peace (Mendocino Township)	Elected 2 Sep 1857, accepted by W. B. Hagans, Chairman of the Board of Supervisors	A	267-269
Wilson, Ben T.	Noonan, George P.; Cook, I. F.; Taylor, John S.; Barham, J. A.	2,000	1 Dec 1886	Constable (Santa Rosa Township)	Elected 2 Nov 1886	3	76-77

Principal Name	Sureties	Amount ($)	Date	Office	Notes	Book	Page(s)
Wilson, Charles K.*	Call, G. W.; Doda, John	1,000	8 Dec 1892	Justice of the Peace (Salt Point Township)	Elected 8 Nov 1892	4	259
Wilson, Henderson	Davis, G. W.; Cattron, William C.	200	11 Oct 1861	Road Master (District No. 2, Santa Rosa Township)	Appointed 12 Sep 1861 by the Board of Supervisors, witness William H. Crowell	B	236
Wilson, Henderson	Crane, George L.; Beaver, Henry	200	27 Feb 1861	Road Overseer (part of Santa Rosa Township lying north of Santa Rosa Creek)	Appointed 21 Feb 1861 by the Board of Supervisors	B	142
Wilson, S. H.	Hopper, Thomas; Farmer, C. C.; Boyce, J. F.; Farmer, E. T.	2,000	10 Jan 1879	Constable (Santa Rosa Township)	Appointed 9 Jan 1879 [by the Board of Supervisors to fill the vacancy caused by the death of W. C. Logan]	1	452-453
Wilson, S. H.	Farmer, Elijah T.; Wilson, H.	3,000	24 Feb 1861	Hospital Keeper	Awarded a $1,500 contract 24 Feb 1861 by the Board of Supervisors for the keeping of the County Hospital for the term of one year	B	148
Wilson, Silvester H.	Farmer, William; Crane, Joel	3,000	24 Feb 1860	Hospital Keeper	Awarded the contract for keeping the County Hospital for the sum of $1,500 for the term of one year by the Board of Supervisors	B	77
Wilson, W. A.*	Miller, J. R.; Wilson, M. A.	1,000	10 Aug 1891	Constable (Russian River Township)	Appointed 20 Jul 1891 by the Board of Supervisors	4	188
Wilson, W. A.*	Mitchell, R. T.; Bell, Henry	1,000	4 Aug 1891	Pound Master (Russian River Pound District)	Appointed 20 Jul 1891 by the Board of Supervisors	4	189
Wilson, William	Rambo, Jacob	200	[14 Sep 1861]	Road Overseer (District No. 2, Analy Township)	Appointed	B	229
Wilson, William H.	Barnes, Aaron, Sr.; Ragle, George J.	1,000	12 Dec 1888	Constable (Analy Township)	Elected 6 Nov 1888	4	31
Wilson, William Lee	Wilson, Henderson; Farmer, John H.	1,000	27 Oct 1869	Constable (Santa Rosa Township)	Elected 1 Sep 1869	C	6
Wilson, William*	Pews, John; Hudspeth, James; McChristian, Owen; Walker, John	1,000	25 Nov 1882	Constable (Analy Township)	Elected 7 Nov 1882	2	181-182
Wines, William F.*	Campbell, John T.; Davis, M. S.; Shelton, A. C.; Oates, James W.; Hopper, Thomas; Ware, A. B.; Overton, A. P.; Taylor, John S.; Carithers, D. N.; Reynolds, W. D.	25,000	21 Nov 1892	Clerk	Elected 8 Nov 1892, witness L. W. Juilliard	4	207
Winkler, Archibald	Singley, James; Keller, George H.	2,000	24 Feb 1852	Constable (Petaluma Township)	Elected, includes oath of office dated 25 Feb 1852	A	45
Winslow, Nelson	Yates, John W.; Bell, Henry; Buel, Samuel; Hubbard, P. G.; West, Samuel; McCollough, S. G.; Kennedy, James; Shipley, R. J.; Burris, Lewis C.	5,000	8 Feb 1858	Justice of the Peace (Russian River Township)	Appointed 2 Nov 1857 by the Board of Supervisors	A	296
Wisecarver, J. R.*	Cummings, Eli; Stites, A. H.	1,000	23 Jan 1875	Road Overseer (Washington Township)	Appointed 7 Jan 1875 by the Board of Supervisors	1	94-95

135

Principal Name	Sureties	Amount ($)	Date	Office	Notes	Book	Page(s)
Wisecarver, Joseph	Cummings, Eli; McMinn, William	1,000	20 Jan 1873	Road Master (Washington Road District)	Appointed 7 Jan 1873 by the Board of Supervisors		
Witham, George F.	Watriss, George E.; Whitman, George W.	1,000	15 Jan 1880	Road Overseer (Sonoma Road District North)	Appointed 7 Jan 1880 [by the Board of Supervisors]		
Wood, Ben S.	Graves, John Q.; Underhill, John G.	5,000	11 Jun 1881	Auditor	Elected 3 Sep 1879, a supplemental bond substituting John Q. Graves and John G. Underhill for A. Kohle and E. Latapie (both died) as sureties on Ben S. Wood's original bond dated 22 Sep 1879, includes several Superior Court documents relating to this matter	1	588-590
Wood, Ben S.	Graves, John Q.; Underhill, John G.	10,000	11 Jun 1881	Recorder & ex officio Auditor	Elected 3 Sep 1879, a supplemental bond substituting John Q. Graves and John G. Underhill for A. Kohle and E. Latapie (both died) as sureties on Ben S. Wood's original bond dated 22 Sep 1879, includes several Superior Court documents relating to this matter	1	586-588
Wood, Ben S.	Rupe, Sam H.; Powell, Ransom; Hassett, John D.; West, Robert; Hopper, David	10,000	16 Sep 1873	Recorder & ex officio Auditor	Elected 3 Sep 1873, witness H. M. Willson	B	711-712
Wood, Ben S.	Taylor, John S.; Ross, Robert; Noonan, George P.; Peterson, A.	5,000	18 Jan 1884	Notary Public	Appointed 11 Jan 1884	2	309-310
Wood, Ben S.	Seawell, James B.; Williams, George F.	5,000	18 Sep 1873	Recorder	Elected 3 Sep 1873, witness H. M. Willson	B	712-714
Wood, Ben S.	Noonan, George P.; Roney, J. M.; Rupe, Sam H.; Seawell, James B.	5,000	20 Sep 1877	Recorder	Elected 5 Sep 1877	1	296-297
Wood, Ben S.	Noonan, George P.; Roney, J. M.; Rupe, Sam H.; Seawell, James B.; Strom, William; Kennedy, George H.	10,000	20 Sep 1877	Recorder & ex officio Auditor	Elected 5 Sep 1877	1	301-303
Wood, Ben S.	Carter, Joseph W.; Mills, E. T.; Ross, H. J.; McMinn, John	5,000	21 Jan 1886	Notary Public	Appointed 12 Jan 1886 [by George Stoneman, Governor of California]	1	600-601
Wood, Ben S.	Noonan, George P.; Kohle, A.; Latapie, E.; Clark, James P.	5,000	22 Sep 1879	Recorder	Elected 3 Sep 1879, witness A. D. Laughlin	1	489-490
Wood, Ben S.	Noonan, George P.; Kohle, A.; Latapie, E.; Clark, James P.	10,000	22 Sep 1879	Recorder & ex officio Auditor	Elected 3 Sep 1879, witness A. D. Laughlin	1	490-492
Wood, Ben S. *	Carter, J. W.; Burris, L. W.; Burger, C. H.; McDonald, M. L.	2,500	12 Jan 1888	Notary Public	Appointed 11 Jan 1888 by R. W. Waterman, Governor of California	3	200-202
Wood, Ben S. *	Carter, J. W.; Burris, L. W.; Burger, C. H.; McDonald, M. L.	5,000	12 Jan 1888	Notary Public	Appointed 11 Jan 1888 by R. W. Waterman, Governor of California	3	215-216
Wood, Ben S. *	Allen, S. I.; McReynolds, James; Reed, W. C.; Brooke, T. J.	5,000	18 Jan 1890	Notary Public	Appointed 11 Jan 1890 by R. W. Waterman, Governor of California	4	73
Wood, J. B.	Matthews, O. B.; Arthur, C. R.; Rupe, Samuel H.; Boggs, A. Leonard; Tate, Thomas H.; Wylie, E. R.; Laughlin, M. N.; Laughlin, James H.; Cavanagh, John; Smyth, Thomas M.; Petray, R. A.; Shinn, S. M.; Dickenson, R. D.; Burriss, L. C.	5,000	[6 Oct 1857]	Surveyor	Elected 2 Sep 1857, accepted by W. B. Hagans, Chairman of the Board of Supervisors	A	248-254

Principal Name	Sureties	Amount ($)	Date	Office	Notes	Book	Page(s)
Wood, John B.	Rupe, Samuel H.; Seawell, William H.; Seawell, James B.; Espey, George T.; Hudson, Thomas W.	5,000	12 Feb 1866	Surveyor	Elected 6 Sep 1865	B	522
Wood, John B.	Rupe, Samuel H.; Powell, Ransom; Hassett, J. D.	5,000	17 Feb 1872	Surveyor	Elected 6 Sep 1871	C	152-153
Wood, John B.	Bailhache, John N.; Rupe, Sam H.; Truitt, J. H.; Seawell, James B.; Norton, L. A.	5,000	26 Sep 1867	Surveyor	Elected 4 Sep 1867	B	579
Wood, John B.	Carder, D. D.; Overton, A. P.; Ellis, J. J.; Rohrer, Cyrus; Matthews, O. B.; Speers, William B.; Rexford, E. A.; Robberson, John S.; Johnson, Fred	5,000	30 Sep 1859	Surveyor	Elected 7 Sep 1859 for the term of two years from the first Monday of October 1859 [3 Oct 1859]	B	41
Wood, John B.	Rupe, Sam H.; Norton, L. A.; Hardin, James A.; Brown, John	5,000	30 Sep 1875	Surveyor	Elected 1 Sep 1875	1	150-152
Wood, John B. *	Norton, L. A.; Rupe, Sam H.; Seawell, William H.	5,000	21 Sep 1869	Surveyor	Elected 1 Sep 1869	B	629
Wooden, Joseph	Gibbs, Henry; Mecham, Harry	200	[15 Nov 1864]	Road Master (District No. 2, Petaluma Township)	Appointed 15 Nov 1864 by the Board of Supervisors, includes oath of office dated 15 Nov 1864	B	462
Woods, J. S.	Rupe, Sam. H.; Neab, Johan; Selling, John	5,000	26 Nov 1856	Justice of the Peace (Sonoma Township)	Elected 4 Nov 1856	A	171
Woodson, W. H.	Gaver, A. P.; Hall, Henry	1,000	3 Dec 1886	Constable (Analy Township)	Elected 2 Nov 1886	3	90-91
Woodward, A. B.	McClellan, M. T.; Fisk, J. C.	1,000	20 Dec 1869	Justice of the Peace (Salt Point Township)	Elected 20 Oct 1869	C	24
Woodworth, P. N.	Fuller, Isaac; Perkins, G. R.	100	3 May 1858	Road Overseer (Annally Township)	Appointed February Term 1858 by the Board of Supervisors		
Woodworth, R. L.	Morse, Amasa; Hasbrouck, A.; McNabb, James H.	5,000	9 Apr 1866	Notary Public	Commissioned 5 Apr 1866 by F. F. Low, Governor of California	B	545
Worth, Claiborne	Sissengood, John; Davis, G. V.; Vassar, W. J.; Menihan, M.	1,000	13 Jan 1879	Road Overseer (Cloverdale Road District)	Appointed 7 Jan 1879 by the Board of Supervisors		
Worth, Claiborne	Brush, W. T.; Hall, M. V.; Murphy, Richard; Davis, G. V.	1,000	17 Jan 1880	Road Overseer (Cloverdale Road District)	Appointed 7 Jan 1880 by the Board of Supervisors		
Worth, Joseph Z.	Berry, S. B.; Kimble, H.	1,000	3 Sep 1883	Constable (Analy Township)	Appointed 3 Sep 1883 [by the Board of Supervisors, vice W. H. Willson, resigned], includes oath of office dated 20 Sep 1883	2	300-301
Worth, Lewis W.	Champlin, Charles; Schell, Theodore L.; Cook, David; Clark, Howard; Shaw, Oliver B.; Green, William; Craig, Oliver W.	5,000	29 Aug 1864	Notary Public	Commissioned 2 May 1864 by Frederic Low, Governor of California, includes oath of office dated 14 Aug 1864	B	459-460
Wratten, George L.	Burris, D.; Duhring, F.	5,000	14 Jul 1876	Notary Public	Appointed 1 Jul 1876, includes oath of office dated 14 Jul 1876	1	221-222

Principal Name	Sureties	Amount ($)	Date	Office	Notes	Book	Page(s)
Wratten, George L.	Vallejo, Mariano G.; Pauli, G. T.	5,000	19 May 1859	Notary Public	Appointed and commissioned 16 May 1859 for the term of two years, witness Peter Campbell, includes oath of office dated 19 May 1859	A	379
Wratten, George L.	Vallejo, M. G.; Brooks, B. S.	5,000	25 May 1861	Notary Public	Appointed & commissioned 17 May 1861	B	156
Wratten, George L.	Synder, J. R.; Hill, William McPherson	5,000	6 Jul 1872	Notary Public	Appointed 2 Jul 1872 by Newton Booth, Governor of California, for the term of two years		
Wratten, George L.	Edwards, A. S.; Poppe, J. A.	5,000	6 Jul 1874	Notary Public	Appointed 1 Jul 1874 by the Governor of California, includes oath of office dated 6 Jul 1874	1	23-24
Wratten, George L.	Goss, Leonard; Monahan, Patrick	5,000	6 Jul 1878	Notary Public	[Appointed] & commissioned 1 Jul 1878 by the Governor of California	1	432-433
Wratten, George L.	Hill, William McPherson; Munday, B. B.	5,000	7 May 1862	Notary Public	Appointed & commissioned 1 May 1862 by Leland Stanford, Governor of California, for the term of two years, includes oath of office dated 7 May 1862	B	261
Wratten, George L.	Munday, B. B.; Tate, Thomas H.	5,000	9 Jul 1857	Notary Public	Appointed and commissioned 7 May 1857, includes oath of office dated 9 Jul 1857	A	187-189
Wright, D. H.	Walker, John; Carrillo, Julio	1,000	1 Oct 1859	Constable (Analy Township)	Elected 7 Sep 1859	B	46
Wright, D. H.	Dougherty, John; Orr, John	1,000	23 Nov 1860	Constable (Annally Township)	Elected 6 Nov 1860	B	114
Wright, Joseph	Farmer, E. T.; Peterson, A. J.; Gray, J. W.; Beacom, Thomas; Atkins, W. G.; Roney, J. M.; Latapie, E.; Pauli, G. T.; Park, A. W.; McReynolds, John; Simons, John S.; McReynolds, James	25,000	8 Sep 1875	Sheriff	Elected 1 Sep 1875	1	113-115
Wright, Joseph	Farmer, E. T.; Peterson, A. J.; Gray, J. W.; Beacom, Thomas; Atkins, W. G.; Roney, J. M.; Latapie, E.; Pauli, G. T.; Park, A. W.; McReynolds, John; Simons, John S.; McReynolds, James; Wright, W. S. M.	30,000	8 Sep 1875	Sheriff & ex officio Tax Collector	Elected 1 Sep 1875	1	115-117
Yarbrough, C. D.	Heald, Thomas T.; McPeak, Anthony	1,000	13 Jan 1873	Road Master (Redwood Road District)	Appointed 7 Jan 1873 by the Board of Supervisors		
Yarbrough, C. D.	McPeak, M. A.; Bohn, Fred	1,000	16 Jan 1880	Road Master (Redwood Road District)	Appointed 8 Jan 1880 [by the Board of Supervisors]		
Yarbrough, C. D.	McPeak, M. A.; Bohn, Fredrick	1,000	21 Feb 1878	Road Overseer (Redwood Road District)	Appointed 7 Feb 1878 [by the Board of Supervisors]	1	407-408
Yarbrough, C. D.	Heald, Thomas T.; Bagley, J. W.	1,000	21 Jan 1874	Road Overseer (Redwood Road District)	Appointed 5 Jan 1874 by the Board of Supervisors		
Yarbrough, C. D.	Lunsford, R. B.; McPeak, M. A.	1,000	24 Dec 1880	Road Overseer (Redwood Township)	Elected 2 Nov 1880	2	78-79
Yates, J. W.	Thompson, J. D.; Wilson, M. A.	200	19 Sep 1863	Road Master (District No. 2, Russian River Township)	Elected 2 Sep 1863	B	381

Principal Name	Sureties	Amount ($)	Date	Office	Notes	Book	Page(s)
Yates, J. W.	Smith, I. P.; Espey, J. H.	2,000	23 Oct 1871	Constable (Russian River Township)	Elected 6 Sep 1871	C	96
Yates, J. W.	Rosenberg, M. J.; Bedwell, Franklin	500	29 Sep 1865	Road Master (Road District No. 2, Russian River Township)	Elected 6 Sep 1865	B	481
Yates, J. William	Thompson, J. D.; West, Samuel	500	16 Nov 1855	Road Overseer (Russian River District No. 7)	Appointed by the Board of Supervisors		
Yates, John W.	Esmond, Charles; Kennedy, G. H.	1,000	18 Mar 1871	Constable (Russian River Township)	Appointed [6 Mar 1871 by the Board of Supervisors to fill the vacancy caused by the removal of G. H. Esmond]	C	70
Yates, John W.	Griffith, John G.; Moore, Thomas W.	1,000	2 Oct 1854	Constable (Russian River Township)	Elected 6 Sep 1854	A	89
Young, Frank W.	Williams, J. M.; Farmer, C. C.; McMinn, John	5,000	[?] Jan 1880	Notary Public	Appointed 10 Jan 1880, witness R. A. Thompson, second page of original bond is missing	1	561-562
Young, George C.	Roberts, Charles; Lawrence, Henry E.	5,000	2 Jun 1887	Notary Public	Appointed & commissioned 31 May 1887 by Washington Bartlett, Governor of California	3	191-192
Young, George C.*	Ayers, William; Lawrence, H. E.	5,000	26 Jun 1889	Notary Public	Appointed & commissioned 22 Jun 1889 by R. W. Waterman, Governor of California	4	61
Young, John	Hassett, Aaron; Allman, John	1,000	23 Nov 1860	Constable (Mendocino Township)	Elected, witness Johnston Ireland	B	96
Young, Michael	St. Clair, F. C.; Hall, L. J.	1,000	17 Feb 1877	Road Overseer (Pine Flat Road District)	Appointed 9 Feb 1877 by the Board of Supervisors, witness W. W. Moreland	1	246-247
Zane, J. M.	Rohrer, Charles F.; Tupper, G. A.	1,000	6 Dec 1888	Justice of the Peace (Sonoma Township)	Elected 6 Nov 1888	3	317-318
Zane, Joel M.	Tupper, G. A.; Rohrer, Charles F.	1,000	24 Nov 1886	Justice of the Peace (Sonoma Township)	Elected 2 Nov 1886	3	38-39
Zane, Joel M.*	Reid, J. B.; Rohrer, Charles F.	1,000	13 Dec 1892	Justice of the Peace (Sonoma Township)	Elected 8 Nov 1892	4	249
Zilhart, Wesley W.	Quinlan, Patrick D.; Fitzpatrick, Andrew	2,000	4 Oct 1873	Constable (Bodega Township)	Elected 3 Sep 1873	B	749-750

www.ingramcontent.com/pod-product-compliance
Lightning Source LLC
Chambersburg PA
CBHW080333270326
41927CB00014B/3207